ArtScroll Mesorah Series®

אֲשֶׁר
יָצַר
וּמַגְדִּיל
יְשׁוּעֵי
מַלְכּוֹ

Rabbi Nosson Scherman / Rabbi Meir Zlotowitz
General Editors

סִידוּר
מִנְחַת שָׁלוֹם
תפילת מנחה ומעריב לחול
וברכת המזון

NUSACH ASHKENAZ / נוסח אשכנז

Published by

Mesorah Publications, ltd

The ArtScroll Weekday
minchah
maariv
and Grace After Meals

*A new translation
and anthologized commentary
by*
Rabbi Nosson Scherman

Co-edited by
Rabbi Meir Zlotowitz

Designed by
Rabbi Sheah Brander

◆ TABLE OF CONTENTS ◆

FIRST EDITION
Sixteen Impressions … May 1999 — January 2022

THE ARTSCROLL® MESORAH SERIES
Minchas Shalom — Weekday Minchah-Maariv — Nusach Ashkenaz
© *Copyright 1999 by MESORAH PUBLICATIONS, Ltd.*
313 Regina Avenue / Rahway, N.J. 07065 / (718) 921-9000 / www.artscroll.com

Typography by CompuScribe at ArtScroll Studios, Ltd.

This gift of prayer and peace
מנחת שלום
is dedicated to the memory of

Stephen E. Levitz

שלום גאזיק ז"ל בן חונא הלוי

*'Shalom, Shalom for the far and near,'
said HASHEM.*   (*Isaiah* 57:19)

A seeker and builder,
   Shalom Gazik made everyone feel near,
no matter how far he may have been.
He was a devoted husband,
son, and brother,
and a loving, dedicated father.

He built homes for Torah and holiness,
and opened his heart to all who needed
hospitality, inspiration, and friendship.

To know him was to admire, love,
and be indebted to him.
He enriched greater Detroit;
his untimely loss impoverishes us all.

תנצב"ה

❧ An Overview /
Inspiration in Sunset*

עַם זוּ יָצַרְתִּי לִי תְּהִלָּתִי יְסַפֵּרוּ

*I have fashioned this nation for Myself, that it may relate
My praise (Isaiah 43:21).*

רַבִּי אֱלִיעֶזֶר אוֹמֵר: הָעוֹשֶׂה תְּפִלָּתוֹ קֶבַע, אֵין תְּפִלָּתוֹ תַּחֲנוּנִים ...
מַאי קֶבַע? ... כָּל שֶׁאֵין מִתְפַּלֵּל עִם דִּמְדּוּמֵי חַמָּה.

*R' Eliezer says: If one makes his prayer a fixed chore, his
prayer is not a [true] supplication ... What is "a fixed
chore"? ... Anyone who does not pray with the [rising or
setting] rays of the sun (Berachos 28b, 29b).*

Israel is a nation with a unique mission, a mission of which *tefillah*
[prayer] is an integral part. By means of its prayers, Israel performs a
task that benefits God Himself, as it were. This dimension of *tefillah*
strikes many as novel, even bizarre, for we have grown up thinking of
prayer as man's need exclusively — that it is our way of asking the
All-Powerful One to provide *our* necessities and preferences. We look to
Him as the Provider of health, wisdom and safety, and the list goes on and
on. We beseech Him, therefore, to answer our prayers with a one-sided
stream of bounty.

All of this is true, but it misses the mark, for *tefillah* in its most significant sense is man's means of fulfilling *God's* need. How can this be? What
need could God have of man's supplications, no matter how sincerely
mouthed and felt?

Ramban (see *Exodus* 29:46 and *Deuteronomy* 32:26) explains that God
in His wisdom desires that there be a nation on earth that will recognize
and proclaim Him as the Creator and Master of all. But instead of looking
to the heavens and perceiving Who created all this, the nations looked up
and prostrated themselves to the heavenly bodies, or looked around and
worshiped the forces of nature, or looked in the mirror, honored their own
lusts and instincts, and deified their own intelligence and power. Which
nation would see God's wisdom revealed in the marvels of His universe,
and accept the Torah as the revelation of His will? Only Israel.

---

* This Overview is based on portions of *Iyun HaSefillah,* by Rabbi Moshe Eisemann.

If ever this tiny nation were permitted to perish at the hand of its myriad enemies, or if it were permitted to grow fat and lax and finally fall into the embrace of its seductive lovers, then who would remain to bear God's banner on earth? Israel had to survive, because God needed it as the vehicle through which He demonstrated His Presence to anyone who was willing to see: the miracles of the Biblical period, the waxing and waning of its fortunes depending on how loyal it was to Him, the long and painful chain of pogrom, expulsion, and renaissance, and — perhaps the greatest miracle of all — the survival of this one defenseless sheep among seventy wolves.

Primarily, this is a responsibility of עַם יִשְׂרָאֵל, the nation of Israel as a whole. True, there is also *Reb Yisrael*, the individual Jew with his personal responsibility to fulfill the commandments and the right to petition God for succor and sustenance. But even in this role, the Jew should consider himself a limb of a national body whose joint success warms him and whose failure afflicts him.

For this reason, when the Sages instituted the standardized formula of *Shemoneh Esrei* (the *Amidah*), they composed it in the plural form. Each person prays as a member of the community, and as such, his own needs for wisdom, health, prosperity or whatever, are joined with those of his people.

There is another indication of the communal nature of our prayers. The Sages required that gratitude for our redemption from Egyptian bondage and the expression of our confidence in the future redemption must immediately precede *Shemoneh Esrei,* and that no interruption of any sort is permitted between the two [סְמִיכַת גְּאֻלָּה לִתְפִלָּה]: The redemption consecrated the entire nation to God so that it would proclaim His praises in its prayers and through its deeds. So it was in the past and so it will be in the future. Prayer is an acknowledgment that God redeemed the entire nations so that it should join in praising Him.

The Sages and the commentators have related the three daily prayers to the times of the day when they are recited. In this regard, R' Shmuel bar Nachman (*Bereishis Rabbah* 68:11) teaches that *Maariv,* the nighttime prayer, is, in effect, a prayer that God rescue us from the darkness of night and all that it represents; *Shacharis,* the morning prayer, is an expression of gratitude that He has shown us the light of a new day. These are straightforward, quite understandable messages. However, his explanation of *Minchah,* the afternoon prayer, seems somewhat cryptic. The afternoon prayer, he says, is an appeal: "Just as You have privileged me to see the sun rise, so may You privilege me to see it set." Why does R' Shmuel

bar Nachman say that it is a "privilege" to see the sun go down? And why is it that *Minchah* seems to be suspended between sunrise and sunset?

Shacharis is the time of bright potential, the time when the sun of promise and expectation is rising higher and higher, the time when man looks ahead to a productive day. *Maariv* is recited at night, but even that is a time of hope that the worst is over, for to paraphrase the Sages, "Had I not been enveloped in darkness I could not have appreciated the light."

But *Minchah* symbolizes the dreariest aspect of life, trepidation and a helplessness to prevent the light and cheer from slipping away. The sun is setting; the darkness is coming. Hope wanes and suffering approaches. It is far worse to be losing what one has laboriously accumulated than to have lost everything and start all over again. The former breeds despair; the latter determination and even optimism.

The *Minchah* prayer was instituted by Isaac, and it represents his personal experience. The concept of Jewish exile began when he was born, because he never enjoyed the princely status and respect accorded Abraham by the Canaanite nations. According to *Ibn Ezra* — a view disputed by most other commentators — Isaac suffered the further degradation of losing the family fortune he had inherited from Abraham. His mature years were darkened by blindness and the rift between his sons Jacob and Esau. Isaac also represents מִדַּת הַדִּין, the *Attribute of Justice*, meaning that he was driven by a powerful urge for self-perfection, that he analyzed his deeds and desires, and tended to refrain from any act that fell short of his high standards.

Given his plight and his mode of service, we would expect to find Isaac morose and depressed, but we do not. His very name was given him by God as a permanent reminder of צְחֹק, the *happy laughter* with which everyone greeted the joyous news that the barren marriage of his elderly parents would be blessed with an offspring. Isaac was conceived in joy, born in joy — and he lived with joy, despite the darkness closing in around him. The way in which Isaac viewed life was transmitted to us in his *Minchah* prayer, for, properly understood, it is Israel's way of giving meaning to, and finding optimism in, every ordeal.

When the sun shines on our lives, it gives us an awareness of God's omnipresent mercy and vigilance, and we thank Him. When its brilliance forsakes us, we seek the reason for His displeasure, but remain aware that even harsh judgment is not haphazard and that it is meant to bring ultimate benefits. Therefore, the Sages teach that one who fails to pray with the rising of the sun has turned his prayers into "a fixed chore" (*Berachos* 29b). By responding to the changing rays he symbolizes that he searches for God's Presence in every manifestation of nature and life. To do other-

wise — to remain constant and impervious to upheaval and change — would be to demonstrate in deed that one's prayer is a fixed chore rather than a heartfelt supplication for God's helpful intervention.

But there is another element in the equation. Sometimes people can be carried away by their emotions and fail to realize that man does not merely react to the buffeting of events. He must respond to a higher motivation; to a more intense awe; to a reverence for God Who demands that man act in accordance with the Divine will. Therefore the Talmud concludes: *In the West* [i.e., *Eretz Yisrael*] *they cursed one who prays only with the rays of the sun. Why? Because sometimes he may miss the proper time* (*Berachos* 29b).

There is a need for man to respond to events, but there is a greater need for him to respond to the will of God. The Torah specifies times for prayer because man cannot rely on his often imperfect awareness of God's Presence in the events. By tying his supplications to the times when God wishes to receive him, man demonstrates that He fears not only the dangers implicit in the receding rays of the sun, but the Cause of all shining and darkening; consequently his prayers are regulated by a higher law than the elements. Thus, man's scheduled prayers remind him of God's eternal Presence, which in turn makes him better able to interpret natural phenomena as manifestations of God's will.

The commentators explain that while each of the Patriarchs prayed three times a day, each instituted for posterity the one prayer with which he was especially identified. Isaac knew that his lifetime would be one of waning graciousness and that he would bequeath to Jacob a period of darkness. Isaac's legacy was an awareness of how to understand and cope with tragedy.

In relating that Isaac's prayer won the blessing of children for his barren wife, Rebecca, the Torah uses an uncommon word for prayer: וַיֶּעְתַּר יִצְחָק לֹה, *Isaac entreated to Hashem* (Genesis 25:21). Reish Lakish comments in the Midrash that the unusual verb וַיֶּעְתַּר comes from the word עֶתֶר, *pitchfork,* implying that Isaac overturned God's decree of barrenness: Just as a pitchfork turns sheaves of grass from one place to another, so does the prayer of the righteous transform God's will from the Attribute of Justice to the Attribute of Mercy.

Sfas Emes explains that Isaac utilized the quality of justice to gain mercy; his "pitchfork-like prayer" took the sheaves of justice and transformed them into mercy, its seeming opposite. In Isaac's prayer from the depths of despair, there was a conscious effort to fight for mercy. Sometimes mercy is undeserved and sometimes it is earned. How can mercy be earned, and if it is indeed deserved, then why is it called mercy?

Sfas Emes explains that even God's "gifts" are not dispensed haphazardly. True, if man is to be measured in the most exacting measure of justice, he cannot claim that he is worthy of God's largess — for what human being can ever survive Divine scrutiny? But God does not expect the impossible from us. We are called upon to recognize His will in the impending darkness, to seek the reasons for our loss of God's favor and to turn back from whatever it is that displeases Him, to try to perceive the justice in His wrath, and to remember in the midst of turmoil that even our current ordeal is part of the Divine plan that will ultimately bring the universe to perfection. Such a realization does not come easily; it is worthy of the teaching of an Isaac. When the Patriarch's offspring absorb his legacy, they are truly worthy of his blessings and God's.

This volume contains the prayers of the afternoon and night, beginning with Isaac's response to God's receding smile. Isaac's prayer was *Minchah,* which means "gift," and a gift it was, a lavish one that God treasured. Isaac showed God and taught us that the Jew perceives a lesson in every event, and even when he cannot understand the teaching, he acknowledges that there is a Creator Whose Providence determines all.

THE NAMES OF GOD

The Four-Letter Name of *Hashem* [יה־ה־ו־ה] indicates that God is timeless and infinite, since the letters of this Name are those of the words הָיָה הֹוֶה וְיִהְיֶה, *He was, He is, and He will be*. This Name appears in some editions with vowel points [יְה־ֹו־ָה] and in others, such as the present edition, without vowels. In either case, this Name is *never* pronounced as it is spelled.

During prayer, or when a blessing is recited, or when Torah verses are read, the Four-Letter Name should be pronounced as if it were spelled אֲדֹנָי, *Adonai*, the Name that identifies God as the Master of All. At other times, it should be pronounced הַשֵׁם, *Hashem*, literally, ''the Name.''

According to the *Shulchan Aruch*, one should have both meanings — the Master of All and the Timeless, Infinite One — in mind when reciting the Four-Letter Name during prayer (*Orach Chaim* Ch. 5). According to *Vilna Gaon*, however, one need have in mind only the meaning of the Name as it is pronounced — the Master of All (ibid.).

When the Name is spelled אֲדֹנָי in the prayer or verse, all agree that one should have in mind that God is the Master of All.

The Name אֱלֹהִים, *God*, refers to Him as the One Who is all-powerful and Who is in direct overlordship of the universe (ibid.). This is also used as a generic name for the angels, a court, rulers, and even idols. However, when the term אֱלֹהִים is used for the God of Israel, it means the One Omniscient God, Who is uniquely identified with His Chosen People.

In this *siddur*, the Four-Letter Name of God is translated ''*Hashem*,'' the pronunciation traditionally used for the Name to avoid pronouncing it unnecessarily. This pronunciation should be used when studying the meanings of the prayers. However, if one prays in English, he should say ''God'' or ''Lord'' or he should pronounce the Name in the proper Hebrew way — *Adonai* — in accord with the ruling of most halachic authorities.

PRONOUNCING THE NAMES OF GOD

The following table gives the pronunciations of the Name when it appears with a prefix.

בְּי־ה־ו־ה — *bă dŏ nai'*
הַי־ה־ו־ה — *hăă dŏ năi'*
וַי־ה־ו־ה — *vă dŏ nai'*
כַּי־ה־ו־ה — *kă dŏ nai'*
לַי־ה־ו־ה — *lă dŏ nai'*
מַי־ה־ו־ה — *mă ă dŏ nai'*
שֶׁי־ה־ו־ה — *she ă dŏ nai'*

Sometimes the Name appears with the vowelization יֱ־ה־ו־ה. This version of the Name is pronounced as if it were spelled אֱלֹהִים, *e lŏ him'*, the Name that refers to God as the One Who is all-powerful. When it appears with a prefix לֱי־ה־ו־ה, it is pronounced *lă lŏ him'*. We have translated this Name as *Hashem/Elohim* to indicate that it refers to the aspects inherent in each of those Names.

MINCHAH

מנחה לחול ﴾

אַשְׁרֵי יוֹשְׁבֵי בֵיתֶךָ, עוֹד יְהַלְלוּךָ סֶּלָה.[1] אַשְׁרֵי הָעָם שֶׁכָּכָה
לּוֹ, אַשְׁרֵי הָעָם שֶׁיהוה אֱלֹהָיו.[2]

תְּהִלָּה לְדָוִד.
אֲרוֹמִמְךָ* אֱלוֹהַי הַמֶּלֶךְ, וַאֲבָרְכָה שִׁמְךָ לְעוֹלָם וָעֶד.

תהלים קמה

﴿ WEEKDAY MINCHAH ﴾ / מנחה לחול ﴿

Minchah corresponds to the *tamid*, the daily afternoon offering in the Temple (*Berachos* 26b), so it is recited only when it was permissible to offer the *tamid*: from half an hour after midday until evening. The preferable time, however, is not before three and a half variable hours after midday (*Orach Chaim* 233:1). A variable hour is one twelfth of the time from sunrise to sunset.

﴿ Ashrei / אַשְׁרֵי ﴾

The Talmud (*Berachos* 4b) teaches that

the Sages assured a share in the World to Come to anyone who recites *Ashrei* properly three times a day. It has this special status because no other psalm possesses both of these virtues: (a) Beginning with the word אֲרוֹמִמְךָ (the first substantive word of the psalm), the initials of the psalm's respective verses follow the order of the *Aleph-Beis*; and (b) it contains the inspiring and reassuring testimony to God's mercy, פּוֹתֵחַ אֶת יָדֶךָ ..., *You open Your hand ... As Zohar* teaches, the recitation of this verse is not considered a *request* that God open His

---

MAARIV

מעריב לחול ﴾

Congregation, then *chazzan*:

וְהוּא רַחוּם יְכַפֵּר עָוֹן וְלֹא יַשְׁחִית, וְהִרְבָּה לְהָשִׁיב אַפּוֹ,
וְלֹא יָעִיר כָּל חֲמָתוֹ.[1] ❖ יהוה הוֹשִׁיעָה, הַמֶּלֶךְ יַעֲנֵנוּ
בְיוֹם קָרְאֵנוּ.[2]

Chazzan bows at בָּרְכוּ and straightens up at 'ה.

בָּרְכוּ אֶת יהוה הַמְבֹרָךְ.

Congregation, followed by *chazzan*, responds, bowing at בָּרוּךְ and straightening up at 'ה.

בָּרוּךְ יהוה הַמְבֹרָךְ לְעוֹלָם וָעֶד.

﴿ WEEKDAY MAARIV ﴾ / מעריב לחול ﴿

Like *Shacharis* and *Minchah*, *Maariv* has its basis in the Temple service. In the Temple, no sacrifices were offered in the evening, but any sacrificial parts that had not been burned during the day could be placed on the Altar and burned at night. Thus, although no sacrificial service was *required* during the night, it was uncommon for the Altar not to be in use. This explains

why *Maariv* began as a voluntary service; unlike *Shacharis* and *Minchah* that took the place of the required *tamid*-offerings, the evening service on the Altar was optional in the sense that it was unnecessary if all the parts could be burned during the day. During Talmudic times, the universal consensus of Jewry adopted *Maariv* as an obligatory service, so it now has the status of *Shacharis* and *Minchah*.

MINCHAH

⊰❙ WEEKDAY MINCHAH ❙⊱

אַשְׁרֵי *Praiseworthy are those who dwell in Your house; may they always praise You, Selah!* [1] *Praiseworthy is the people for whom this is so, praiseworthy is the people whose God is HASHEM.* [2]

Psalm 145   *A psalm of praise by David:*

א *I will exalt You,* • *my God the King, and I will bless Your Name forever and ever.*

(1) Psalms 84:5. (2) 144:15.

hand for us; rather it is purely a recitation of praise.

Psalm 145 begins with the verse תְּהִלָה לְדָוִד; the two preliminary verses, each beginning with the word אַשְׁרֵי, are affixed to תְּהִלָה לְדָוִד for two reasons: (a) By expressing the idea that those who can dwell in God's house of prayer and service are praiseworthy, these verses set the stage for the succeeding psalms of praise, for we, the praiseworthy ones, are about to laud the

God in Whose house we dwell; and (b) the word אַשְׁרֵי is found three times in these verses. This alludes to the Talmudic dictum that one who recites Psalm 145 three times a day is assured of a share in the World to Come; thus, those who do so are indeed אַשְׁרֵי, *praiseworthy.*

תְּהִלָה ... אֲרוֹמִמְךָ — *A psalm ... I will exalt You.* Beginning with the word אֲרוֹמִמְךָ, the initials of the respective verses follow the order of the *Aleph-Beis.* According to

MAARIV

⊰❙ WEEKDAY MAARIV ❙⊱

Congregation, then chazzan:

וְהוּא *He, the Merciful One, is forgiving of iniquity and does not destroy. Frequently He withdraws His anger, not arousing His entire rage.* [1]

Chazzan — HASHEM, *save! May the King answer us on the day we call.* [2]

Chazzan bows at "Bless" and straightens up at "HASHEM."

Bless HASHEM, the blessed One.

Congregation, followed by chazzan, responds, bowing at "Blessed" and straightening up at "HASHEM."

Blessed is HASHEM, the blessed One, for all eternity.

(1) Psalms 78:38. (2) 20:10.

As a general rule, no אָמֵן, *Amen,* or other prayer response may be recited between *Borchu* and *Shemoneh Esrei,* but there are exceptions. The main exception is "between chapters" [בֵּין הַפְּרָקִים] of the *Shema* blessings — i.e., after each of the blessings, and between the three chapters of *Shema.* At those points, every אָמֵן (but not בָּרוּךְ הוּא וּבָרוּךְ שְׁמוֹ) may be said.

Some responses are permitted at any point in the *Shema* blessings. They are: (a) In

Kaddish, עָלְמַיָּא ... רַבָּא שְׁמֵהּ יְהֵא אָמֵן and the response אָמֵן בְּעָלְמָא ... דַּאֲמִירָן; and (b) the response to בָּרְכוּ.

No interruptions whatever are permitted during the two verses of שְׁמַע and שְׁמַע.

The ideal time for *Maariv* is after dark. However, if one will not have a *minyan* later, he may recite *Maariv* as much as one and a quarter variable hours before sunset, in which case he must repeat the three chapters of *Shema* after dark.

בְּכָל יוֹם אֲבָרְכֶךָּ,* וַאֲהַלְלָה שִׁמְךָ לְעוֹלָם וָעֶד. גָּדוֹל יהוה וּמְהֻלָּל מְאֹד, וְלִגְדֻלָּתוֹ אֵין חֵקֶר.* דּוֹר לְדוֹר יְשַׁבַּח מַעֲשֶׂיךָ, וּגְבוּרֹתֶיךָ יַגִּידוּ.

Abuduraham the *Aleph-Beis* structure symbolizes that we praise God with every sound available to the organs of speech. *Midrash Tadshei* records that the Psalmists and Sages used the *Aleph-Beis* formula in chapters that they wanted people to follow more easily or to memorize.

בְּכָל יוֹם אֲבָרְכֶךָּ — *Every day I will bless You.* True, no mortal can pretend to know God's essence, but each of us is equipped to appreciate life, health, sustenance, sunshine, rainfall and so on. For these and their daily renewal, we give daily blessings (*Siach Yitzchak*).

ברכות קריאת שמע

בָּרוּךְ אַתָּה יהוה אֱלֹהֵינוּ מֶלֶךְ הָעוֹלָם, אֲשֶׁר בִּדְבָרוֹ* מַעֲרִיב עֲרָבִים, בְּחָכְמָה פּוֹתֵחַ שְׁעָרִים, וּבִתְבוּנָה מְשַׁנֶּה עִתִּים, וּמַחֲלִיף אֶת הַזְּמַנִּים, וּמְסַדֵּר אֶת הַכּוֹכָבִים בְּמִשְׁמְרוֹתֵיהֶם בָּרָקִיעַ כִּרְצוֹנוֹ. בּוֹרֵא יוֹם וָלָיְלָה, גּוֹלֵל אוֹר מִפְּנֵי חֹשֶׁךְ וְחֹשֶׁךְ מִפְּנֵי אוֹר. וּמַעֲבִיר יוֹם וּמֵבִיא לָיְלָה, וּמַבְדִּיל בֵּין יוֹם וּבֵין לָיְלָה, יהוה צְבָאוֹת שְׁמוֹ. ❖ אֵל חַי וְקַיָּם, תָּמִיד יִמְלוֹךְ עָלֵינוּ, לְעוֹלָם וָעֶד. בָּרוּךְ אַתָּה יהוה, הַמַּעֲרִיב עֲרָבִים. (.Cong – אָמֵן)

אַהֲבַת עוֹלָם* בֵּית יִשְׂרָאֵל עַמְּךָ אָהַבְתָּ. תּוֹרָה וּמִצְוֹת, חֻקִּים וּמִשְׁפָּטִים, אוֹתָנוּ לִמַּדְתָּ. עַל כֵּן יהוה אֱלֹהֵינוּ, בְּשָׁכְבֵנוּ וּבְקוּמֵנוּ נָשִׂיחַ בְּחֻקֶּיךָ, וְנִשְׂמַח בְּדִבְרֵי תוֹרָתֶךָ, וּבְמִצְוֹתֶיךָ לְעוֹלָם וָעֶד. ❖ כִּי הֵם חַיֵּינוּ, וְאֹרֶךְ יָמֵינוּ, וּבָהֶם נֶהְגֶּה יוֹמָם וָלָיְלָה. וְאַהֲבָתְךָ, אַל תָּסִיר מִמֶּנּוּ לְעוֹלָמִים. בָּרוּךְ אַתָּה יהוה, אוֹהֵב עַמּוֹ יִשְׂרָאֵל. (.Cong – אָמֵן)

ברכות קריאת שמע / Blessings of the Shema

The nighttime Blessings of the *Shema* are similar in theme to those of the morning, except that there are three in the morning and four in the evening. The total of seven is based on the verse (*Psalms* 119:164): *Seven*

times a day I praise You (Berachos 11a, Rashi). The first of the evening blessings describes God's control over nature, seasons, and the cycles of light. The second speaks of God's gift of the Torah, the very essence of Israel's survival. The third refers to the Exodus, but with emphasis on the

---

MINCHAH

ב *Every day I will bless You, • and I will laud Your Name forever and ever.*

ג *HASHEM is great and exceedingly lauded,
and His greatness is beyond investigation. •*

ד *Each generation will praise Your deeds to the next
and of Your mighty deeds they will tell;*

וְלִגְדֻלָּתוֹ אֵין חֵקֶר — *And His greatness is beyond investigation.* Much though we may try, we can understand neither God's essence nor His ways through human analysis, for He is infinite. We *must* rely on the traditions that have come to us from earlier generations, as the next verse suggests (*Rama*).

MAARIV

BLESSINGS OF THE SHEMA

בָּרוּךְ *Blessed are You, HASHEM, our God, King of the universe, Who by His word• brings on evenings, with wisdom opens gates, with understanding alters periods, changes the seasons, and orders the stars in their heavenly constellations as He wills. He creates day and night, removing light before darkness and darkness before light. He causes day to pass and brings night, and separates between day and night — HASHEM, Master of Legions, is His Name.* Chazzan– *May the living and enduring God continuously reign over us, for all eternity. Blessed are You, HASHEM, Who brings on evenings.* (Cong.– Amen.)

אַהֲבַת *[With] an eternal love• have You loved the House of Israel, Your nation. Torah and commandments, decrees and ordinances have You taught us. Therefore HASHEM, our God, upon our retiring and arising, we will discuss Your decrees and we will rejoice with the words of Your Torah and with Your commandments for all eternity.* Chazzan– *For they are our life and the length of our days and about them we will meditate day and night. May You not remove Your love from us forever. Blessed are You, HASHEM, Who loves His people Israel.* (Cong.– Amen.)

---

future redemption. The fourth stresses God's protection of His people from the terrors and dangers of night and slumber.

בָּרוּךְ אַתָּה . . . אֲשֶׁר בִּדְבָרוֹ — *Blessed are You . . . Who by His word.* The command of God created day just as it created night, for every moment of the day and night has a purpose in God's plan. This recognition of God's everpresent will is especially important at night, which represents the period of fear, failure, and exile (*R' Hirsch*).

אַהֲבַת עוֹלָם — *[With] an eternal love.* This blessing is an ecstatic expression of gratitude to God for the gift of Torah. Only after acknowledging our dependence on, and love for, the Torah, can we go on to express our undivided loyalty and dedication to ה אֶחָד, HASHEM, the One and Only God, Who gave us this most precious gift.

The blessing begins with an expression of an axiom of Jewish existence: God loves us. The fact that He chose to give us His Torah proves that it is the vehicle for our national fulfillment. Therefore we dedicate ourselves to study it — constantly, joyously, and devotedly (*Siach Yitzchak*).

MINCHAH

הֲדַר כְּבוֹד הוֹדֶךָ וְדִבְרֵי נִפְלְאֹתֶיךָ אָשִׂיחָה.

וֶעֱזוּז נוֹרְאֹתֶיךָ יֹאמֵרוּ, וּגְדוּלָּתְךָ אֲסַפְּרֶנָּה.

זֵכֶר רַב טוּבְךָ יַבִּיעוּ, וְצִדְקָתְךָ יְרַנֵּנוּ.

חַנּוּן וְרַחוּם* יהוה, אֶרֶךְ אַפַּיִם וּגְדָל חָסֶד.

חַנּוּן וְרַחוּם — *Gracious and Merciful.* Because God is *merciful,* He is אֶרֶךְ אַפַּיִם, *slow to anger,* so that punishment is delayed as long

as possible to allow time for repentance. And because He is *gracious,* He is גְּדָל חָסֶד, *great in bestowing kindness (Siach Yitzchak).*

MAARIV

שְׁמַע

Immediately before its recitation concentrate on fulfilling the positive commandment of reciting the *Shema* twice daily. It is important to enunciate each word clearly and not to run words together. For this reason, vertical lines have been placed between two words that are prone to be slurred into one and are not separated by a comma or a hyphen.

When praying without a *minyan,* begin with the following three-word formula:

אֵל מֶלֶךְ נֶאֱמָן.*

Recite the first verse aloud, with the right hand covering the eyes, and concentrate intensely upon accepting God's absolute sovereignty.

שְׁמַע | יִשְׂרָאֵל,* | יהוה | אֱלֹהֵינוּ, | יהוה | אֶחָד*׃¹

בָּרוּךְ שֵׁם* כְּבוֹד מַלְכוּתוֹ לְעוֹלָם וָעֶד. — *In an undertone*

While reciting the first paragraph (דברים ו:ה-ט), concentrate on accepting the commandment to love God.

וְאָהַבְתָּ* | אֵת | יהוה | אֱלֹהֶיךָ, | בְּכָל־לְבָבְךָ, | וּבְכָל־נַפְשְׁךָ,
וּבְכָל־מְאֹדֶךָ׃ | וְהָיוּ הַדְּבָרִים הָאֵלֶּה, אֲשֶׁר | אָנֹכִי

◄§ שְׁמַע / THE SHEMA §►

The recitation of the three paragraphs of *Shema* is required by the Torah, and one must have in mind that he is about to fulfill this commandment. Although one should try to concentrate on the meaning of all three paragraphs, one must concentrate at least on the meaning of the first verse (שְׁמַע) and the second verse (בָּרוּךְ שֵׁם) because the recitation of *Shema* represents fulfillment of the paramount commandment of acceptance of God's absolute sovereignty (קַבָּלַת עוֹל מַלְכוּת שָׁמַיִם). By declaring that God is One, Unique, and Indivisible, we subordinate every facet of our personalities, possessions — our very lives — to His will.

אֵל מֶלֶךְ נֶאֱמָן — *God, trustworthy King.* He is אֵל, *God,* the All-powerful source of all mercy; He is the מֶלֶךְ, *King,* Who rules, leads, and exercises supervision over all; and He is נֶאֱמָן, *trustworthy,* i.e., fair, apportioning no more suffering nor less good than one deserves *(Anaf Yosef).*

שְׁמַע יִשְׂרָאֵל — *Hear, O Israel.* Although the commentators find many layers of profound meaning in this seminal verse, one should have at least the following points in mind during its recitation:

□ At this point in history, HASHEM is only אֱלֹהֵינוּ, *our God,* for He is not acknowledged universally. Ultimately, however, all will recognize Him as ה' אֶחָד, *the One and Only*

MINCHAH

ה The splendrous glory of Your power
   and Your wondrous deeds I shall discuss.
ו And of Your awesome power they will speak,
   and Your greatness I shall relate.
ז A recollection of Your abundant goodness they will utter
   and of Your righteousness they will sing exultantly.
ח Gracious and merciful• is HASHEM,
   slow to anger, and great in [bestowing] kindness.

MAARIV

THE SHEMA

Immediately before its recitation concentrate on fulfilling the positive commandment of
reciting the *Shema* twice daily. It is important to enunciate each word clearly and not to run
words together.

When praying without a *minyan*, begin with the following three-word formula:
God, trustworthy King.•

Recite the first verse aloud, with the right hand covering the eyes,
and concentrate intensely upon accepting God's absolute sovereignty.

Hear, O Israel:• HASHEM is our God, HASHEM, the One and Only.•[1]

In an undertone: *Blessed is the Name• of His glorious kingdom for all eternity.*

While reciting the first paragraph (*Deuteronomy 6:5-9*),
concentrate on accepting the commandment to love God.

וְאָהַבְתָּ *You shall love• HASHEM, your God, with all your heart, with all
your soul and with all your resources. Let these matters that I*

(1) *Deuteronomy 6:4.*

God (Rashi; Aruch HaShulchan 61:4).

□ ה׳ — HASHEM. God is the Eternal One,
Who was, is, and always will be [הָיָה הֹוֶה
וְיִהְיֶה], and He is אָדוֹן, *Master*, of all.

□ אֱלֹהֵינוּ — *Our God.* He is all-Powerful
(*Orach Chaim 5*).

אֶחָד — *The One [and Only].* The word has
two connotations: (a) There is no God other
than HASHEM (*Rashbam*); and, (b) though we
perceive God in many roles — kind, angry,
merciful, wise, judging, and so on — these
different attitudes are not contradictory,
even though human intelligence does not
comprehend their harmony. *Harav Gedaliah
Schorr* likened this concept to a ray of light
seen through a prism. Though one sees a
myriad of different colors, they are all a
single ray of light. So, too, God's many man-

ifestations are truly one.

In saying the word אֶחָד, *the One and Only*,
draw out the second syllable (חָ) a bit and
emphasize the final consonant (ד). While
drawing out the ד — a letter with the numerical value of eight — bear in mind that God
is Master of the earth and the seven heavens. While clearly enunciating the final ד —
which has the numerical value of four —
bear in mind that God is Master in all four
directions, meaning everywhere.

◆§ בָּרוּךְ שֵׁם — *Blessed is the Name.* Having
proclaimed God as our King, we are grateful
for the privilege of serving the One Whose
kingdom is eternal and unbounded (*Etz
Yosef*).

◆§ וְאָהַבְתָּ — *You shall love.* One should learn
to fulfill the commandments out of love,

MINCHAH

טוֹב יהוה לַכֹּל, וְרַחֲמָיו עַל כָּל מַעֲשָׂיו.

יוֹדְוּךָ יהוה כָּל מַעֲשֶׂיךָ, וַחֲסִידֶיךָ יְבָרְכְוּכָה.

כְּבוֹד מַלְכוּתְךָ יֹאמֵרוּ, וּגְבוּרָתְךָ יְדַבֵּרוּ.

לְהוֹדִיעַ לִבְנֵי הָאָדָם גְּבוּרֹתָיו, וּכְבוֹד הֲדַר מַלְכוּתוֹ.

MAARIV

מְצַוְּךָ הַיּוֹם,* עַל־לְבָבֶךָ:* וְשִׁנַּנְתָּם לְבָנֶיךָ, וְדִבַּרְתָּ בָּם, בְּשִׁבְתְּךָ
בְּבֵיתֶךָ, וּבְלֶכְתְּךָ בַדֶּרֶךְ, וּבְשָׁכְבְּךָ וּבְקוּמֶךָ: וּקְשַׁרְתָּם לְאוֹת ׀
עַל־יָדֶךָ, וְהָיוּ לְטֹטָפֹת ׀ בֵּין ׀ עֵינֶיךָ: וּכְתַבְתָּם ׀ עַל־מְזֻזוֹת
בֵּיתֶךָ, וּבִשְׁעָרֶיךָ:

While reciting the second paragraph (דברים יא:יג-כא), concentrate on
accepting all the commandments and the concept of reward and punishment.

וְהָיָה,* אִם־שָׁמֹעַ ׀ תִּשְׁמְעוּ אֶל־מִצְוֹתַי, אֲשֶׁר ׀ אָנֹכִי
מְצַוֶּה ׀ אֶתְכֶם הַיּוֹם, לְאַהֲבָה אֶת־יהוה ׀ אֱלֹהֵיכֶם
וּלְעָבְדוֹ, בְּכָל־לְבַבְכֶם, וּבְכָל־נַפְשְׁכֶם: וְנָתַתִּי מְטַר־אַרְצְכֶם
בְּעִתּוֹ, יוֹרֶה וּמַלְקוֹשׁ, וְאָסַפְתָּ דְגָנֶךָ וְתִירֹשְׁךָ וְיִצְהָרֶךָ:
וְנָתַתִּי ׀ עֵשֶׂב ׀ בְּשָׂדְךָ לִבְהֶמְתֶּךָ, וְאָכַלְתָּ וְשָׂבָעְתָּ: הִשָּׁמְרוּ*
לָכֶם, פֶּן־יִפְתֶּה לְבַבְכֶם, וְסַרְתֶּם וַעֲבַדְתֶּם ׀ אֱלֹהִים ׀ אֲחֵרִים,
וְהִשְׁתַּחֲוִיתֶם לָהֶם: וְחָרָה ׀ אַף־יהוה בָּכֶם, וְעָצַר ׀ אֶת־
הַשָּׁמַיִם, וְלֹא־יִהְיֶה מָטָר, וְהָאֲדָמָה לֹא תִתֵּן אֶת־יְבוּלָהּ,
וַאֲבַדְתֶּם* ׀ מְהֵרָה מֵעַל ׀ הָאָרֶץ הַטֹּבָה ׀ אֲשֶׁר ׀ יהוה נֹתֵן
לָכֶם: וְשַׂמְתֶּם ׀ אֶת־דְּבָרַי ׀ אֵלֶּה, עַל־לְבַבְכֶם וְעַל־
נַפְשְׁכֶם, וּקְשַׁרְתֶּם ׀ אֹתָם לְאוֹת ׀ עַל־יֶדְכֶם, וְהָיוּ לְטוֹטָפֹת

---

rather than fear — and certainly not out of
habit. The Mishnah (Berachos 9:5) explains
that one should serve God with all his emotions and desires (with all your heart), even
to the point of giving up his life for God (with
all your soul), and even at the cost of his
wealth (with all your resources).

אֲשֶׁר אָנֹכִי מְצַוְּךָ הַיּוֹם — That I command you
today. But have they all been commanded
today? This teaches that although the Torah
was given thousands of years ago, we are

not to regard the commandments as an ancient rite that we follow out of loyalty and
habit. Rather, we are to regard them with as
much freshness and enthusiasm as if God
had given them this very day (Sifre).

עַל לְבָבֶךָ — Upon your heart. Always be
conscious of the demands of God and His
Torah. Then, you will convey them to your
children and speak of them, i.e., try to
study, concentrate, and review wherever
you are.

MINCHAH

ט *HASHEM is good to all; His mercies are on all His works.*

י *All Your works shall thank You, HASHEM,*
and Your devout ones will bless You.

כ *Of the glory of Your kingdom they will speak,*
and of Your power they will tell;

ל *To inform human beings of His mighty deeds,*
and the glorious splendor of His kingdom.

MAARIV

command you today• *be upon your heart.• Teach them thoroughly to your children and speak of them while you sit in your home, while you walk on the way, when you retire and when you arise. Bind them•* *as a sign upon your arm and let them be tefillin between your eyes. And write them on the doorposts of your house and upon your gates.*

While reciting the second paragraph (*Deuteronomy* 11:13-21), concentrate on accepting all the commandments and the concept of reward and punishment.

וְהָיָה *And it will come to pass•* *that if you continually hearken to My commandments that I command you today, to love HASHEM, your God, and to serve Him, with all your heart and with all your soul — then I will provide rain for your land in its proper time, the early and late rains, that you may gather in your grain, your wine, and your oil. I will provide grass in your field for your cattle and you will eat and be satisfied. Beware•* *lest your heart be seduced and you turn astray and serve gods of others and bow to them.•* *Then the wrath of HASHEM will blaze against you. He will restrain the heaven so there will be no rain and the ground will not yield its produce. And you will swiftly be banished•* *from the goodly land which HASHEM gives you. Place these words of Mine upon your heart and upon your soul; bind them for a sign upon your arm and let them be tefillin*

וּקְשַׁרְתֶּם — *Bind them.* Tefillin on the arm, next to the heart, and on the head consecrate one's physical, emotional, and intellectual powers to God's service (*Ramban*). The *mezuzah* on the doorpost consecrates one's home to Him.

וְהָיָה ⸗ — *And it will come to pass.* Unlike the first paragraph of *Shema*, this one specifies the duty to perform מִצְוֹתַי, *My commandments*, and teaches that when the nation is righteous, it will be rewarded with success and prosperity. When it sins, it must expect poverty and exile.

וְאָכַלְתָּ וְשָׂבָעְתָּ. הִשָּׁמְרוּ — *And you will eat and*

be satisfied. Beware . . . Prosperity is often the greatest challenge to religious devotion. People who are rich in wealth but poor in sophistication often succumb to temptation (*Rashi*).

יִפְתֶּה . . . וְהִשְׁתַּחֲוִיתֶם לָהֶם — *Be seduced . . . and bow to them*, i.e., to strange gods. An imperceptible, seemingly innocent surrender to temptation can be the beginning of a course that will end in idolatry (*Rashi*).

וְלֹא יִהְיֶה מָטָר . . . וַאֲבַדְתֶּם — *So there will be no rain . . . And you will . . . be banished.* First will come famine. If that does not bring repentance, exile will follow (*Vilna Gaon*).

MINCHAH

מַלְכוּתְךָ מַלְכוּת כָּל עֹלָמִים, וּמֶמְשַׁלְתְּךָ בְּכָל דּוֹר וָדֹר.
סוֹמֵךְ יהוה* לְכָל הַנֹּפְלִים, וְזוֹקֵף לְכָל הַכְּפוּפִים.

סוֹמֵךְ ה׳ — *HASHEM supports.* No verse in *Ashrei* begins with a נ, because in the context of this verse that speaks of God supporting the fallen, the letter נ can be taken as an allusion to נְפִילָה, Israel's future *downfall*, ח״ו, and the Psalmist refused to use a letter that could suggest such tragedy. Nevertheless, knowing that downfalls would take place, the Psalmist comforted Israel by saying *God supports all the fallen ones.* This is an implied guarantee that even when a dreaded downfall hap-

MAARIV

בֵּין ו עֵינֶיךָ: וְלִמַּדְתֶּם ו אֹתָם ו אֶת־בְּנֵיכֶם, לְדַבֵּר בָּם,
בְּשִׁבְתְּךָ* בְּבֵיתֶךָ, וּבְלֶכְתְּךָ בַדֶּרֶךְ, וּבְשָׁכְבְּךָ וּבְקוּמֶךָ:
וּכְתַבְתָּם ו עַל־מְזוּזוֹת בֵּיתֶךָ, וּבִשְׁעָרֶיךָ: לְמַעַן ו יִרְבּוּ ו יְמֵיכֶם
וִימֵי בְנֵיכֶם, עַל הָאֲדָמָה ו אֲשֶׁר נִשְׁבַּע ו יהוה לַאֲבֹתֵיכֶם לָתֵת
לָהֶם, כִּימֵי הַשָּׁמַיִם ו עַל־הָאָרֶץ:*

במדבר טו:לז-מא

וַיֹּאמֶר ו יהוה* ו אֶל־מֹשֶׁה לֵּאמֹר: דַּבֵּר ו אֶל־בְּנֵי ו יִשְׂרָאֵל,
וְאָמַרְתָּ ו אֲלֵהֶם, וְעָשׂוּ לָהֶם צִיצִת, עַל־כַּנְפֵי
בִגְדֵיהֶם לְדֹרֹתָם, וְנָתְנוּ ו עַל־צִיצִת הַכָּנָף, פְּתִיל תְּכֵלֶת:*
וְהָיָה לָכֶם ו לְצִיצִת, וּרְאִיתֶם ו אֹתוֹ, וּזְכַרְתֶּם ו אֶת־כָּל־
מִצְוֹת ו יהוה, וַעֲשִׂיתֶם ו אֹתָם, וְלֹא־תָתוּרוּ ו אַחֲרֵי
לְבַבְכֶם וְאַחֲרֵי ו עֵינֵיכֶם, אֲשֶׁר־אַתֶּם זֹנִים ו אַחֲרֵיהֶם:
לְמַעַן תִּזְכְּרוּ, וַעֲשִׂיתֶם ו אֶת־כָּל־מִצְוֹתָי, וִהְיִיתֶם קְדֹשִׁים
לֵאלֹהֵיכֶם: אֲנִי יהוה ו אֱלֹהֵיכֶם, אֲשֶׁר

Concentrate on fulfilling the commandment to remember the Exodus from Egypt.

הוֹצֵאתִי ו אֶתְכֶם ו מֵאֶרֶץ מִצְרַיִם,
לִהְיוֹת לָכֶם לֵאלֹהִים, אֲנִי ו יהוה ו אֱלֹהֵיכֶם: אֱמֶת* —

Although the word אֱמֶת belongs to the next paragraph,
it is appended to the conclusion of the previous one.

יהוה אֱלֹהֵיכֶם אֱמֶת, — *Chazzan repeats*

וְלִמַּדְתֶּם ... בְּשִׁבְתְּךָ — *Teach them ... while you sit.* In giving the command to educate children in the Torah, the verse speaks in the plural (וְלִמַּדְתֶּם), while the other words in the verse (בְּשִׁבְתְּךָ and so on) are in the singular. This alludes to a *communal* responsibility to arrange for the Torah education of children (*Iyun Tefillah*).

MINCHAH

מ *Your kingdom is a kingdom spanning all eternities,*
   and Your dominion is throughout every generation.

ס *HASHEM supports*• *all the fallen ones and straightens all the bent.*

---

pens, the people can look forward to His support (*Berachos* 4b). *Maharsha* comments that by omitting a direct mention of downfall, the Psalmist implies that even

when Israel *does* suffer reverses, those reverses will never be complete. Rather, as the next verse declares, God will support the fallen.

MAARIV

between your eyes. Teach them to your children, to discuss them, while you sit• *in your home, while you walk on the way, when you retire and when you arise. And write them on the doorposts of your house and upon your gates. In order to prolong your days and the days of your children upon the ground that HASHEM has sworn to your ancestors to give them, like the days of the heaven on the earth.*•

Numbers 15:37-41

וַיֹּאמֶר *And HASHEM said*• *to Moses saying: Speak to the Children of Israel and say to them that they are to make themselves tzitzis on the corners of their garments, throughout their generations. And they are to place upon the tzitzis of each corner a thread of techeiles.*• *And it shall constitute tzitzis for you, that you may see it and remember all the commandments of HASHEM and perform them; and not explore after your heart and after your eyes after which you stray. So that you may remember and perform all My commandments; and be holy to your God.*

Concentrate on fulfilling the commandment of remembering the Exodus from Egypt.

I am HASHEM, your God, Who has removed you from the land of Egypt to be a God to you; I am HASHEM your God — it is true• —

Although the word אֱמֶת, *"true,"* belongs to the next paragraph, it is appended to the conclusion of the previous one.

Chazzan repeats: **HASHEM, your God, is true,**

כִּימֵי הַשָּׁמַיִם עַל הָאָרֶץ — *Like the days of the heaven on the earth.* Eretz Yisrael is the eternal heritage of the Jewish people, just as heaven will always remain above the earth. Alternatively, just as heaven always showers blessings upon the earth in the form of life-giving rain, so too Israel will be blessed in the land God has sworn to it.

וַיֹּאמֶר ה׳ — *And HASHEM said.* The third paragraph of *Shema* is recited to fulfill the commandment to recall the Exodus every day. By freeing Israel from Egypt, God laid

claim to the nation's eternal allegiance. No Jew is free to absolve himself of that obligation (*Rashi*).

פְּתִיל תְּכֵלֶת — *A thread of techeiles.* Techeiles is sky-blue wool dyed with the secretion of an amphibian called *chilazon.* For many centuries the identity of the animal has been unknown. Even in the absence of the *techeiles* thread, however, the commandment of *tzitzis* remains binding (*Menachos* 38a).

אֱמֶת — *True.* The law that one may not interrupt between the last words of the

---

MINCHAH

עֵינֵי כֹל אֵלֶיךָ יְשַׂבֵּרוּ,* וְאַתָּה נוֹתֵן לָהֶם אֶת אָכְלָם בְּעִתּוֹ.

פּוֹתֵחַ* אֶת יָדֶךָ, Concentrate intently while reciting the verse,

וּמַשְׂבִּיעַ לְכָל חַי רָצוֹן.

עֵינֵי כֹל אֵלֶיךָ יְשַׂבֵּרוּ — *The eyes of all look to You with hope.* Even animals instinctively rely upon God for their sustenance [how much more so should man recognize the beneficence of his Maker!] (Radak).

פּוֹתֵחַ — *[You] open.* When reciting this verse, one must have in mind the translation of the words because this declaration of God's universal goodness is one of the two reasons the Sages required the thrice-daily recita-

---

MAARIV

וֶאֱמוּנָה* כָּל זֹאת, וְקַיָּם עָלֵינוּ, כִּי הוּא יהוה אֱלֹהֵינוּ וְאֵין זוּלָתוֹ, וַאֲנַחְנוּ יִשְׂרָאֵל עַמּוֹ. הַפּוֹדֵנוּ מִיַּד מְלָכִים, מַלְכֵּנוּ הַגּוֹאֲלֵנוּ מִכַּף כָּל הֶעָרִיצִים. הָאֵל הַנִּפְרָע לָנוּ מִצָּרֵינוּ, וְהַמְשַׁלֵּם גְּמוּל לְכָל אֹיְבֵי נַפְשֵׁנוּ. הָעֹשֶׂה גְדוֹלוֹת עַד אֵין חֵקֶר, וְנִפְלָאוֹת עַד אֵין מִסְפָּר.[1] הַשָּׂם נַפְשֵׁנוּ בַּחַיִּים, וְלֹא נָתַן לַמּוֹט רַגְלֵנוּ.[2] הַמַּדְרִיכֵנוּ עַל בָּמוֹת אוֹיְבֵינוּ, וַיָּרֶם קַרְנֵנוּ עַל כָּל שׂוֹנְאֵינוּ. הָעֹשֶׂה לָּנוּ נִסִּים וּנְקָמָה בְּפַרְעֹה, אוֹתוֹת וּמוֹפְתִים בְּאַדְמַת בְּנֵי חָם. הַמַּכֶּה בְעֶבְרָתוֹ כָּל בְּכוֹרֵי מִצְרָיִם, וַיּוֹצֵא אֶת עַמּוֹ יִשְׂרָאֵל מִתּוֹכָם לְחֵרוּת עוֹלָם. הַמַּעֲבִיר בָּנָיו בֵּין גִּזְרֵי יַם סוּף, אֶת רוֹדְפֵיהֶם וְאֶת שׂוֹנְאֵיהֶם בִּתְהוֹמוֹת טִבַּע. וְרָאוּ בָנָיו גְּבוּרָתוֹ, שִׁבְּחוּ וְהוֹדוּ לִשְׁמוֹ. ✦ וּמַלְכוּתוֹ בְרָצוֹן קִבְּלוּ עֲלֵיהֶם. מֹשֶׁה וּבְנֵי יִשְׂרָאֵל לְךָ עָנוּ שִׁירָה בְּשִׂמְחָה רַבָּה, וְאָמְרוּ כֻלָּם:

מִי כָמֹכָה בָּאֵלִם יהוה, מִי כָּמֹכָה נֶאְדָּר בַּקֹּדֶשׁ, נוֹרָא תְהִלֹּת,* עֹשֵׂה פֶלֶא.[3]

Shema and אֱמֶת is of ancient origin. The reason is so that we declare, as did the prophet [Jeremiah 10:10], יהוה אֱלֹהִים אֱמֶת, *HASHEM, God, is true* (Berachos 14a).

אֱמֶת וֶאֱמוּנָה — *True and faithful.* This paragraph continues our fulfillment of the obligation to recall the Exodus in the evening. The morning blessing of אֱמֶת וְיַצִּיב, *True and certain,* concentrates on God's

kindness in having redeemed us from Egypt, while אֱמֶת וֶאֱמוּנָה, *True and faithful,* recited at night, symbolizes exile and stresses our faith that God will redeem us from this exile just as He did at the time of the Exodus (Berachos 12a; Rashi and Tosafos).

הַשָּׂם נַפְשֵׁנוּ בַּחַיִּים — *Who set our soul in life.* A reference to the night in Egypt when all

MINCHAH

ע The eyes of all look to You with hope•
and You give them their food in its proper time;

פ You open• Your hand,
and satisfy the desire of every living thing.

Concentrate intently while reciting
the verse You open . . .

tion of this psalm. One who forgot to concentrate on the translation must recite the
verse again (Tur and Shulchan Aruch 51:7).

This verse should be recited with great joy at
the knowledge that God cares for every creature (Yesod V'Shoresh HaAvodah).

MAARIV

וֶאֱמוּנָה and faithful• is all this, and it is firmly established for us that
He is HASHEM our God, and there is none but Him, and we are
Israel, His people. He redeems us from the power of kings, our King Who
delivers us from the hand of all the cruel tyrants. He is the God Who
exacts vengeance for us from our foes and Who brings just retribution
upon all enemies of our soul; Who performs great deeds that are beyond
comprehension, and wonders beyond number. [1] Who set our soul in life•
and did not allow our foot to falter. [2] Who led us upon the heights of our
enemies and raised our pride above all who hate us; Who wrought for us
miracles and vengeance upon Pharaoh; signs and wonders on the land
of the offspring of Ham; Who struck with His anger all the firstborn of
Egypt and removed His people Israel from their midst to eternal freedom;
Who brought His children through the split parts of the Sea of Reeds
while those who pursued them and hated them He caused to sink into
the depths. When His children perceived His power, they lauded and
gave grateful praise to His Name. Chazzan— And His Kingship they
accepted upon themselves willingly. Moses and the Children of Israel
raised their voices to You in song, with abundant gladness — and said
unanimously:

Who is like You among the heavenly powers, HASHEM!
Who is like You, mighty in holiness,
too awesome for praise, • doing wonders! [3]

(1) Job 9:10. (2) Psalms 66:9. (3) Exodus 15:11.

non-Jewish firstborn died, but Jewish souls
were preserved (Abudraham). This also implies God's protection from the murderous
designs of our enemies in all generations
(Siach Yitzchak).

נוֹרָא תְהִלֹּת — Too awesome for praise. We
are too terrified to attempt a complete

assessment of His greatness, because whatever we say is insufficient (Rashi).

Rambam comments that it is impossible
for people to praise God adequately; the
only way to laud Him is by simply recount-
ing His awe-inspiring deeds. Thus he would
render this phrase: [God's] awesomeness
constitutes His praises.

MINCHAH

צַדִּיק יהוה בְּכָל דְּרָכָיו, וְחָסִיד בְּכָל מַעֲשָׂיו.

קָרוֹב יהוה לְכָל קֹרְאָיו, לְכֹל אֲשֶׁר יִקְרָאֻהוּ בֶאֱמֶת.

MAARIV

✧ מַלְכוּתְךָ רָאוּ בָנֶיךָ בּוֹקֵעַ יָם לִפְנֵי מֹשֶׁה, זֶה אֵלִי עָנוּ וְאָמְרוּ:

יהוה יִמְלֹךְ לְעֹלָם וָעֶד.²

✧ וְנֶאֱמַר: כִּי פָדָה יהוה אֶת יַעֲקֹב, וּגְאָלוֹ מִיַּד חָזָק מִמֶּנּוּ.³
בָּרוּךְ אַתָּה יהוה, גָּאַל יִשְׂרָאֵל. (.אָמֵן – Cong)

הַשְׁכִּיבֵנוּ∗ יהוה אֱלֹהֵינוּ לְשָׁלוֹם, וְהַעֲמִידֵנוּ מַלְכֵּנוּ
לְחַיִּים, וּפְרוֹשׂ עָלֵינוּ סֻכַּת שְׁלוֹמֶךָ, וְתַקְּנֵנוּ
בְּעֵצָה טוֹבָה מִלְּפָנֶיךָ, וְהוֹשִׁיעֵנוּ לְמַעַן שְׁמֶךָ. וְהָגֵן בַּעֲדֵנוּ,
וְהָסֵר מֵעָלֵינוּ אוֹיֵב, דֶּבֶר, וְחֶרֶב, וְרָעָב, וְיָגוֹן, וְהָסֵר שָׂטָן
מִלְּפָנֵינוּ וּמֵאַחֲרֵינוּ, וּבְצֵל כְּנָפֶיךָ תַּסְתִּירֵנוּ,⁴ כִּי אֵל שׁוֹמְרֵנוּ
וּמַצִּילֵנוּ אָתָּה, כִּי אֵל מֶלֶךְ חַנּוּן וְרַחוּם אָתָּה.⁵ ✧ וּשְׁמוֹר
צֵאתֵנוּ וּבוֹאֵנוּ לְחַיִּים וּלְשָׁלוֹם מֵעַתָּה וְעַד עוֹלָם.⁶ בָּרוּךְ אַתָּה
יהוה, שׁוֹמֵר עַמּוֹ יִשְׂרָאֵל לָעַד. (.אָמֵן – Cong)

Some congregations omit the following on the conclusion of the Sabbath and Yom Tov
and on Chol HaMoed. They continue with Half-*Kaddish* (p. 28).

בָּרוּךְ יהוה לְעוֹלָם,∗ אָמֵן וְאָמֵן.⁷ בָּרוּךְ יהוה מִצִּיּוֹן, שֹׁכֵן
יְרוּשָׁלָ͏ִם, הַלְלוּיָהּ.⁸ בָּרוּךְ יהוה אֱלֹהִים אֱלֹהֵי
יִשְׂרָאֵל, עֹשֵׂה נִפְלָאוֹת לְבַדּוֹ. וּבָרוּךְ שֵׁם כְּבוֹדוֹ לְעוֹלָם,
וְיִמָּלֵא כְבוֹדוֹ אֶת כָּל הָאָרֶץ, אָמֵן וְאָמֵן.⁹ יְהִי כְבוֹד יהוה
לְעוֹלָם, יִשְׂמַח יהוה בְּמַעֲשָׂיו.¹⁰ יְהִי שֵׁם יהוה מְבֹרָךְ מֵעַתָּה וְעַד
עוֹלָם.¹¹ כִּי לֹא יִטֹּשׁ יהוה אֶת עַמּוֹ בַּעֲבוּר שְׁמוֹ הַגָּדוֹל, כִּי הוֹאִיל
יהוה לַעֲשׂוֹת אֶתְכֶם לוֹ לְעָם.¹² וַיַּרְא כָּל הָעָם וַיִּפְּלוּ עַל פְּנֵיהֶם,

---

◈ הַשְׁכִּיבֵנוּ ◈ — *Lay us down.* The Talmud (*Be-rachos* 4a) describes this blessing as an extension of the previous blessing of redemption [גְּאוּלָה אֲרִיכְתָּא]. Whereas the theme of

the earlier blessing was God's redemption of Israel from Egypt [and the allusion to the future redemption], this one describes Him as our Savior from the dangers and afflic-

---

MINCHAH

צ Righteous is HASHEM in all His ways
and magnanimous in all His deeds.

ק HASHEM is close to all who call upon Him —
to all who call upon Him sincerely.

MAARIV

Chazzan— Your children beheld Your majesty, as You split the sea before
Moses, "This is my God!"[1] they exclaimed, then they said:

"HASHEM shall reign for all eternity!"[2]

Chazzan— And it is further said: "For HASHEM has redeemed Jacob and
delivered him from a power mightier than he."[3] Blessed are You, HASHEM,
Who redeemed Israel.   (Cong.— Amen.)

הַשְׁכִּיבֵנוּ Lay us down• to sleep, HASHEM, our God, in peace, raise us
erect, our King, to life; and spread over us the shelter of Your
peace. Set us aright with good counsel from before Your Presence, and save
us for Your Name's sake. Shield us, remove from us foe, plague, sword,
famine, and woe; and remove spiritual impediment from before us and
behind us, and in the shadow of Your wings shelter us[4] — for God Who
protects and rescues us are You; for God, the Gracious and Compassionate King, are You.[5] Chazzan— Safeguard our going and coming, for
life and for peace from now to eternity.[6] Blessed are You, HASHEM, Who
protects His people Israel forever.   (Cong.— Amen.)

Some congregations omit the following on the conclusion of the Sabbath and Yom Tov
and on Chol HaMoed. They continue with Half-Kaddish (p. 28).

בָּרוּךְ Blessed is HASHEM forever,• Amen and Amen.[7] Blessed is
HASHEM from Zion, Who dwells in Jerusalem, Halleluyah![8]
Blessed is HASHEM, God, the God of Israel, Who alone does wondrous
things. Blessed is His glorious Name forever, and may all the earth be
filled with His glory, Amen and Amen.[9] May the glory of HASHEM endure
forever, let HASHEM rejoice in His works.[10] Blessed be the Name of
HASHEM from this time and forever.[11] For HASHEM will not cast off His
people for the sake of His Great Name, for HASHEM has vowed to make
you His own people.[12] Then the entire people saw and fell on their faces

---

(1) Exodus 15:2. (2) 15:18. (3) Jeremiah 31:10. (4) Cf. Psalms 17:8.
(5) Cf. Nehemiah 9:31. (6) Cf. Psalms 121:8. (7) 89:53. (8) 135:21.
(9) 72:18-19. (10) 104:31. (11) 113:2. (12) I Samuel 12:22.

---

tions associated with the terrors of night,
literally and figuratively (Seder HaYom).

בָּרוּךְ ה׳ לְעוֹלָם — Blessed is HASHEM forever. This collection of Scriptural verses

---

MINCHAH

רְצוֹן יְרֵאָיו יַעֲשֶׂה, וְאֶת שַׁוְעָתָם יִשְׁמַע וְיוֹשִׁיעֵם.
שׁוֹמֵר יהוה אֶת כָּל אֹהֲבָיו, וְאֵת כָּל הָרְשָׁעִים יַשְׁמִיד.
∗ תְּהִלַּת יהוה יְדַבֶּר פִּי, וִיבָרֵךְ כָּל בָּשָׂר שֵׁם קָדְשׁוֹ לְעוֹלָם
וָעֶד. וַאֲנַחְנוּ נְבָרֵךְ יָהּ מֵעַתָּה וְעַד עוֹלָם, הַלְלוּיָהּ.[1]

MAARIV

וַיֹּאמְרוּ, יהוה הוּא הָאֱלֹהִים, יהוה הוּא הָאֱלֹהִים.[1] וְהָיָה יהוה
לְמֶלֶךְ עַל כָּל הָאָרֶץ, בַּיּוֹם הַהוּא יִהְיֶה יהוה אֶחָד וּשְׁמוֹ אֶחָד.[2]
יְהִי חַסְדְּךָ יהוה עָלֵינוּ, כַּאֲשֶׁר יִחַלְנוּ לָךְ.[3] הוֹשִׁיעֵנוּ יהוה
אֱלֹהֵינוּ, וְקַבְּצֵנוּ מִן הַגּוֹיִם, לְהֹדוֹת לְשֵׁם קָדְשֶׁךָ, לְהִשְׁתַּבֵּחַ
בִּתְהִלָּתֶךָ.[4] כָּל גּוֹיִם אֲשֶׁר עָשִׂיתָ יָבוֹאוּ וְיִשְׁתַּחֲווּ לְפָנֶיךָ אֲדֹנָי,
וִיכַבְּדוּ לִשְׁמֶךָ.[5] וַאֲנַחְנוּ עַמְּךָ וְצֹאן מַרְעִיתֶךָ, נוֹדֶה לְּךָ לְעוֹלָם, לְדוֹר
וָדֹר נְסַפֵּר תְּהִלָּתֶךָ.[6] בָּרוּךְ יהוה בַּיּוֹם. בָּרוּךְ יהוה בַּלַּיְלָה.
בָּרוּךְ יהוה בְּשָׁכְבֵנוּ. בָּרוּךְ יהוה בְּקוּמֵנוּ. כִּי בְיָדְךָ נַפְשׁוֹת
הַחַיִּים וְהַמֵּתִים. אֲשֶׁר בְּיָדוֹ נֶפֶשׁ כָּל חָי, וְרוּחַ כָּל בְּשַׂר אִישׁ.[7]
בְּיָדְךָ אַפְקִיד רוּחִי, פָּדִיתָה אוֹתִי, יהוה אֵל אֱמֶת.[8] אֱלֹהֵינוּ
שֶׁבַּשָּׁמַיִם, יַחֵד שִׁמְךָ, וְקַיֵּם מַלְכוּתְךָ תָּמִיד, וּמְלוֹךְ עָלֵינוּ
לְעוֹלָם וָעֶד.

יִרְאוּ עֵינֵינוּ וְיִשְׂמַח לִבֵּנוּ וְתָגֵל נַפְשֵׁנוּ בִּישׁוּעָתְךָ בֶּאֱמֶת,
בֶּאֱמֹר לְצִיּוֹן מָלַךְ אֱלֹהָיִךְ.[9] יהוה מֶלֶךְ,[10] יהוה מָלָךְ,[11]
יהוה יִמְלֹךְ לְעֹלָם וָעֶד.[12] ∗ כִּי הַמַּלְכוּת שֶׁלְּךָ הִיא, וּלְעוֹלְמֵי
עַד תִּמְלוֹךְ בְּכָבוֹד, כִּי אֵין לָנוּ מֶלֶךְ אֶלָּא אָתָּה. בָּרוּךְ אַתָּה
יהוה, הַמֶּלֶךְ בִּכְבוֹדוֹ תָּמִיד יִמְלוֹךְ עָלֵינוּ לְעוֹלָם וָעֶד, וְעַל כָּל
מַעֲשָׂיו. (אָמֵן.) —Cong.

---

was introduced during the Geonic era. At that time most people gathered in the fields for prayers (apparently on the way from their farms to their homes). In order to shorten the service so that it could be completed before dark, this collection of verses was substituted for *Shemoneh Esrei*, which would be recited

---

MINCHAH

ר *The will of those who fear Him He will do;*
and their cry He will hear, and save them.

שׁ *HASHEM protects all who love Him; but all the wicked He will destroy.*

ת ❖ *May my mouth declare the praise of HASHEM*
and may all flesh bless His Holy Name forever and ever.
We will bless God from this time and forever, Halleluyah! [1]

---

(1) *Psalms* 115:18.

MAARIV

---

and said, "HASHEM — only He is God! HASHEM — only He is God!" [1] *Then HASHEM will be King over all the world, on that day HASHEM will be One and His Name will be One.* [2] *May Your kindness, HASHEM, be upon us, just as we awaited You.* [3] *Save us, HASHEM, our God, gather us from the nations, to thank Your Holy Name and to glory in Your praise!* [4] *All the nations that You made will come and bow before You, My Lord, and shall glorify Your Name. For You are great and work wonders; You alone, O God.* [5] *Then we, Your people and the sheep of Your pasture, shall thank You forever; for generation after generation we will relate Your praise.* [6] *Blessed is HASHEM by day; blessed is HASHEM by night; Blessed is HASHEM when we retire; Blessed is HASHEM when we arise. For in Your hand are the souls of the living and the dead. He in Whose hand is the soul of all the living and the spirit of every human being.* [7] *In Your hand I shall entrust my spirit, You redeemed me, HASHEM, God of truth.* [8] *Our God, Who is in heaven, bring unity to Your Name; establish Your kingdom forever and reign over us for all eternity.*

יְרָאוּ *May our eyes see, our heart rejoice and our soul exult in Your salvation in truth, when Zion is told, "Your God has reigned!"* [9] *HASHEM reigns,* [10] *HASHEM has reigned,* [11] *HASHEM will reign for all eternity.* [12] *Chazzan— For the kingdom is Yours and You will reign for all eternity in glory, for we have no King but You. Blessed are You, HASHEM, the King in His glory — He shall constantly reign over us forever and ever, and over all His creatures.*   (Cong.— Amen.)

---

(1) *I Kings* 18:39. (2) *Zechariah* 14:9. (3) *Psalms* 33:22. (4) 106:47.
(5) 86:9-10. (6) 79:13. (7) *Job* 12:10. (8) *Psalms* 31:6.
(9) Cf. *Isaiah* 52:7. (10) *Psalms* 10:16. (11) 93:1 et al. (12) *Exodus* 15:18.

---

later by each individual in the safety of his home. Another version has it that these verses were added in order to allow latecomers more time to catch up to the congregation. Whichever the reason, it was retained even after the practice of praying in the fields was discontinued.

The chazzan recites חֲצִי קַדִּישׁ:

יִתְגַּדַּל וְיִתְקַדַּשׁ שְׁמֵהּ רַבָּא. (.cong – אָמֵן) בְּעָלְמָא דִּי בְרָא כִרְעוּתֵהּ. וְיַמְלִיךְ מַלְכוּתֵהּ, בְּחַיֵּיכוֹן וּבְיוֹמֵיכוֹן וּבְחַיֵּי דְכָל בֵּית יִשְׂרָאֵל, בַּעֲגָלָא וּבִזְמַן קָרִיב. וְאִמְרוּ: אָמֵן.

(.Cong – אָמֵן. יְהֵא שְׁמֵהּ רַבָּא מְבָרַךְ לְעָלַם וּלְעָלְמֵי עָלְמַיָּא.)

יְהֵא שְׁמֵהּ רַבָּא מְבָרַךְ לְעָלַם וּלְעָלְמֵי עָלְמַיָּא.

יִתְבָּרַךְ וְיִשְׁתַּבַּח וְיִתְפָּאַר וְיִתְרוֹמַם וְיִתְנַשֵּׂא וְיִתְהַדָּר וְיִתְעַלֶּה וְיִתְהַלָּל שְׁמֵהּ דְּקֻדְשָׁא בְּרִיךְ הוּא (.Cong – בְּרִיךְ הוּא) – לְעֵלָּא מִן כָּל

[from Rosh Hashanah to Yom Kippur substitute — לְעֵלָּא (וּ)לְעֵלָּא מִכָּל] בִּרְכָתָא וְשִׁירָתָא תֻּשְׁבְּחָתָא וְנֶחֱמָתָא דַּאֲמִירָן בְּעָלְמָא. וְאִמְרוּ: אָמֵן. (.Cong–אָמֵן.)

On a Fast Day at Minchah: After *Ashrei* and Half-*Kaddish* have been recited, if seven members of the *minyan* are fasting, the Torah and *Haftarah* are read. Turn to page 110.

◆§ שמונה עשרה – עמידה ◆

Take three steps backward, then three steps forward. Remain standing with feet together while reciting *Shemoneh Esrei*. Recite it with quiet devotion and without any interruption. Although it should not be audible to others, one must pray loudly enough to hear himself. See Laws (pp. 123-126) for a brief summary of its laws including how to rectify the omission of phrases that are added at particular times of the year.

כִּי שֵׁם יהוה אֶקְרָא, הָבוּ גֹדֶל לֵאלֹהֵינוּ.[1]

אֲדֹנָי שְׂפָתַי תִּפְתָּח, וּפִי יַגִּיד תְּהִלָּתֶךָ.[2]

אבות

Bend the knees at בָּרוּךְ; bow at אַתָּה; straighten up at 'ה.

בָּרוּךְ אַתָּה יהוה אֱלֹהֵינוּ וֵאלֹהֵי אֲבוֹתֵינוּ,* אֱלֹהֵי אַבְרָהָם, אֱלֹהֵי יִצְחָק, וֵאלֹהֵי יַעֲקֹב, הָאֵל הַגָּדוֹל הַגִּבּוֹר וְהַנּוֹרָא, אֵל עֶלְיוֹן, גּוֹמֵל חֲסָדִים טוֹבִים, וְקוֹנֵה הַכֹּל, וְזוֹכֵר חַסְדֵי אָבוֹת,* וּמֵבִיא גוֹאֵל* לִבְנֵי בְנֵיהֶם, לְמַעַן שְׁמוֹ בְּאַהֲבָה.

From Rosh Hashanah to Yom Kippur add [if forgotten, do not repeat *Shemoneh Esrei*]:

זָכְרֵנוּ לְחַיִּים, מֶלֶךְ חָפֵץ בַּחַיִּים,

וְכָתְבֵנוּ בְּסֵפֶר הַחַיִּים, לְמַעַנְךָ אֱלֹהִים חַיִּים.

◆§ שְׁמוֹנֶה עֶשְׂרֵה / **SHEMONEH ESREI** ◆

Shemoneh Esrei has three sections: (a) In the first three blessings, the suppliant pays homage to God, like a slave praising his master before he dares make a request; (b) the middle section of thirteen blessings contains the suppliant's requests; (c) in the last three blessings, he takes leave, expressing gratitude and confidence in his Master's graciousness (*Berachos* 34a).

Even the middle section is not merely a catalogue of selfish requests. In each blessing, we acknowledge God's mastery before making the request. Thus, each blessing is an affirmation of God's power (*Vilna Gaon*).

◆§ אבות / **Patriarchs**

The first blessing, אבות, *Patriarchs*, recalls the greatness of our forefathers in whose merit God pledged to help Israel throughout history, even if we are unworthy.

The *chazzan* recites Half-*Kaddish*:

יִתְגַּדַּל *May His great Name grow exalted and sanctified* (Cong.— *Amen.*) *in the world that He created as He willed. May He give reign to His kingship in your lifetimes and in your days, and in the lifetimes of the entire Family of Israel, swiftly and soon. Now respond: Amen.*

(Cong. — *Amen. May His great Name be blessed forever and ever.*)

May His great Name be blessed forever and ever.

Blessed, praised, glorified, exalted, extolled, mighty, upraised, and lauded be the Name of the Holy One, Blessed is He, (Cong.— *Blessed is He*) — [From Rosh Hashanah to Yom Kippur add: *exceedingly*] *beyond any blessing and song, praise and consolation that are uttered in the world. Now respond: Amen.* (Cong. — *Amen.*)

> **On a Fast Day at Minchah:** After *Ashrei* and Half-*Kaddish* have been recited, if seven members of the *minyan* are fasting, the Torah and *Haftarah* are read. Turn to page 110.

◆§ SHEMONEH ESREI — AMIDAH §◆

Take three steps backward, then three steps forward. Remain standing with feet together while reciting *Shemoneh Esrei*. Recite it with quiet devotion and without any interruption. Although it should not be audible to others, one must pray loudly enough to hear himself. See Laws (pp. 123-126) for a brief summary of its laws including how to rectify the omission of phrases that are added at particular times of the year.

When I call out the Name of HASHEM, ascribe greatness to our God.[1]

My Lord, open my lips, that my mouth may declare Your praise.[2]

PATRIARCHS

Bend the knees at "*Blessed*"; bow at "*You*"; straighten up at "*HASHEM.*"

בָּרוּךְ *Blessed are You,* • HASHEM, *our God and the God of our fore-fathers,* • *God of Abraham, God of Isaac, and God of Jacob; the great, mighty, and awesome God, the supreme God, Who bestows beneficial kindnesses and creates everything, Who recalls the kindnesses of the Patriarchs and brings a Redeemer* • *to their children's children, for His Name's sake, with love.*

> From Rosh Hashanah to Yom Kippur add [if forgotten, do not repeat Shemoneh Esrei]:
> *Remember us for life, O King Who desires life, and inscribe us in the Book of Life — for Your sake, O Living God.*

(1) *Deuteronomy* 32:3. (2) *Psalms* 51:17.

בָּרוּךְ אַתָּה — *Blessed are You.* [Since God is perfect by definition, what benefit can man's blessing confer upon Him?]

❑ This is a declaration of fact: God *is* blessed in the sense that He is perfect and complete (*Sefer HaChinuch* 430).

❑ God is the *Source* of inexhaustible blessing, and He has created the world in order to do good to His creatures. Since this is His will, we pray for the Redemption, when man will be worthy of His utmost blessing (*Rashba; R' Bachya*).

אֱלֹהֵינוּ וֵאלֹהֵי אֲבוֹתֵינוּ — *Our God and the God of our forefathers.* First we call Him *our God* because we are obligated to serve Him and know Him to the limit of our capacity. But there is much about His ways that we cannot understand. In response to such doubts we proclaim that He is *the God of our forefathers*, and we have faith in the tradition they transmitted (*Dover Shalom*).

וּמֵבִיא גוֹאֵל — *And brings a Redeemer.* The phrase is in present tense. Every event, no matter how terrible it may seem, is a step

Bend the knees at בָּרוּךְ; bow at אַתָּה; straighten up at 'ה.

מֶלֶךְ עוֹזֵר וּמוֹשִׁיעַ וּמָגֵן. בָּרוּךְ אַתָּה יהוה, מָגֵן אַבְרָהָם.

גבורות

אַתָּה גִּבּוֹר לְעוֹלָם אֲדֹנָי, מְחַיֵּה מֵתִים* אַתָּה, רַב לְהוֹשִׁיעַ.

Between Shemini Atzeres and Pesach add [If forgotten, see Laws §7]:

מַשִּׁיב הָרוּחַ וּמוֹרִיד הַגֶּשֶׁם [נ״א הַגָּשֶׁם].

מְכַלְכֵּל חַיִּים בְּחֶסֶד, מְחַיֵּה מֵתִים בְּרַחֲמִים רַבִּים, סוֹמֵךְ נוֹפְלִים, וְרוֹפֵא חוֹלִים, וּמַתִּיר אֲסוּרִים, וּמְקַיֵּם אֱמוּנָתוֹ לִישֵׁנֵי עָפָר. מִי כָמוֹךָ בַּעַל גְּבוּרוֹת, וּמִי דּוֹמֶה לָּךְ, מֶלֶךְ מֵמִית וּמְחַיֶּה וּמַצְמִיחַ יְשׁוּעָה.

From Rosh Hashanah to Yom Kippur add [if forgotten, do not repeat Shemoneh Esrei]:

מִי כָמוֹךָ אַב הָרַחֲמִים, זוֹכֵר יְצוּרָיו לְחַיִּים בְּרַחֲמִים.

וְנֶאֱמָן אַתָּה לְהַחֲיוֹת מֵתִים. בָּרוּךְ אַתָּה יהוה, מְחַיֵּה הַמֵּתִים.

During the *chazzan's* repetition at Minchah, *Kedushah* (below) is recited here.

קדושה

Stand with feet together and avoid any interruptions.
Rise on toes when saying קָדוֹשׁ, קָדוֹשׁ, קָדוֹשׁ; בָּרוּךְ כְּבוֹד (of בָּרוּךְ); and יִמְלֹךְ.

נְקַדֵּשׁ אֶת שִׁמְךָ בָּעוֹלָם, כְּשֵׁם שֶׁמַּקְדִּישִׁים אוֹתוֹ בִּשְׁמֵי — Cong.
מָרוֹם, כַּכָּתוּב עַל יַד נְבִיאֶךָ, וְקָרָא זֶה אֶל זֶה וְאָמַר: then *chazzan*

קָדוֹשׁ קָדוֹשׁ קָדוֹשׁ יהוה צְבָאוֹת, מְלֹא כָל הָאָרֶץ כְּבוֹדוֹ.¹ — All

לְעֻמָּתָם בָּרוּךְ יֹאמֵרוּ: — Chazzan

בָּרוּךְ כְּבוֹד יהוה, מִמְּקוֹמוֹ.² — All

וּבְדִבְרֵי קָדְשְׁךָ כָּתוּב לֵאמֹר: — Chazzan

יִמְלֹךְ יהוה לְעוֹלָם, אֱלֹהַיִךְ צִיּוֹן לְדֹר וָדֹר, הַלְלוּיָהּ.³ — All

— Chazzan only concludes לְדוֹר וָדוֹר נַגִּיד גָּדְלֶךָ וּלְנֵצַח נְצָחִים קְדֻשָּׁתְךָ
נַקְדִּישׁ, וְשִׁבְחֲךָ אֱלֹהֵינוּ מִפִּינוּ לֹא יָמוּשׁ לְעוֹלָם וָעֶד, כִּי אֵל מֶלֶךְ גָּדוֹל
וְקָדוֹשׁ אָתָּה. בָּרוּךְ אַתָּה יהוה, הָאֵל הַקָּדוֹשׁ.

הַמֶּלֶךְ הַקָּדוֹשׁ — From Rosh Hashanah to Yom Kippur substitute

Chazzan continues . . . אַתָּה חוֹנֵן (p. 32).

---

toward the ultimate redemption by the Messiah (*Siach Yitzchak*).

God's Might / גבורות ـ₪

מְחַיֵּה מֵתִים — *The Resuscitator of the dead.* The concept that God restores life is found three times in this section, alluding to the three kinds of resuscitation: man's awakening every morning after deathlike slumber; the rain that has the life-sustaining quality of making vegetation grow; and the literal resuscitation of the dead that will take place in the Messianic age (*Abudraham*).

Kedushah / קדושה ـ₪

Kedushah, Sanctification, expresses the

Bend the knees at "Blessed"; bow at "You"; straighten up at "HASHEM."

O King, Helper, Savior, and Shield. Blessed are You, HASHEM, Shield of Abraham.

GOD'S MIGHT

אַתָּה *You are eternally mighty, my Lord, the Resuscitator of the dead•
are You; abundantly able to save,*

Between Shemini Atzeres and Pesach, add [if forgotten, see Laws §7]:

Who makes the wind blow and makes the rain descend;

*Who sustains the living with kindness, resuscitates the dead with
abundant mercy, supports the fallen, heals the sick, releases the
confined, and maintains His faith to those asleep in the dust. Who is like
You, O Master of mighty deeds, and who is comparable to You, O King
Who causes death and restores life and makes salvation sprout!*

From Rosh Hashanah to Yom Kippur add [if forgotten, do not repeat Shemoneh Esrei]:
Who is like You, Merciful Father, Who recalls His creatures mercifully for life!

*And You are faithful to resuscitate the dead. Blessed are You, HASHEM,
Who resuscitates the dead.*

During the chazzan's repetition at Minchah, Kedushah (below) is recited here.

KEDUSHAH

Stand with feet together and avoid any interruptions.
Rise on toes when saying Holy, holy, holy; Blessed is; and HASHEM shall reign.

Cong. נְקַדֵּשׁ *We shall sanctify Your Name in this world, just as they*
then   *sanctify it in heaven above, as it is written by Your prophet,*
chazzan — *"And one [angel] will call another and say:*

All — *'Holy, holy, holy is HASHEM, Master of Legions, the whole world is
filled with His glory.'* "[1]

Chazzan — *Those facing them say: "Blessed":*

All — *"Blessed is the glory of HASHEM from His place."* [2]

Chazzan — *And in Your holy Writings the following is written:*

All — *"HASHEM shall reign forever — your God, O Zion — from generation
to generation, Halleluyah!"* [3]

Chazzan only concludes: *From generation to generation we shall relate Your
greatness and for infinite eternities we shall proclaim Your holiness. Your praise,
our God, shall not leave our mouth forever and ever, for You, O God, are a great
and holy King. Blessed are You, HASHEM,* °*the holy God.*

From Rosh Hashanah to Yom Kippur substitute: °*the holy King.*

Chazzan continues אַתָּה חוֹנֵן, *You graciously endow . . . (p. 32).*

---

(1) Isaiah 6:3. (2) Ezekiel 3:12. (3) Psalms 146:10.

concept that God is exalted above and separated from the limitations of material existence. When a minyan (quorum of ten) is
present, it becomes the representative of
the nation and echoes the angels who sing

God's praises by proclaiming His holiness
and glory. We do this by reciting Kedushah, a prayer based on that of the angels
themselves, and with feet together, in the
manner of the angels (Ezekiel 1:7).

קדושת השם

אַתָּה קָדוֹשׁ וְשִׁמְךָ קָדוֹשׁ, וּקְדוֹשִׁים בְּכָל יוֹם יְהַלְלוּךָ סֶּלָה. בָּרוּךְ אַתָּה יהוה, °הָאֵל הַקָּדוֹשׁ.

°הַמֶּלֶךְ הַקָּדוֹשׁ – From Rosh Hashanah to Yom Kippur substitute [If forgotten, repeat *Shemoneh Esrei*. See *Laws* §6.]

בינה

אַתָּה חוֹנֵן לְאָדָם דַּעַת, וּמְלַמֵּד לֶאֱנוֹשׁ בִּינָה.

At the conclusion of the Sabbath and of Festivals, add:

אַתָּה חוֹנַנְתָּנוּ לְמַדַּע תּוֹרָתֶךָ, וַתְּלַמְּדֵנוּ לַעֲשׂוֹת חֻקֵּי רְצוֹנֶךָ, וַתַּבְדֵּל יהוה אֱלֹהֵינוּ בֵּין קֹדֶשׁ לְחוֹל, בֵּין אוֹר לְחוֹשֶׁךְ, בֵּין יִשְׂרָאֵל לָעַמִּים, בֵּין יוֹם הַשְּׁבִיעִי לְשֵׁשֶׁת יְמֵי הַמַּעֲשֶׂה. אָבִינוּ מַלְכֵּנוּ הָחֵל עָלֵינוּ הַיָּמִים הַבָּאִים לִקְרָאתֵנוּ לְשָׁלוֹם, חֲשׂוּכִים מִכָּל חֵטְא, וּמְנֻקִּים מִכָּל עָוֹן וּמְדֻבָּקִים בְּיִרְאָתֶךָ. וְ . . .

חָנֵּנוּ מֵאִתְּךָ דֵּעָה בִּינָה וְהַשְׂכֵּל. בָּרוּךְ אַתָּה יהוה, חוֹנֵן הַדָּעַת.

תשובה

הֲשִׁיבֵנוּ אָבִינוּ לְתוֹרָתֶךָ, וְקָרְבֵנוּ מַלְכֵּנוּ לַעֲבוֹדָתֶךָ, וְהַחֲזִירֵנוּ בִּתְשׁוּבָה שְׁלֵמָה לְפָנֶיךָ. בָּרוּךְ אַתָּה יהוה, הָרוֹצֶה בִּתְשׁוּבָה.

סליחה

Strike the left side of the chest with the right fist while reciting the words חָטָאנוּ and פָשָׁעְנוּ.

סְלַח לָנוּ אָבִינוּ כִּי חָטָאנוּ, מְחַל לָנוּ מַלְכֵּנוּ כִּי פָשָׁעְנוּ, כִּי מוֹחֵל וְסוֹלֵחַ אָתָּה. בָּרוּךְ אַתָּה יהוה, חַנּוּן הַמַּרְבֶּה לִסְלוֹחַ.

גאולה

רְאֵה בְעָנְיֵנוּ,* וְרִיבָה רִיבֵנוּ, וּגְאָלֵנוּ מְהֵרָה לְמַעַן שְׁמֶךָ, כִּי גּוֹאֵל חָזָק אָתָּה. בָּרוּךְ אַתָּה יהוה, גּוֹאֵל יִשְׂרָאֵל.

At *Minchah* of a fast day, the *chazzan* recites עֲנֵנוּ at this point. See *Laws* §9.

עֲנֵנוּ יהוה עֲנֵנוּ, בְּיוֹם צוֹם תַּעֲנִיתֵנוּ, כִּי בְצָרָה גְדוֹלָה אֲנָחְנוּ. אַל תֵּפֶן אֶל רִשְׁעֵנוּ, וְאַל תַּסְתֵּר פָּנֶיךָ מִמֶּנּוּ, וְאַל תִּתְעַלַּם מִתְּחִנָּתֵנוּ. הֱיֵה נָא קָרוֹב לְשַׁוְעָתֵנוּ, יְהִי נָא חַסְדְּךָ לְנַחֲמֵנוּ, טֶרֶם נִקְרָא אֵלֶיךָ עֲנֵנוּ, כַּדָּבָר שֶׁנֶּאֱמַר: וְהָיָה טֶרֶם יִקְרָאוּ וַאֲנִי אֶעֱנֶה, עוֹד הֵם מְדַבְּרִים וַאֲנִי אֶשְׁמָע.² כִּי אַתָּה יהוה הָעוֹנֶה בְּעֵת צָרָה, פּוֹדֶה וּמַצִּיל בְּכָל עֵת צָרָה וְצוּקָה. בָּרוּךְ אַתָּה יהוה, הָעוֹנֶה בְּעֵת צָרָה.

HOLINESS OF GOD'S NAME

אַתָּה *You are holy and Your Name is holy, and holy ones praise You every day, forever. Blessed are You, HASHEM, °the holy God.*

From Rosh Hashanah to Yom Kippur substitute: °*the holy King.*
[If forgotten, repeat Shemoneh Esrei. See Laws §6.]

INSIGHT

אַתָּה *You graciously endow man with wisdom and teach insight to a frail mortal.*

At the conclusion of the Sabbath and of Festivals, add:

אַתָּה *You have graced us with intelligence to study Your Torah and You have taught us to perform the decrees You have willed. HASHEM, our God, You have distinguished between the sacred and the secular, between light and darkness, between Israel and the peoples, between the seventh day and the six days of labor. Our Father, our King, begin for us the days approaching us for peace, free from all sin, cleansed from all iniquity and attached to fear of You. And . . .*

Endow us graciously from Yourself with wisdom, insight, and discernment. Blessed are You, HASHEM, gracious Giver of wisdom.

REPENTANCE

הֲשִׁיבֵנוּ *Bring us back, our Father, to Your Torah, and bring us near, our King, to Your service, and influence us to return in perfect repentance before You. Blessed are You, HASHEM, Who desires repentance.*

FORGIVENESS

Strike the left side of the chest with the right fist while reciting the words "erred" and "sinned."

סְלַח *Forgive us, our Father, for we have erred; pardon us, our King, for we have willfully sinned; for You pardon and forgive. Blessed are You, HASHEM, the gracious One Who pardons abundantly.*

REDEMPTION

רְאֵה *Behold our affliction,* • *take up our grievance, and redeem us*[1] *speedily for Your Name's sake, for You are a powerful Redeemer. Blessed are You, HASHEM, Redeemer of Israel.*

At Minchah of a fast day, the chazzan recites "Answer us" at this point. See Laws §9.

עֲנֵנוּ *Answer us, HASHEM, answer us, on this day of our fast, for we are in great distress. Do not pay attention to our wickedness; do not hide Your Face from us, and do not ignore our supplication. Please be near to our outcry; please let Your kindness comfort us — before we call to You answer us, as it is said: "And it will be that before they call, I will answer; while they yet speak, I will hear."*[2] *For You, HASHEM, are the One Who responds in time of distress, Who redeems and rescues in every time of distress and woe. Blessed are You, HASHEM, Who responds in time of distress.*

(1) Cf. Psalms 119:153-154. (2) Isaiah 65:24.

סְלִיחָה / Forgiveness

סְלִיחָה, *forgiveness,* means not even harboring resentment or ill-will, but מְחִילָה, *pardon,* means giving up the right to punish for a wrong (*Abudraham*).

גְּאוּלָה / Redemption

רְאֵה בְעָנְיֵנוּ — *Behold our affliction.* Though Israel suffers because of its own sins, our enemies have no right to claim that they are merely doing God's work, because they

רפואה

רְ**פָאֵנוּ** יהוה וְנֵרָפֵא,* הוֹשִׁיעֵנוּ וְנִוָּשֵׁעָה, כִּי תְהִלָּתֵנוּ אָתָּה,[1]
וְהַעֲלֵה רְפוּאָה שְׁלֵמָה לְכָל מַכּוֹתֵינוּ, °°כִּי אֵל מֶלֶךְ
רוֹפֵא נֶאֱמָן וְרַחֲמָן אָתָּה. בָּרוּךְ אַתָּה יהוה, רוֹפֵא חוֹלֵי עַמּוֹ
יִשְׂרָאֵל.

ברכת השנים

In the following blessing, וְתֵן בְּרָכָה is recited from Chol HaMoed Pesach through Minchah of December 4th (or 5th in the year before a civil leap year); וְתֵן טַל וּמָטָר לִבְרָכָה is recited from Maariv of December 4th (or 5th) until Pesach. [If the wrong phrase was recited, see Laws §8.]

בָּרֵךְ עָלֵינוּ יהוה אֱלֹהֵינוּ אֶת הַשָּׁנָה הַזֹּאת וְאֶת כָּל מִינֵי
תְבוּאָתָהּ לְטוֹבָה,

[וְתֵן בְּרָכָה / וְתֵן טַל וּמָטָר לִבְרָכָה]

עַל פְּנֵי הָאֲדָמָה, וְשַׂבְּעֵנוּ מִטּוּבֶךָ, וּבָרֵךְ שְׁנָתֵנוּ כַּשָּׁנִים
הַטּוֹבוֹת. בָּרוּךְ אַתָּה יהוה, מְבָרֵךְ הַשָּׁנִים.

קיבוץ גליות

תְּקַע בְּשׁוֹפָר גָּדוֹל לְחֵרוּתֵנוּ, וְשָׂא נֵס לְקַבֵּץ גָּלֻיּוֹתֵינוּ,
וְקַבְּצֵנוּ יַחַד מֵאַרְבַּע כַּנְפוֹת הָאָרֶץ.[2] בָּרוּךְ אַתָּה
יהוה, מְקַבֵּץ נִדְחֵי עַמּוֹ יִשְׂרָאֵל.

דין

הָשִׁיבָה שׁוֹפְטֵינוּ כְּבָרִאשׁוֹנָה, וְיוֹעֲצֵינוּ כְּבַתְּחִלָּה,[3] וְהָסֵר
מִמֶּנּוּ יָגוֹן וַאֲנָחָה, וּמְלוֹךְ עָלֵינוּ אַתָּה יהוה לְבַדְּךָ
בְּחֶסֶד וּבְרַחֲמִים, וְצַדְּקֵנוּ בַּמִּשְׁפָּט. בָּרוּךְ אַתָּה יהוה, °מֶלֶךְ
אוֹהֵב צְדָקָה וּמִשְׁפָּט.

°הַמֶּלֶךְ הַמִּשְׁפָּט. — From Rosh Hashanah to Yom Kippur substitute
[If forgotten, do not repeat Shemoneh Esrei. See Laws §6.]

°°At this point one may interject a prayer for one who is ill:
יְהִי רָצוֹן מִלְּפָנֶיךָ, יהוה אֱלֹהַי וֵאלֹהֵי אֲבוֹתַי,
שֶׁתִּשְׁלַח מְהֵרָה רְפוּאָה שְׁלֵמָה מִן הַשָּׁמַיִם, רְפוּאַת הַנֶּפֶשׁ וּרְפוּאַת הַגּוּף
לַחוֹלֶה — for a male (patient's name) בֶּן (mother's name) בְּתוֹךְ שְׁאָר חוֹלֵי יִשְׂרָאֵל.
לַחוֹלָה — for a female (patient's name) בַּת (mother's name) בְּתוֹךְ שְׁאָר חוֹלֵי יִשְׂרָאֵל.
Continue— כִּי אֵל ...

cause Israel to suffer much more than necessary (Etz Yosef).

רְפָאֵנוּ ה׳ וְנֵרָפֵא — Heal us, HASHEM — then we will be healed. Sometimes human beings

HEALTH AND HEALING

רְפָאֵנוּ Heal us, HASHEM — then we will be healed; • save us — then we will be saved, for You are our praise. [1] Bring complete recovery for all our ailments, ° ° for You are God, King, the faithful and compassionate Healer. Blessed are You, HASHEM, Who heals the sick of His people Israel.

YEAR OF PROSPERITY

In the following blessing, "give a blessing" is recited from Chol HaMoed Pesach through Minchah of December 4th (or 5th in the year before a civil leap year); "give dew and rain" is recited from Maariv of December 4th (or 5th) until Pesach. [If the wrong phrase was recited, see Laws §8.]

בָּרֵךְ Bless on our behalf — O HASHEM, our God — this year and all its kinds of crops for the best, and

[give a blessing / give dew and rain for a blessing]

on the face of the earth, and satisfy us from Your bounty, and bless our year like the best years. Blessed are You, HASHEM, Who blesses the years.

INGATHERING OF EXILES

תְּקַע Sound the great shofar for our freedom, raise the banner to gather our exiles and gather us together from the four corners of the earth. [2] Blessed are You, HASHEM, Who gathers in the dispersed of His people Israel.

RESTORATION OF JUSTICE

הָשִׁיבָה Restore our judges as in earliest times and our counselors as at first; [3] remove from us sorrow and groan; and reign over us — You, HASHEM, alone — with kindness and compassion, and justify us through judgment. Blessed are You, HASHEM, °the King Who loves righteousness and judgment.

From Rosh Hashanah to Yom Kippur substitute: °the King of Judgment.
[If forgotten, do not repeat Shemoneh Esrei. See Laws §6.]

°°At this point one may interject a prayer for one who is ill:
May it be Your will, HASHEM, my God, and the God of my forefathers, that You quickly send a complete recovery from heaven, spiritual healing and physical healing to the patient (name) son/daughter of (mother's name) among the other patients of Israel.
Continue: for You are God . . .

(1) Cf. Jeremiah 17:14. (2) Cf. Isaiah 11:12. (3) Cf. 1:26.

or angels are God's agents to heal illness, but in that case, the cure may be only partial or temporary. [Or the pain or other symptoms may be relieved, while the illness itself remains uncured (Siach Yitzchak). But if God Himself undertakes to cure the patient, we are confident that it will not be a temporary nor a partial measure: *then we will be healed* (Etz Yosef from Zohar).]

בִּרְכַּת הַשָּׁנִים / Year of Prosperity

We request a blessing on our general business activities and then go on to ask for

abundant crops. Even in bad times some people prosper, and even in good times some farms and businesses fail. We ask not only for general prosperity, but that we be enabled to share in it (R' S.R. Hirsch).

קִבּוּץ גָּלִיּוֹת / Ingathering of Exiles

This blessing differs from the earlier one of גְּאֻלָה, Redemption, in three ways: (a) The earlier blessing refers to God's *daily* help in all sorts of crises and suffering, while this one refers to the *future* Redemption from exile; (b) the earlier blessing refers only to

ברכת המינים

וְלַמַּלְשִׁינִים אַל תְּהִי תִקְוָה, וְכָל הָרִשְׁעָה כְּרֶגַע תֹּאבֵד, וְכָל אֹיְבֶיךָ מְהֵרָה יִכָּרֵתוּ, וְהַזֵּדִים מְהֵרָה תְעַקֵּר וּתְשַׁבֵּר וּתְמַגֵּר וְתַכְנִיעַ בִּמְהֵרָה בְיָמֵינוּ. בָּרוּךְ אַתָּה יהוה, שׁוֹבֵר אֹיְבִים וּמַכְנִיעַ זֵדִים.

צדיקים

עַל הַצַּדִּיקִים וְעַל הַחֲסִידִים, וְעַל זִקְנֵי עַמְּךָ בֵּית יִשְׂרָאֵל, וְעַל פְּלֵיטַת סוֹפְרֵיהֶם, וְעַל גֵּרֵי הַצֶּדֶק עָלֵינוּ, יֶהֱמוּ רַחֲמֶיךָ יהוה אֱלֹהֵינוּ, וְתֵן שָׂכָר טוֹב לְכָל הַבּוֹטְחִים בְּשִׁמְךָ בֶּאֱמֶת, וְשִׂים חֶלְקֵנוּ עִמָּהֶם לְעוֹלָם, וְלֹא נֵבוֹשׁ כִּי בְךָ בָּטָחְנוּ. בָּרוּךְ אַתָּה יהוה, מִשְׁעָן וּמִבְטָח לַצַּדִּיקִים.

בנין ירושלים

וְלִירוּשָׁלַיִם עִירְךָ בְּרַחֲמִים תָּשׁוּב, וְתִשְׁכּוֹן בְּתוֹכָהּ כַּאֲשֶׁר דִּבַּרְתָּ, וּבְנֵה אוֹתָהּ בְּקָרוֹב בְּיָמֵינוּ בִּנְיַן עוֹלָם, וְכִסֵּא דָוִד מְהֵרָה לְתוֹכָהּ תָּכִין. °°בָּרוּךְ אַתָּה יהוה, בּוֹנֵה יְרוּשָׁלָיִם.

°°During *Minchah* of Tishah B'Av substitute the following conclusion.
[If forgotten, do not repeat *Shemoneh Esrei*.]

נַחֵם יהוה אֱלֹהֵינוּ אֶת אֲבֵלֵי צִיּוֹן, וְאֶת אֲבֵלֵי יְרוּשָׁלַיִם, וְאֶת הָעִיר הָאֲבֵלָה וְהַחֲרֵבָה וְהַבְּזוּיָה וְהַשּׁוֹמֵמָה. הָאֲבֵלָה מִבְּלִי בָנֶיהָ, וְהַחֲרֵבָה מִמְּעוֹנוֹתֶיהָ, וְהַבְּזוּיָה מִכְּבוֹדָהּ, וְהַשּׁוֹמֵמָה מֵאֵין יוֹשֵׁב. וְהִיא יוֹשֶׁבֶת וְרֹאשָׁהּ חָפוּי כְּאִשָּׁה עֲקָרָה שֶׁלֹּא יָלָדָה. וַיְבַלְּעוּהָ לִגְיוֹנוֹת, וַיִּירָשׁוּהָ עוֹבְדֵי זָרִים, וַיַּטִּילוּ אֶת עַמְּךָ יִשְׂרָאֵל לֶחָרֶב, וַיַּהַרְגוּ בְזָדוֹן חֲסִידֵי עֶלְיוֹן. עַל כֵּן צִיּוֹן בְּמַר תִּבְכֶּה, וִירוּשָׁלַיִם תִּתֵּן קוֹלָהּ. לִבִּי לִבִּי עַל חַלְלֵיהֶם, מֵעַי מֵעַי עַל חַלְלֵיהֶם, כִּי אַתָּה יהוה בָּאֵשׁ הִצַּתָּהּ, וּבָאֵשׁ אַתָּה עָתִיד לִבְנוֹתָהּ, כָּאָמוּר: וַאֲנִי אֶהְיֶה לָּהּ, נְאֻם יהוה, חוֹמַת אֵשׁ סָבִיב, וּלְכָבוֹד אֶהְיֶה בְתוֹכָהּ.[1] בָּרוּךְ אַתָּה יהוה, מְנַחֵם צִיּוֹן וּבוֹנֵה יְרוּשָׁלָיִם.

---

physical salvation, while this one is a plea for *spiritual* deliverance; (c) this one specifies not only freedom from oppression, but the ingathering of all exiles to *Eretz Yisrael*.

בְּרְכַּת הַמִּינִים / Against Heretics
Chronologically, this is the *nineteenth* blessing of *Shemoneh Esrei*; it was insti-

tuted in Yavneh, during the tenure of Rabban Gamliel II as *Nassi* of Israel, some time after the destruction of the Second Temple. The blessing was composed in response to the threats of such heretical Jewish sects as the Sadducees, Boethusians, Essenes, and the early Christians, who tried to lead Jews astray through

AGAINST HERETICS

וְלַמַּלְשִׁינִים *And for slanderers let there be no hope; and may all wickedness perish in an instant; and may all Your enemies be cut down speedily. May You speedily uproot, smash, cast down, and humble the wanton sinners — speedily in our days. Blessed are You, Hashem, Who breaks enemies and humbles wanton sinners.*

THE RIGHTEOUS

עַל הַצַּדִּיקִים *On the righteous, on the devout, on the elders of Your people the Family of Israel, on the remnant of their scholars, on the righteous converts and on ourselves — may Your compassion be aroused, Hashem, our God, and give goodly reward to all who sincerely believe in Your Name. Put our lot with them forever, and we will not feel ashamed, for we trust in You. Blessed are You, Hashem, Mainstay and Assurance of the righteous.*

REBUILDING JERUSALEM

וְלִירוּשָׁלַיִם *And to Jerusalem, Your city, may You return in compassion, and may You rest within it, as You have spoken. May You rebuild it soon in our days as an eternal structure, and may You speedily establish the throne of David within it.* °°*Blessed are You, Hashem, the Builder of Jerusalem.*

°°*During Minchah of Tishah B'Av substitute the following conclusion.*
[If forgotten, do not repeat Shemoneh Esrei.]

נַחֵם *O Hashem, our God, console the mourners of Zion and the mourners of Jerusalem, and the city that is mournful, ruined, scorned, and desolate: mournful without her children, ruined without her abodes, scorned without her glory, and desolate without inhabitant. She sits with covered head like a barren woman who never gave birth. Legions have devoured her, and idolaters have conquered her; they have cast Your people Israel to the sword and wantonly murdered the devout servants of the Supreme One. Therefore, Zion weeps bitterly and Jerusalem raises her voice. My heart, my heart — [it aches] for their slain! My innards, my innards — [they ache] for their slain! For You Hashem, with fire You consumed her and with fire You will rebuild her, as it is said: "I will be for her, the words of Hashem, a wall of fire around and I will be glorious in her midst."[1] Blessed are You, Hashem, Who consoles Zion and rebuilds Jerusalem.*

---

(1) Zechariah 2:9.

example and persuasion, and who used their political power to oppress observant Jews and to slander them to the anti-Semitic Roman government.

Despite the disappearance from within Israel of the particular sects against whom it was directed, this blessing is always relevant, because there are still nonbelievers and heretics who endanger the spiritual continuity of Israel (Yaaros D'vash).

צַדִּיקִים / **The Righteous**
These four categories of people — righteous, devout, elders, scholars — are the leaders of the nation. Because the nation needs them, the Sages instituted a special prayer for their welfare (R' Yehudah ben Yakar).

בִּנְיַן יְרוּשָׁלַיִם / **Rebuilding Jerusalem**
After having sought God's blessing on Israel's leaders and righteous people, we

מלכות בית דוד

אֶת צֶמַח דָּוִד עַבְדְּךָ מְהֵרָה תַצְמִיחַ, וְקַרְנוֹ תָּרוּם בִּישׁוּעָתֶךָ, כִּי לִישׁוּעָתְךָ קִוִּינוּ כָּל הַיּוֹם. בָּרוּךְ אַתָּה יהוה, מַצְמִיחַ קֶרֶן יְשׁוּעָה.

קבלת תפלה

שְׁמַע קוֹלֵנוּ יהוה אֱלֹהֵינוּ, חוּס וְרַחֵם עָלֵינוּ, וְקַבֵּל בְּרַחֲמִים וּבְרָצוֹן אֶת תְּפִלָּתֵנוּ, כִּי אֵל שׁוֹמֵעַ תְּפִלּוֹת וְתַחֲנוּנִים אָתָּה. וּמִלְּפָנֶיךָ מַלְכֵּנוּ, רֵיקָם אַל תְּשִׁיבֵנוּ, °°

°°On a fast day, one who is fasting adds the following.
[If forgotten, do not repeat *Shemoneh Esrei*. See Laws §9.]

עֲנֵנוּ יהוה עֲנֵנוּ, בְּיוֹם צוֹם תַּעֲנִיתֵנוּ, כִּי בְצָרָה גְדוֹלָה אֲנָחְנוּ. אַל תֵּפֶן אֶל רִשְׁעֵנוּ, וְאַל תַּסְתֵּר פָּנֶיךָ מִמֶּנּוּ, וְאַל תִּתְעַלַּם מִתְּחִנָּתֵנוּ. הֱיֵה נָא קָרוֹב לְשַׁוְעָתֵנוּ, יְהִי נָא חַסְדְּךָ לְנַחֲמֵנוּ, טֶרֶם נִקְרָא אֵלֶיךָ עֲנֵנוּ, כַּדָּבָר שֶׁנֶּאֱמַר: וְהָיָה טֶרֶם יִקְרָאוּ וַאֲנִי אֶעֱנֶה, עוֹד הֵם מְדַבְּרִים וַאֲנִי אֶשְׁמָע. כִּי אַתָּה יהוה הָעוֹנֶה בְּעֵת צָרָה, פּוֹדֶה וּמַצִּיל בְּכָל עֵת צָרָה וְצוּקָה.
(p. 40) . . . כִּי אַתָּה שׁוֹמֵעַ תְּפִלַּת — Continue

°°During the silent *Shemoneh Esrei* one may insert
either or both of these personal prayers.

For forgiveness:	For livelihood:
אָנָּא יהוה, חָטָאתִי עָוִיתִי וּפָשַׁעְתִּי לְפָנֶיךָ, מִיּוֹם הֱיוֹתִי עַל הָאֲדָמָה עַד הַיּוֹם הַזֶּה (וּבִפְרָט בַּחֵטְא ....). אָנָּא יהוה, עֲשֵׂה לְמַעַן שִׁמְךָ הַגָּדוֹל, וּתְכַפֶּר לִי עַל עֲוֹנַי וַחֲטָאַי וּפְשָׁעַי שֶׁחָטָאתִי וְשֶׁעָוִיתִי וְשֶׁפָּשַׁעְתִּי לְפָנֶיךָ, מֵעוֹרְרִי עַד הַיּוֹם הַזֶּה. וּתְמַלֵּא כָּל הַשְּׁמוֹת שֶׁפָּגַמְתִּי בְּשִׁמְךָ הַגָּדוֹל.	**אַתָּה** הוּא יהוה הָאֱלֹהִים, הַזָּן וּמְפַרְנֵס וּמְכַלְכֵּל מִקַּרְנֵי רְאֵמִים עַד בֵּיצֵי כִנִּים. הַטְרִיפֵנִי לֶחֶם חֻקִּי, וְהַמְצֵא לִי וּלְכָל בְּנֵי בֵיתִי מְזוֹנוֹתַי קֹדֶם שֶׁאֶצְטָרֵךְ לָהֶם, בְּנַחַת וְלֹא בְצַעַר, בְּהֶתֵּר וְלֹא בְאִסּוּר, בְּכָבוֹד וְלֹא בְבִזָּיוֹן, לְחַיִּים וּלְשָׁלוֹם, מִשֶּׁפַע בְּרָכָה וְהַצְלָחָה, וּמִשֶּׁפַע בְּרָכָה עֶלְיוֹנָה, כְּדֵי שֶׁאוּכַל לַעֲשׂוֹת רְצוֹנֶךָ וְלַעֲסוֹק בְּתוֹרָתֶךָ וּלְקַיֵּם מִצְוֹתֶיךָ. וְאַל תַּצְרִיכֵנִי לִידֵי מַתְּנַת בָּשָׂר וָדָם. וִיקֻיַּם בִּי מִקְרָא שֶׁכָּתוּב: פּוֹתֵחַ אֶת יָדֶךָ, וּמַשְׂבִּיעַ לְכָל חַי רָצוֹן.[2] וְכָתוּב: הַשְׁלֵךְ עַל יהוה יְהָבְךָ, וְהוּא יְכַלְכְּלֶךָ.[3] (p. 40) . . . כִּי אַתָּה שׁוֹמֵעַ תְּפִלַּת — Continue

---

מַלְכוּת בֵּית דָּוִד / Davidic Reign — In this blessing we are taught that the ultimate salvation of the Jewish people is possible only through the Davidic Messiah.

seek His blessing for the Holy City. No blessing is complete until the seat of holiness, Jerusalem, is rebuilt in all its grandeur (*Iyun Tefillah*).

DAVIDIC REIGN

אֶת צֶמַח *The offspring of Your servant David may You speedily cause to flourish, and enhance his pride through Your salvation, for we hope for Your salvation all day long. Blessed are You, HASHEM, Who causes the pride of salvation to flourish.*

ACCEPTANCE OF PRAYER

שְׁמַע קוֹלֵנוּ *Hear our voice, HASHEM, our God, pity and be compassionate to us, and accept — with compassion and favor — our prayer, for God Who hears prayers and supplications are You. From before Yourself, our King, turn us not away empty-handed,* °°

°°On a fast day, one who is fasting adds the following.
[If forgotten, do not repeat *Shemoneh Esrei*. See Laws §9.]

עֲנֵנוּ *Answer us, HASHEM, answer us, on this day of our fast, for we are in great distress. Do not pay attention to our wickedness; do not hide Your Face from us, and do not ignore our supplication. Please be near to our outcry; please let Your kindness comfort us — before we call to You answer us, as it is said: "And it will be that before they call, I will answer; while they yet speak; I will hear."[1] For You, HASHEM, are the One Who responds in time of distress, Who redeems and rescues in every time of distress and woe.*

Continue: *for You hear the prayer . . .* (p. 40).

°°During the silent *Shemoneh Esrei* one may insert
either or both of these personal prayers.

For forgiveness:

אָנָּא *Please, O HASHEM, I have erred, been iniquitous, and willfully sinned before You, from the day I have existed on earth until this very day (and especially with the sin of . . .). Please, HASHEM, act for the sake of Your Great Name and grant me atonement for my iniquities, my errors, and my willful sins through which I have erred, been iniquitous, and willfully sinned before You, from my youth until this day. And make whole all the Names that I have blemished in Your Great Name.*

For livelihood:

אַתָּה *It is You, HASHEM, the God Who nourishes, sustains, and supports, from the horns of re'eimim to the eggs of lice. Provide me with my allotment of bread; and bring forth for me and all members of my household, my food, before I have need for it; in contentment but not in pain, in a permissible but not a forbidden manner, in honor but not in disgrace, for life and for peace; from the flow of blessing and success and from the flow of the Heavenly spring, so that I be enabled to do Your will and engage in Your Torah and fulfill Your commandments. Make me not needful of people's largesse; and may there be fulfilled in me the verse that states, "You open Your hand and satisfy the desire of every living thing,"[2] and that states, "Cast your burden upon HASHEM and He will support you."[3]*

Continue: *for You hear the prayer . . .* (p. 40).

---

(1) Isaiah 65:24. (2) Psalms 145:16. (3) 55:23.

⋖ קַבָּלַת תְּפִלָּה / Acceptance of Prayer

[In the middle section of *Shemoneh Esrei* we have asked God to grant us our specific needs. We now close the section with a general plea that He take note of all our needs and grant our requests.]

⋖ Personal Prayers

In this blessing, one may add specific, personal requests for any private or general need in any language or style, for the feelings and devotion of the supplicant are more important than the form of the prayer.

כִּי אַתָּה שׁוֹמֵעַ תְּפִלַּת עַמְּךָ יִשְׂרָאֵל בְּרַחֲמִים. בָּרוּךְ אַתָּה יהוה, שׁוֹמֵעַ תְּפִלָּה.

עבודה

רְצֵה יהוה אֱלֹהֵינוּ בְּעַמְּךָ יִשְׂרָאֵל וּבִתְפִלָּתָם, וְהָשֵׁב אֶת הָעֲבוֹדָה לִדְבִיר בֵּיתֶךָ. וְאִשֵּׁי יִשְׂרָאֵל וּתְפִלָּתָם בְּאַהֲבָה תְקַבֵּל בְּרָצוֹן, וּתְהִי לְרָצוֹן תָּמִיד עֲבוֹדַת יִשְׂרָאֵל עַמֶּךָ.

On Rosh Chodesh and Chol HaMoed add the following:
(During the *chazzan's* repetition, the congregation responds אָמֵן as indicated.)

אֱלֹהֵינוּ וֵאלֹהֵי אֲבוֹתֵינוּ, יַעֲלֶה, וְיָבֹא, וְיַגִּיעַ, וְיֵרָאֶה, וְיֵרָצֶה, וְיִשָּׁמַע, וְיִפָּקֵד, וְיִזָּכֵר זִכְרוֹנֵנוּ וּפִקְדוֹנֵנוּ, וְזִכְרוֹן אֲבוֹתֵינוּ, וְזִכְרוֹן מָשִׁיחַ בֶּן דָּוִד עַבְדֶּךָ, וְזִכְרוֹן יְרוּשָׁלַיִם עִיר קָדְשֶׁךָ, וְזִכְרוֹן כָּל עַמְּךָ בֵּית יִשְׂרָאֵל לְפָנֶיךָ, לִפְלֵיטָה לְטוֹבָה לְחֵן וּלְחֶסֶד וּלְרַחֲמִים, לְחַיִּים וּלְשָׁלוֹם, בְּיוֹם

on Succos: חַג הַסֻּכּוֹת on Pesach: חַג הַמַּצּוֹת on Rosh Chodesh: רֹאשׁ הַחֹדֶשׁ

הַזֶּה. זָכְרֵנוּ יהוה אֱלֹהֵינוּ בּוֹ לְטוֹבָה (.Cong – אָמֵן), וּפָקְדֵנוּ בוֹ לִבְרָכָה (.Cong – אָמֵן), וְהוֹשִׁיעֵנוּ בוֹ לְחַיִּים (.Cong – אָמֵן). וּבִדְבַר יְשׁוּעָה וְרַחֲמִים, חוּס וְחָנֵּנוּ וְרַחֵם עָלֵינוּ וְהוֹשִׁיעֵנוּ, כִּי אֵלֶיךָ עֵינֵינוּ, כִּי אֵל מֶלֶךְ חַנּוּן וְרַחוּם אָתָּה.[1]

[If forgotten, repeat *Shemoneh Esrei*. See Laws §11.]

וְתֶחֱזֶינָה עֵינֵינוּ בְּשׁוּבְךָ לְצִיּוֹן בְּרַחֲמִים. בָּרוּךְ אַתָּה יהוה, הַמַּחֲזִיר שְׁכִינָתוֹ לְצִיּוֹן.

הודאה

Bow at מוֹדִים; straighten up at ה'. In his repetition the *chazzan* should recite the entire מוֹדִים aloud, while the congregation recites מוֹדִים דְּרַבָּנָן softly.

מוֹדִים אֲנַחְנוּ לָךְ, שָׁאַתָּה הוּא יהוה אֱלֹהֵינוּ וֵאלֹהֵי אֲבוֹתֵינוּ לְעוֹלָם וָעֶד. צוּר חַיֵּינוּ, מָגֵן יִשְׁעֵנוּ אַתָּה הוּא לְדוֹר וָדוֹר. נוֹדֶה לְּךָ* וּנְסַפֵּר

מוֹדִים דְּרַבָּנָן

מוֹדִים אֲנַחְנוּ לָךְ, שָׁאַתָּה הוּא יהוה אֱלֹהֵינוּ וֵאלֹהֵי אֲבוֹתֵינוּ, אֱלֹהֵי כָל בָּשָׂר, יוֹצְרֵנוּ, יוֹצֵר בְּרֵאשִׁית. בְּרָכוֹת וְהוֹדָאוֹת לְשִׁמְךָ הַגָּדוֹל וְהַקָּדוֹשׁ, עַל שֶׁהֶחֱיִיתָנוּ וְקִיַּמְתָּנוּ. כֵּן תְּחַיֵּנוּ וּתְקַיְּמֵנוּ, וְתֶאֱסוֹף גָּלֻיּוֹתֵינוּ לְחַצְרוֹת קָדְשֶׁךָ, לִשְׁמוֹר חֻקֶּיךָ וְלַעֲשׂוֹת רְצוֹנֶךָ, וּלְעָבְדְּךָ בְּלֵבָב שָׁלֵם, עַל שֶׁאֲנַחְנוּ מוֹדִים לָךְ. בָּרוּךְ אֵל הַהוֹדָאוֹת.

עֲבוֹדָה / Temple Service
This begins the final section of *Shemoneh Esrei*. Like a servant who is grateful for having had the opportunity to express himself before his master, we thank God for hearing us out.

*for You hear the prayer of Your people Israel with compassion. Blessed are
You, HASHEM, Who hears prayer.*

TEMPLE SERVICE

רְצֵה **Be favorable,** HASHEM, our God, toward Your people Israel and their
prayer and restore the service to the Holy of Holies of Your Temple.
The fire-offerings of Israel and their prayer accept with love and favor, and
may the service of Your people Israel always be favorable to You.

On Rosh Chodesh and Chol HaMoed add the following:
(During the chazzan's repetition, the congregation responds Amen as indicated.)

אֱלֹהֵינוּ **Our God and God of our forefathers,** may there rise, come, reach, be
noted, be favored, be heard, be considered, and be remembered — the
remembrance and consideration of ourselves; the remembrance of our forefathers; the remembrance of Messiah, son of David, Your servant; the remembrance
of Jerusalem, the City of Your Holiness; and the remembrance of Your entire people
the Family of Israel — before You for deliverance, for goodness, for grace, for
kindness, and for compassion, for life, and for peace on this day of

| on Rosh Chodesh: | on Pesach: | on Succos: |
| Rosh Chodesh. | the Festival of Matzos. | the Succos Festival. |

Remember us on it, HASHEM, our God, for goodness (Cong.—Amen); consider us
on it for blessing (Cong.—Amen); and help us on it for life (Cong.—Amen). In the
matter of salvation and compassion, pity, be gracious and compassionate with us
and help us, for our eyes are turned to You, because You are God, the gracious and
compassionate King.[1]   [If forgotten, repeat Shemoneh Esrei. See Laws §11.]

וְתֶחֱזֶינָה **May our eyes behold** Your return to Zion in compassion.
Blessed are You, HASHEM, Who restores His Presence to Zion.

THANKSGIVING [MODIM]

Bow at "We gratefully thank You"; straighten up at "HASHEM." In his repetition the chazzan
recites the entire Modim aloud, while the congregation recites Modim of the Rabbis softly.

מוֹדִים **We gratefully
thank You,** for it
is You Who are HASHEM,
our God and the God of
our forefathers for all eternity; Rock of our lives,
Shield of our salvation
are You from generation
to generation. We shall
thank You• and relate

MODIM OF THE RABBIS

מוֹדִים **We gratefully thank You,** for it is You Who
are HASHEM, our God and the God of our
forefathers, the God of all flesh, our Molder, the
Molder of the universe. Blessings and thanks are due
Your great and holy Name for You have given us life
and sustained us. So may You continue to give us
life and sustain us and gather our exiles to the
Courtyards of Your Sanctuary, to observe Your decrees, to do Your will and to serve You wholeheartedly. [We thank You] for inspiring us to thank You.
Blessed is the God of thanksgivings.

---

(1) Cf. Nehemiah 9:31.

הוֹדָאָה ❧ / Thanksgiving [Modim]
נוֹדֶה לְךָ — We shall thank You. Having begun
the blessing by describing God's greatness

and our relationship to Him, we now specify
what we thank Him for.

תְּהִלָּתֶךָ[1] עַל חַיֵּינוּ הַמְּסוּרִים בְּיָדֶךָ, וְעַל נִשְׁמוֹתֵינוּ הַפְּקוּדוֹת
לָךְ, וְעַל נִסֶּיךָ שֶׁבְּכָל יוֹם עִמָּנוּ, וְעַל נִפְלְאוֹתֶיךָ* וְטוֹבוֹתֶיךָ
שֶׁבְּכָל עֵת, עֶרֶב וָבֹקֶר וְצָהֳרָיִם. הַטּוֹב כִּי לֹא כָלוּ רַחֲמֶיךָ,
וְהַמְרַחֵם כִּי לֹא תַמּוּ חֲסָדֶיךָ,[2] מֵעוֹלָם קִוִּינוּ לָךְ.

On Chanukah and Purim add the following:

(וְ)עַל הַנִּסִּים, וְעַל הַפֻּרְקָן, וְעַל הַגְּבוּרוֹת, וְעַל הַתְּשׁוּעוֹת, וְעַל
הַמִּלְחָמוֹת, שֶׁעָשִׂיתָ לַאֲבוֹתֵינוּ בַּיָּמִים הָהֵם בַּזְּמַן הַזֶּה.

On Purim:	On Chanukah:
בִּימֵי מָרְדְּכַי וְאֶסְתֵּר בְּשׁוּשַׁן הַבִּירָה, כְּשֶׁעָמַד עֲלֵיהֶם הָמָן הָרָשָׁע, בִּקֵּשׁ לְהַשְׁמִיד לַהֲרֹג וּלְאַבֵּד אֶת כָּל הַיְּהוּדִים, מִנַּעַר וְעַד זָקֵן, טַף וְנָשִׁים בְּיוֹם אֶחָד, בִּשְׁלוֹשָׁה עָשָׂר לְחֹדֶשׁ שְׁנֵים עָשָׂר, הוּא חֹדֶשׁ אֲדָר, וּשְׁלָלָם לָבוֹז.[5] וְאַתָּה בְּרַחֲמֶיךָ הָרַבִּים הֵפַרְתָּ אֶת עֲצָתוֹ, וְקִלְקַלְתָּ אֶת מַחֲשַׁבְתּוֹ, וַהֲשֵׁבוֹתָ לּוֹ גְּמוּלוֹ בְּרֹאשׁוֹ, וְתָלוּ אוֹתוֹ וְאֶת בָּנָיו עַל הָעֵץ.	**בִּימֵי** מַתִּתְיָהוּ בֶּן יוֹחָנָן כֹּהֵן גָּדוֹל חַשְׁמוֹנַאי וּבָנָיו, כְּשֶׁעָמְדָה מַלְכוּת יָוָן הָרְשָׁעָה עַל עַמְּךָ יִשְׂרָאֵל, לְהַשְׁכִּיחָם תּוֹרָתֶךָ,* וּלְהַעֲבִירָם מֵחֻקֵּי רְצוֹנֶךָ. וְאַתָּה בְּרַחֲמֶיךָ הָרַבִּים, עָמַדְתָּ לָהֶם בְּעֵת צָרָתָם, רַבְתָּ אֶת רִיבָם, דַּנְתָּ אֶת דִּינָם, נָקַמְתָּ אֶת נִקְמָתָם.[3] מָסַרְתָּ גִבּוֹרִים בְּיַד חַלָּשִׁים, וְרַבִּים בְּיַד מְעַטִּים, וּטְמֵאִים בְּיַד טְהוֹרִים, וּרְשָׁעִים בְּיַד צַדִּיקִים, וְזֵדִים בְּיַד עוֹסְקֵי תוֹרָתֶךָ. וּלְךָ עָשִׂיתָ שֵׁם גָּדוֹל וְקָדוֹשׁ בְּעוֹלָמֶךָ, וּלְעַמְּךָ יִשְׂרָאֵל עָשִׂיתָ תְּשׁוּעָה גְדוֹלָה וּפֻרְקָן כְּהַיּוֹם הַזֶּה. וְאַחַר כֵּן בָּאוּ בָנֶיךָ לִדְבִיר בֵּיתֶךָ, וּפִנּוּ אֶת הֵיכָלֶךָ, וְטִהֲרוּ אֶת מִקְדָּשֶׁךָ, וְהִדְלִיקוּ נֵרוֹת בְּחַצְרוֹת קָדְשֶׁךָ, וְקָבְעוּ שְׁמוֹנַת יְמֵי חֲנֻכָּה אֵלּוּ, לְהוֹדוֹת וּלְהַלֵּל לְשִׁמְךָ הַגָּדוֹל.

[If forgotten, do not repeat Shemoneh Esrei. See Laws §12.]

וְעַל כֻּלָּם יִתְבָּרַךְ וְיִתְרוֹמַם שִׁמְךָ מַלְכֵּנוּ תָּמִיד לְעוֹלָם וָעֶד.

From Rosh Hashanah to Yom Kippur add [if forgotten, do not repeat Shemoneh Esrei]:

וּכְתוֹב לְחַיִּים טוֹבִים כָּל בְּנֵי בְרִיתֶךָ.

עַל הַנִּסִּים / **Chanukah — Purim**

This declaration of thanks for the miracles of Chanukah and Purim is inserted in this section of Shemoneh Esrei that is likewise devoted to expressions of gratitude.

חֲנוּכָה / **Chanukah**

לְהַשְׁכִּיחָם תּוֹרָתֶךָ — To make them forget Your

נִסֶּיךָ ... נִפְלְאוֹתֶיךָ — Your miracles ... Your wonders. We thank God for both miracles, the extraordinary events everyone recognizes as the results of God's intervention, and wonders, the familiar things that we have grown accustomed to, such as breathing, raining, and growing (Etz Yosef).

Your praise [1] *— for our lives, which are committed to Your power and for our souls that are entrusted to You; for Your miracles that are with us every day; and for Your wonders• and favors in every season — evening, morning, and afternoon. The Beneficent One, for Your compassions were never exhausted, and the Compassionate One, for Your kindnesses never ended* [2] *— always have we put our hope in You.*

On Chanukah and Purim add the following:

(וְ)עַל הַנִּסִּים *(And) for the miracles, and for the salvation, and for the mighty deeds, and for the victories, and for the battles which You performed for our forefathers in those days, at this time.*

On Chanukah:

בִּימֵי *In the days of Mattisyahu, the son of Yochanan, the High Priest, the Hasmonean, and his sons — when the wicked Greek kingdom rose up against Your people Israel to make them forget Your Torah• and compel them to stray from the statutes of Your Will — You in Your great mercy stood up for them in the time of their distress. You took up their grievance, judged their claim, and avenged their wrong.* [3] *You delivered the strong into the hands of the weak, the many into the hands of the few, the impure into the hands of the pure, the wicked into the hands of the righteous, and the wanton into the hands of the diligent students of Your Torah. For Yourself You made a great and holy Name in Your world, and for Your people Israel you worked a great victory* [4] *and salvation as this very day. Thereafter, Your children came to the Holy of Holies of Your House, cleansed Your Temple, purified the site of Your Holiness and kindled lights in the Courtyards of Your Sanctuary; and they established these eight days of Chanukah to express thanks and praise to Your great Name.*

On Purim:

בִּימֵי *In the days of Mordechai and Esther, in Shushan, the capital, when Haman, the wicked, rose up against them and sought to destroy, to slay, and to exterminate all the Jews, young and old, infants and women, on the same day, on the thirteenth of the twelfth month which is the month of Adar, and to plunder their possessions.* [5] *But You, in Your abundant mercy, nullified his counsel and frustrated his intention and caused his design to return upon his own head and they hanged him and his sons on the gallows.*

[If forgotten, do not repeat Shemoneh Esrei. See Laws §12.]

For all these, may Your Name be blessed and exalted, our King, continually forever and ever.

From Rosh Hashanah to Yom Kippur add [if forgotten, do not repeat Shemoneh Esrei]:
And inscribe all the children of Your covenant for a good life.

---

(1) Cf. *Psalms* 79:13. (2) Cf. *Lamentations* 3:22. (3) Cf. *Jeremiah* 51:36. (4) Cf. *I Samuel* 19:5. (5) *Esther* 3:13.

Torah. The Syrian-Greeks knew that the key to the Jewish religion is the study of Torah; if Torah study were neglected, then the decline of ritual observance would be inevitable and swift. Therefore, they concentrated first on causing Torah to be forgotten, knowing that the deterioration of observance would soon follow (*R' Hirsch*).

פּוּרִים / Purim

The paragraph describing the miracle of Purim is far briefer than that describing Chanukah. The danger of Purim was straightforward — the extermination of the nation — and requires no elaboration. The peril of Chanukah was more subtle. It involved assimilation and impurity. The

Bend the knees at בָּרוּך; bow at אַתָּה; straighten up at ה'.

וְכָל הַחַיִּים* יוֹדוּךָ סֶּלָה, וִיהַלְלוּ אֶת שִׁמְךָ בֶּאֱמֶת, הָאֵל יְשׁוּעָתֵנוּ וְעֶזְרָתֵנוּ סֶלָה. בָּרוּךְ אַתָּה יהוה, הַטּוֹב שִׁמְךָ וּלְךָ נָאֶה לְהוֹדוֹת.

ON PUBLIC FAST DAYS AT MINCHAH: The *chazzan* recites בְּרְכַּת כֹּהֲנִים during his repetition except in a house of mourning. The *chazzan* faces right at וִישְׁמְרֶךָ; faces left at פָּנָיו אֵלֶיךָ וִיחֻנֶּךָּ; faces the Ark for the rest of the blessings.

אֱלֹהֵינוּ וֵאלֹהֵי אֲבוֹתֵינוּ, בָּרְכֵנוּ בַבְּרָכָה הַמְשֻׁלֶשֶׁת בַּתּוֹרָה הַכְּתוּבָה עַל יְדֵי מֹשֶׁה עַבְדֶּךָ, הָאֲמוּרָה מִפִּי אַהֲרֹן וּבָנָיו, כֹּהֲנִים עַם קְדוֹשֶׁךָ,

כָּאָמוּר: יְבָרֶכְךָ יהוה, וְיִשְׁמְרֶךָ.	(Cong.— כֵּן יְהִי רָצוֹן.)
יָאֵר יהוה פָּנָיו אֵלֶיךָ, וִיחֻנֶּךָּ.	(Cong.— כֵּן יְהִי רָצוֹן.)
יִשָּׂא יהוה פָּנָיו אֵלֶיךָ, וְיָשֵׂם לְךָ שָׁלוֹם.¹	(Cong.— כֵּן יְהִי רָצוֹן.)

שלום

שָׁלוֹם רָב עַל יִשְׂרָאֵל עַמְּךָ תָּשִׂים לְעוֹלָם, כִּי אַתָּה הוּא מֶלֶךְ אָדוֹן לְכָל הַשָּׁלוֹם. וְטוֹב בְּעֵינֶיךָ לְבָרֵךְ אֶת עַמְּךָ יִשְׂרָאֵל בְּכָל עֵת וּבְכָל שָׁעָה בִּשְׁלוֹמֶךָ. °בָּרוּךְ אַתָּה יהוה, הַמְבָרֵךְ אֶת עַמּוֹ יִשְׂרָאֵל בַּשָּׁלוֹם.

On public fast days substitute at Minchah:

שִׂים שָׁלוֹם, טוֹבָה, וּבְרָכָה, חֵן, וָחֶסֶד וְרַחֲמִים, עָלֵינוּ וְעַל כָּל יִשְׂרָאֵל עַמֶּךָ. בָּרְכֵנוּ אָבִינוּ, כֻּלָּנוּ כְּאֶחָד בְּאוֹר פָּנֶיךָ, כִּי בְאוֹר פָּנֶיךָ נָתַתָּ לָּנוּ, יהוה אֱלֹהֵינוּ, תּוֹרַת חַיִּים וְאַהֲבַת חֶסֶד, וּצְדָקָה, וּבְרָכָה, וְרַחֲמִים, וְחַיִּים, וְשָׁלוֹם. וְטוֹב בְּעֵינֶיךָ לְבָרֵךְ אֶת עַמְּךָ יִשְׂרָאֵל בְּכָל עֵת וּבְכָל שָׁעָה בִּשְׁלוֹמֶךָ. °בָּרוּךְ אַתָּה יהוה, הַמְבָרֵךְ אֶת עַמּוֹ יִשְׂרָאֵל בַּשָּׁלוֹם.

° *From Rosh Hashanah to Yom Kippur substitute the following:*

בְּסֵפֶר חַיִּים בְּרָכָה וְשָׁלוֹם, וּפַרְנָסָה טוֹבָה, נִזָּכֵר וְנִכָּתֵב לְפָנֶיךָ, אֲנַחְנוּ וְכָל עַמְּךָ בֵּית יִשְׂרָאֵל, לְחַיִּים טוֹבִים וּלְשָׁלוֹם. בָּרוּךְ אַתָּה יהוה,

Authorities differ regarding the conclusion of this blessing.

הַמְבָרֵךְ אֶת עַמּוֹ יִשְׂרָאֵל בַּשָּׁלוֹם. / עֹשֵׂה הַשָּׁלוֹם.

[If forgotten, do not repeat *Shemoneh Esrei*. See Laws §5.]

THE *CHAZZAN'S* REPETITION ENDS HERE. INDIVIDUALS CONTINUE BELOW:

יִהְיוּ לְרָצוֹן* אִמְרֵי פִי וְהֶגְיוֹן לִבִּי לְפָנֶיךָ, יהוה צוּרִי וְגֹאֲלִי.²

unaware do not perceive danger unless it is starkly physical in nature. Therefore, a more elaborate explanation is required (R' Hirsch). וְכָל הַחַיִּים ◆ — *Everything alive.* This prayer refers specifically to the universal praise

that will come with the restoration of the Divine service in the rebuilt Temple.

◆ **Peace / שָׁלוֹם**

The consensus of commentators is that שָׁלוֹם רָב, *abundant peace,* is the standard

Bend the knees at "Blessed"; bow at "You"; straighten up at "HASHEM."

Everything alive* will gratefully acknowledge You, Selah! and praise Your Name sincerely, O God of our salvation and help, Selah! Blessed are You, HASHEM, Your Name is "The Beneficent One" and to You it is fitting to give thanks.

ON PUBLIC FAST DAYS AT MINCHAH: The chazzan recites the Priestly Blessing during his repetition except in a house of mourning.

אֱלֹהֵינוּ *Our God and the God of our forefathers, bless us with the three-verse blessing in the Torah that was written by the hand of Moses, Your servant, that was said by Aaron and his sons, the Kohanim, Your holy people, as it is said:*

May HASHEM bless you and safeguard you.   (Cong.— So may it be.)

May HASHEM illuminate His countenance for you and be gracious to you.
(Cong.— So may it be.)

May HASHEM turn His countenance to you and establish peace for you. [1]
(Cong.— So may it be.)

PEACE

שָׁלוֹם *Establish abundant peace upon Your people Israel forever, for You are King, Master of all peace. May it be good in Your eyes to bless Your people Israel at every time and at every hour, with Your peace.* °Blessed are You, HASHEM, Who blesses His people Israel with peace.

On public fast days substitute at Minchah:

שִׂים *Establish peace, goodness, blessing, graciousness, kindness, and compassion upon us and upon all of Your people Israel. Bless us, our Father, all of us as one, with the light of Your countenance, for with the light of Your countenance You gave us, HASHEM, our God, the Torah of life and a love of kindness, righteousness, blessing, compassion, life, and peace. And may it be good in Your eyes to bless Your people Israel at every time and at every hour, with Your peace.* °Blessed are You, HASHEM, Who blesses His people Israel with peace.

° From Rosh Hashanah to Yom Kippur substitute the following:
In the book of life, blessing, and peace, and good livelihood, may we be remembered and inscribed before You — we and Your entire people the Family of Israel — for a good life and for peace. Blessed are You, HASHEM,
Authorities differ regarding the conclusion of this blessing.
Who blesses His people Israel with peace. / Who makes the peace.
[If forgotten, do not repeat Shemoneh Esrei. See Laws §5.]

THE CHAZZAN'S REPETITION ENDS HERE. INDIVIDUALS CONTINUE:

May the expressions of my mouth and the thoughts of my heart find favor* before You, HASHEM, my Rock and my Redeemer. [2]

---

(1) Numbers 6:24-26. (2) Psalms 19:15.

text of this blessing during *Minchah*, and that שִׂים, *Establish peace*, is recited only at times when the Priestly Blessings are recited, because it alludes to those blessings.

וְיִהְיוּ לְרָצוֹן ◆◆ — *May . . . find favor.* We conclude *Shemoneh Esrei* with this brief prayer that our prayers find favor before God. Kabbalistic literature stresses that due to its great sanctity it be recited slowly and fervently.

אֱלֹהַי, נְצוֹר לְשׁוֹנִי מֵרָע, וּשְׂפָתַי מִדַּבֵּר מִרְמָה,[1] וְלִמְקַלְלַי נַפְשִׁי תִדּוֹם, וְנַפְשִׁי כֶּעָפָר לַכֹּל תִּהְיֶה. פְּתַח לִבִּי בְּתוֹרָתֶךָ, וּבְמִצְוֹתֶיךָ תִּרְדּוֹף נַפְשִׁי. וְכָל הַחוֹשְׁבִים עָלַי רָעָה, מְהֵרָה הָפֵר עֲצָתָם וְקַלְקֵל מַחֲשַׁבְתָּם. עֲשֵׂה לְמַעַן שְׁמֶךָ, עֲשֵׂה לְמַעַן יְמִינֶךָ, עֲשֵׂה לְמַעַן קְדֻשָּׁתֶךָ, עֲשֵׂה לְמַעַן תּוֹרָתֶךָ. לְמַעַן יֵחָלְצוּן יְדִידֶיךָ, הוֹשִׁיעָה יְמִינְךָ וַעֲנֵנִי.[2]

Some recite verses pertaining to their names here. See page 120.

An individual who wishes to accept a fast upon himself recites the following declaration at this point during *Minchah* (or later while it is still daytime) on the day before the fast:

רִבּוֹן כָּל הָעוֹלָמִים, הֲרֵי אֲנִי לְפָנֶיךָ בְּתַעֲנִית נְדָבָה לְמָחָר. יְהִי רָצוֹן מִלְּפָנֶיךָ, יְהוָה אֱלֹהַי וֵאלֹהֵי אֲבוֹתַי, שֶׁתְּקַבְּלֵנִי בְּאַהֲבָה וּבְרָצוֹן, וְתָבֹא לְפָנֶיךָ תְּפִלָּתִי, וְתַעֲנֶה עֲתִירָתִי בְּרַחֲמֶיךָ הָרַבִּים. כִּי אַתָּה שׁוֹמֵעַ תְּפִלַּת כָּל פֶּה.

At *Minchah* on the afternoon of an individual's fast, he recites the following:

רִבּוֹן כָּל הָעוֹלָמִים, גָּלוּי וְיָדוּעַ לְפָנֶיךָ, בִּזְמַן שֶׁבֵּית הַמִּקְדָּשׁ קַיָּם אָדָם חוֹטֵא וּמֵבִיא קָרְבָּן, וְאֵין מַקְרִיבִים מִמֶּנּוּ אֶלָּא חֶלְבּוֹ וְדָמוֹ, וְאַתָּה בְּרַחֲמֶיךָ הָרַבִּים מְכַפֵּר. וְעַכְשָׁו יָשַׁבְתִּי בְּתַעֲנִית, וְנִתְמַעֵט חֶלְבִּי וְדָמִי. יְהִי רָצוֹן מִלְּפָנֶיךָ שֶׁיְּהֵא מְעוּט חֶלְבִּי וְדָמִי שֶׁנִּתְמַעֵט הַיּוֹם, כְּאִלּוּ הִקְרַבְתִּיו לְפָנֶיךָ עַל גַּב הַמִּזְבֵּחַ, וְתִרְצֵנִי.

יִהְיוּ לְרָצוֹן אִמְרֵי פִי וְהֶגְיוֹן לִבִּי לְפָנֶיךָ, יְהוָה צוּרִי וְגֹאֲלִי.[3] עֹשֶׂה שָׁלוֹם בִּמְרוֹמָיו, הוּא יַעֲשֶׂה שָׁלוֹם °הַשָּׁלוֹם° עָלֵינוּ, וְעַל כָּל יִשְׂרָאֵל. וְאִמְרוּ: אָמֵן.

Bow. Take three steps back. Bow left and say ... עֹשֶׂה
bow right and say ... הוּא
bow forward and say עָל
כָּל ... אָמֵן.

°**הַשָּׁלוֹם**°—From Rosh Hashanah to Yom Kippur some say

יְהִי רָצוֹן מִלְּפָנֶיךָ, יְהוָה אֱלֹהֵינוּ וֵאלֹהֵי אֲבוֹתֵינוּ, שֶׁיִּבָּנֶה בֵּית הַמִּקְדָּשׁ בִּמְהֵרָה בְיָמֵינוּ, וְתֵן חֶלְקֵנוּ בְּתוֹרָתֶךָ. וְשָׁם נַעֲבָדְךָ בְּיִרְאָה, כִּימֵי עוֹלָם וּכְשָׁנִים קַדְמוֹנִיּוֹת. וְעָרְבָה לַיהוָה מִנְחַת יְהוּדָה וִירוּשָׁלָיִם, כִּימֵי עוֹלָם וּכְשָׁנִים קַדְמוֹנִיּוֹת.[4]

THE INDIVIDUAL'S RECITATION OF *SHEMONEH ESREI* ENDS HERE.

Remain standing in place until the *chazzan* reaches *Kedushah* — or at least until the *chazzan* begins his repetition — then take three steps forward. The *chazzan* himself, or one praying alone, should remain in place for a few moments before taking three steps forward.

⚓ **אֱלֹהַי, נְצוֹר / Concluding Prayers**
Many Talmudic Sages composed supplications that they would recite at the conclu-

sion of *Shemoneh Esrei*, some of which are cited in *Berachos* 16b-17a. The prayer now in universal use is based on that of Mar, son

אֱלֹהַי *My God, guard my tongue from evil and my lips from speaking deceitfully.* [1] *To those who curse me, let my soul be silent; and let my soul be like dust to everyone. Open my heart to Your Torah, then my soul will pursue Your commandments. As for all those who design evil against me, speedily nullify their counsel and disrupt their design. Act for Your Name's sake; act for Your right hand's sake; act for Your sanctity's sake; act for Your Torah's sake. That Your beloved ones may be given rest; let Your right hand save, and respond to me.* [2]

Some recite verses pertaining to their names here. See page 120.

An individual who wishes to accept a fast upon himself recites the following declaration at this point during *Minchah* (or later while it is still daytime) on the day before the fast:

רבּוֹן *Master of all the worlds, I come before You [to accept] a voluntary fast for tomorrow. May it be Your will, HASHEM, my God and the God of my forefathers, that You accept me with love and favor, that my prayer come before You, and that You answer my entreaty in Your abundant mercy, for You hear the prayer of every mouth.*

At *Minchah* on the afternoon of an individual's fast, he recites the following:

רבּוֹן *Master of all the worlds, it is revealed and known before You that in the time when the Holy Temple existed, if someone sinned, he brought an offering — yet nothing of it was offered [on the Altar] except for its fat and blood, yet You in Your abundant mercy would atone. Now I have engaged in a fast and my own fat and blood have been diminished. May it be Your will that the diminution of my fat and blood that was diminished today should be as if I had offered it upon the Altar and may You show me favor.*

May the expressions of my mouth and the thoughts of my heart find

Bow. Take three steps back. Bow left and say, "He Who ..."; bow right and say, "may He ..."; bow forward and say, "and upon ..."

favor before You, HASHEM, my Rock and my Redeemer. [3] *He Who makes peace in His heights, may He make peace upon us, and upon all Israel. Now respond: Amen.*

יְהִי רָצוֹן *May it be Your will, HASHEM, our God and the God of our forefathers, that the Holy Temple be rebuilt, speedily in our days. Grant us our share in Your Torah, and may we serve You there with reverence, as in days of old and in former years. Then the offering of Judah and Jerusalem will be pleasing to HASHEM, as in days of old and in former years.* [4]

THE INDIVIDUAL'S RECITATION OF *SHEMONEH ESREI* ENDS HERE.

Remain standing in place until the *chazzan* reaches *Kedushah* — or at least until the *chazzan* begins his repetition — then take three steps forward. The *chazzan* himself, or one praying alone, should remain in place for a few moments before taking three steps forward.

(1) Cf. *Psalms* 34:14. (2) 60:7; 108:7. (3) 19:15. (4) *Malachi* 3:4.

---

of Rabina (ibid. 18a).

While one is reciting אֱלֹהַי, נְצוֹר, he may not respond to blessings and the like except for the exceptions given below. In the case of those exceptions, it is preferable to recite יִהְיוּ לְרָצוֹן before responding, but if there is not enough time to do so, the responses

should be said anyway. The responses are: *Borchu,* the *amen* after הָאֵל הַקָּדוֹשׁ and שׁוֹמֵעַ תְּפִלָּה; אָמֵן יְהֵא שְׁמֵהּ רַבָּא and the last *amen* of the Half-*Kaddish*; and in *Kedushah* the two verses קָדוֹשׁ and בָּרוּךְ כְּבוֹד; and the three words מוֹדִים אֲנַחְנוּ לָךְ. (See *Orach Chaim* Ch. 122.)

MINCHAH

On most weekdays *Minchah* continues with *Tachanun*, whether or not a *minyan* is present. However, *Tachanun* is omitted in the evening in the event that *Minchah* begins late. On most fast days and from Rosh Hashanah to Yom Kippur insert אֲבִינוּ מַלְכֵּנוּ (p. 106) before *Tachanun*. See page 126 for days when *Tachanun* is omitted. On those days, the *chazzan* goes directly to Full *Kaddish* (p. 56); individuals go on to עָלֵינוּ.

נפילת אפים

Recite until יָבֹשׁוּ רָגַע with the head resting on the left arm, preferably while seated.

וַיֹּאמֶר דָּוִד אֶל גָּד, צַר לִי מְאֹד, נִפְּלָה נָּא בְיַד יהוה, כִּי רַבִּים רַחֲמָיו, וּבְיַד אָדָם אַל אֶפֹּלָה.[1]

רַחוּם וְחַנּוּן חָטָאתִי לְפָנֶיךָ. יהוה מָלֵא רַחֲמִים, רַחֵם עָלַי וְקַבֵּל תַּחֲנוּנָי.

תהלים ו:ב-יא

יהוה אַל בְּאַפְּךָ תוֹכִיחֵנִי, וְאַל בַּחֲמָתְךָ תְיַסְּרֵנִי. חָנֵּנִי יהוה, כִּי אֻמְלַל אָנִי, רְפָאֵנִי יהוה, כִּי נִבְהֲלוּ עֲצָמָי. וְנַפְשִׁי נִבְהֲלָה מְאֹד, וְאַתָּה יהוה, עַד מָתָי. שׁוּבָה יהוה, חַלְּצָה נַפְשִׁי, הוֹשִׁיעֵנִי לְמַעַן חַסְדֶּךָ. כִּי אֵין בַּמָּוֶת זִכְרֶךָ, בִּשְׁאוֹל מִי יוֹדֶה

MAARIV FOR THE CONCLUSION OF THE SABBATH

IF A FESTIVAL (OR EREV PESACH) FALLS BEFORE THE COMING SABBATH, THE *CHAZZAN* RECITES THE FULL *KADDISH* (P. 56) AND THE SERVICE CONTINUES THERE.

The chazzan recites חֲצִי קַדִּישׁ

יִתְגַּדַּל וְיִתְקַדַּשׁ שְׁמֵהּ רַבָּא. (.Cong אָמֵן.) בְּעָלְמָא דִּי בְרָא כִרְעוּתֵהּ. וְיַמְלִיךְ מַלְכוּתֵהּ, בְּחַיֵּיכוֹן וּבְיוֹמֵיכוֹן וּבְחַיֵּי דְכָל בֵּית יִשְׂרָאֵל, בַּעֲגָלָא וּבִזְמַן קָרִיב, וְאִמְרוּ: אָמֵן.

(.Cong — אָמֵן. יְהֵא שְׁמֵהּ רַבָּא מְבָרַךְ לְעָלַם וּלְעָלְמֵי עָלְמַיָּא.)

יְהֵא שְׁמֵהּ רַבָּא מְבָרַךְ לְעָלַם וּלְעָלְמֵי עָלְמַיָּא.

יִתְבָּרַךְ וְיִשְׁתַּבַּח וְיִתְפָּאַר וְיִתְרוֹמַם וְיִתְנַשֵּׂא וְיִתְהַדָּר וְיִתְעַלֶּה וְיִתְהַלָּל שְׁמֵהּ דְּקֻדְשָׁא בְּרִיךְ הוּא (.Cong — בְּרִיךְ הוּא) — לְעֵלָּא מִן כָּל [substitute From Rosh Hashanah to Yom Kippur ° לְעֵלָּא (וּ)לְעֵלָּא מִכָּל] בִּרְכָתָא וְשִׁירָתָא תֻּשְׁבְּחָתָא וְנֶחֱמָתָא דַּאֲמִירָן בְּעָלְמָא, וְאִמְרוּ: אָמֵן. (.Cong — אָמֵן.)

וִיהִי נֹעַם אֲדֹנָי אֱלֹהֵינוּ עָלֵינוּ, וּמַעֲשֵׂה יָדֵינוּ כּוֹנְנָה עָלֵינוּ, וּמַעֲשֵׂה יָדֵינוּ כּוֹנְנֵהוּ.[1]

MINCHAH

On most weekdays *Minchah* continues with *Tachanun*, whether or not a *minyan* is present. However, *Tachanun* is omitted in the evening in the event that *Minchah* begins late. On most fast days and from Rosh Hashanah to Yom Kippur insert *Avinu Malkeinu* (p. 106) before *Tachanun*. See page 126 for days when *Tachanun* is omitted. On those days, the *chazzan* goes directly to Full *Kaddish* (p. 56); individuals go on to *Aleinu*.

TACHANUN / PUTTING DOWN THE HEAD

Recite until "instantly shamed" with the head resting on the left arm, preferably while seated.

וַיֹּאמֶר דָּוִד *And David said to Gad, "I am exceedingly distressed. Let us fall into HASHEM's hand for His mercies are abundant, but let me not fall into human hands."* [1]

O compassionate and gracious One, I have sinned before You. HASHEM, Who is full of mercy, have mercy on me and accept my supplications.

Psalms 6:2-11

'ה *HASHEM, do not rebuke me in Your anger, nor chastise me in Your rage. Favor me, HASHEM, for I am feeble; heal me, HASHEM, for my bones shudder. My soul is utterly confounded, and You, HASHEM, how long? Desist, HASHEM, release my soul; save me as befits Your kindness. For there is no mention of You in death; in the Lower World who will thank*

(1) *II Samuel* 24:14.

נְפִילַת אַפַּיִם / **Putting Down the Head**

Tachanun consists mainly of *Psalms* 6:2-11, which begin ה׳ אַל בְּאַפְּךָ. However, two verses, both of which reflect the theme of

Tachanun, are inserted to introduce the primary psalm.

The act of נְפִילַת אַפַּיִם, *putting down the head*, i.e., "burying" one's face in submis-

MAARIV FOR THE CONCLUSION OF THE SABBATH

IF A FESTIVAL (OR EREV PESACH) FALLS BEFORE THE COMING SABBATH, THE *CHAZZAN* RECITES THE FULL *KADDISH* (P. 56) AND THE SERVICE CONTINUES THERE.

The *chazzan* recites Half-Kaddish:

יִתְגַּדַּל *May His great Name grow exalted and sanctified (Cong.— Amen.) in the world that He created as He willed. May He give reign to His kingship in your lifetimes and in your days, and in the lifetimes of the entire Family of Israel, swiftly and soon. Now respond: Amen.*

(Cong.— Amen. May His great Name be blessed forever and ever.)
May His great Name be blessed forever and ever.

Blessed, praised, glorified, exalted, extolled, mighty, upraised, and lauded be the Name of the Holy One, Blessed is He, (Cong.— Blessed is He) — [From Rosh Hashanah to Yom Kippur add: exceedingly] beyond any blessing and song, praise and consolation that are uttered in the world. Now respond: Amen. (Cong.— Amen.)

וִיהִי *May the pleasantness of my Lord, our God, be upon us — may He establish our handiwork for us; our handiwork, may He establish.* [1]

(1) *Psalms* 90:17.

MINCHAH

לְךָ. יָגַעְתִּי בְּאַנְחָתִי, אֶשְׂחֶה בְכָל לַיְלָה מִטָּתִי, בְּדִמְעָתִי עַרְשִׂי
אַמְסֶה. עָשְׁשָׁה מִכַּעַס עֵינִי, עָתְקָה בְּכָל צוֹרְרָי. סוּרוּ מִמֶּנִּי כָּל
פְּעֲלֵי אָוֶן, כִּי שָׁמַע יהוה קוֹל בִּכְיִי. שָׁמַע יהוה תְּחִנָּתִי, יהוה
תְּפִלָּתִי יִקָּח. יֵבְשׁוּ וְיִבָּהֲלוּ מְאֹד כָּל אֹיְבָי, יָשֻׁבוּ יֵבְשׁוּ רָגַע.

sive supplication, is based on the behavior of Moses, Aaron and Joshua. These three cast themselves down before God in times of stress and tragedy (Numbers 16:22; Joshua 7:6).

This portion of *Tachanun* is recited with the head down and resting on the left arm, and preferably in a sitting position. The head should not rest on the bare arm; rather the arm should be covered with a

MAARIV FOR THE CONCLUSION OF THE SABBATH

תהלים צא

יֹשֵׁב בְּסֵתֶר עֶלְיוֹן, בְּצֵל שַׁדַּי יִתְלוֹנָן. אֹמַר לַיהוה, מַחְסִי
וּמְצוּדָתִי, אֱלֹהַי אֶבְטַח בּוֹ. כִּי הוּא יַצִּילְךָ מִפַּח יָקוּשׁ,
מִדֶּבֶר הַוּוֹת. בְּאֶבְרָתוֹ יָסֶךְ לָךְ, וְתַחַת כְּנָפָיו תֶּחְסֶה, צִנָּה
וְסֹחֵרָה אֲמִתּוֹ. לֹא תִירָא מִפַּחַד לָיְלָה, מֵחֵץ יָעוּף יוֹמָם.
מִדֶּבֶר בָּאֹפֶל יַהֲלֹךְ, מִקֶּטֶב יָשׁוּד צָהֳרָיִם. יִפֹּל מִצִּדְּךָ אֶלֶף,
וּרְבָבָה מִימִינֶךָ, אֵלֶיךָ לֹא יִגָּשׁ. רַק בְּעֵינֶיךָ תַבִּיט, וְשִׁלֻּמַת
רְשָׁעִים תִּרְאֶה. כִּי אַתָּה יהוה מַחְסִי, עֶלְיוֹן שַׂמְתָּ מְעוֹנֶךָ. לֹא
תְאֻנֶּה אֵלֶיךָ רָעָה, וְנֶגַע לֹא יִקְרַב בְּאָהֳלֶךָ. כִּי מַלְאָכָיו יְצַוֶּה
לָּךְ, לִשְׁמָרְךָ בְּכָל דְּרָכֶיךָ. עַל כַּפַּיִם יִשָּׂאוּנְךָ, פֶּן תִּגֹּף בָּאֶבֶן
רַגְלֶךָ. עַל שַׁחַל וָפֶתֶן תִּדְרֹךְ, תִּרְמֹס כְּפִיר וְתַנִּין. כִּי בִי חָשַׁק
וַאֲפַלְּטֵהוּ, אֲשַׂגְּבֵהוּ כִּי יָדַע שְׁמִי. יִקְרָאֵנִי וְאֶעֱנֵהוּ, עִמּוֹ אָנֹכִי
בְצָרָה, אֲחַלְּצֵהוּ וַאֲכַבְּדֵהוּ. ❖ אֹרֶךְ יָמִים אַשְׂבִּיעֵהוּ, וְאַרְאֵהוּ
בִּישׁוּעָתִי. אֹרֶךְ יָמִים אַשְׂבִּיעֵהוּ, וְאַרְאֵהוּ בִּישׁוּעָתִי.

The verses in bold type are the *Kedushah* of the angels.
It is preferable that the congregation recite them aloud and in unison.

וְאַתָּה קָדוֹשׁ יוֹשֵׁב תְּהִלּוֹת יִשְׂרָאֵל.[1] וְקָרָא זֶה אֶל זֶה
וְאָמַר: **קָדוֹשׁ, קָדוֹשׁ, קָדוֹשׁ, יהוה צְבָאוֹת,**
מְלֹא כָל הָאָרֶץ כְּבוֹדוֹ.[2] וּמְקַבְּלִין דֵּין מִן דֵּין וְאָמְרִין:
קַדִּישׁ בִּשְׁמֵי מְרוֹמָא עִלָּאָה בֵּית שְׁכִינְתֵּהּ, קַדִּישׁ עַל
אַרְעָא עוֹבַד גְּבוּרְתֵּהּ, קַדִּישׁ לְעָלַם וּלְעָלְמֵי עָלְמַיָּא, יהוה

MINCHAH

You? I am wearied with my sigh, every night I drench my bed, with my tears I soak my couch. My eye is dimmed because of anger, aged by my tormentors. Depart from me, all evildoers, for HASHEM will accept my prayer. Let all my foes be shamed and utterly confounded, they will regret and be instantly shamed.

sleeve, *tallis,* or even a cloth. This posture is an indication of the feelings of despair and guilt that combine with the undying hope that God's mercy will rescue the supplicant no matter how hopeless his plight. Since Joshua cast himself down in

the presence of the Holy Ark, the act of falling on the face is done only in the presence of a Torah scroll, i.e., an Ark containing a Torah scroll. If a Torah is not present, *Tachanun* is recited with the head held erect.

MAARIV FOR THE CONCLUSION OF THE SABBATH

Psalm 91

יֹשֵׁב *Whoever sits in the refuge of the Most High, he shall dwell in the shadow of the Almighty. I will say of HASHEM, "He is my refuge and my fortress, my God, I will trust in Him." For He will deliver you from the ensnaring trap, from devastating pestilence. With His pinion He will cover you, and beneath His wings you will be protected; shield and armor is His truth. You shall not fear the terror of night; nor the arrow that flies by day; nor the pestilence that walks in gloom; nor the destroyer who lays waste at noon. Let a thousand encamp at your side and a myriad at your right hand, but to you they shall not approach. You will merely peer with your eyes and you will see the retribution of the wicked. Because [you said,] "You, HASHEM, are my refuge," you have made the Most High your dwelling place. No evil will befall you, nor will any plague come near your tent. He will charge His angels for you, to protect you in all your ways. On your palms they will carry you, lest you strike your foot against a stone. Upon the lion and the viper you will tread; you will trample the young lion and the serpent. For he has yearned for Me and I will deliver him; I will elevate him because he knows My Name. He will call upon Me and I will answer him, I am with him in distress; I will release him and I will honor him.* Chazzan— *With long life will I satisfy him, and I will show him My salvation. With long life will I satisfy him, and I will show him My salvation.*

וְאַתָּה קָדוֹשׁ *You are the Holy One, enthroned upon the praises of Israel.*[1] *And one [angel] will call another and say:*

"Holy, holy, holy is HASHEM, Master of Legions, the whole world is filled with His glory."[2] *And they receive permission from one another and say: "Holy in the most exalted heaven, the abode of His Presence; holy on earth, product of His strength; holy forever and ever is HASHEM,*

(1) *Psalms* 22:4. (2) *Isaiah* 6:3.

MINCHAH

Sit up erect and recite:

שׁוֹמֵר יִשְׂרָאֵל, שְׁמוֹר שְׁאֵרִית יִשְׂרָאֵל, וְאַל יֹאבַד יִשְׂרָאֵל, הָאֹמְרִים שְׁמַע יִשְׂרָאֵל.

שׁוֹמֵר גּוֹי אֶחָד, שְׁמוֹר שְׁאֵרִית עַם אֶחָד, וְאַל יֹאבַד גּוֹי אֶחָד, הַמְיַחֲדִים שִׁמְךָ, יהוה אֱלֹהֵינוּ יהוה אֶחָד.

שׁוֹמֵר גּוֹי קָדוֹשׁ, שְׁמוֹר שְׁאֵרִית עַם קָדוֹשׁ, וְאַל יֹאבַד גּוֹי קָדוֹשׁ, הַמְשַׁלְּשִׁים בְּשָׁלֹשׁ קְדֻשּׁוֹת לְקָדוֹשׁ.

מִתְרַצֶּה בְּרַחֲמִים וּמִתְפַּיֵּס בְּתַחֲנוּנִים, הִתְרַצֵּה וְהִתְפַּיֵּס לְדוֹר עָנִי, כִּי אֵין עוֹזֵר. אָבִינוּ מַלְכֵּנוּ, חָנֵּנוּ וַעֲנֵנוּ, כִּי אֵין בָּנוּ מַעֲשִׂים, עֲשֵׂה עִמָּנוּ צְדָקָה וָחֶסֶד וְהוֹשִׁיעֵנוּ.

MAARIV FOR THE CONCLUSION OF THE SABBATH

צְבָאוֹת, מַלְיָא כָל אַרְעָא זִיו יְקָרֵהּ.¹
❖ וַתִּשָּׂאֵנִי רוּחַ, וָאֶשְׁמַע אַחֲרַי קוֹל רַעַשׁ גָּדוֹל: **בָּרוּךְ כְּבוֹד יהוה מִמְּקוֹמוֹ.²** וּנְטָלַתְנִי רוּחָא, וְשִׁמְעֵת בַּתְרַי קָל זִיעַ סַגִּיא דִּמְשַׁבְּחִין וְאָמְרִין: בְּרִיךְ יְקָרָא דַיהוה מֵאֲתַר בֵּית שְׁכִינְתֵּהּ.³

יהוה יִמְלֹךְ לְעֹלָם וָעֶד.⁴ יהוה מַלְכוּתֵהּ קָאֵם לְעָלַם וּלְעָלְמֵי עָלְמַיָּא.⁵

יהוה אֱלֹהֵי אַבְרָהָם יִצְחָק וְיִשְׂרָאֵל אֲבֹתֵינוּ, שָׁמְרָה זֹּאת לְעוֹלָם, לְיֵצֶר מַחְשְׁבוֹת לְבַב עַמֶּךָ, וְהָכֵן לְבָבָם אֵלֶיךָ.⁶ וְהוּא רַחוּם, יְכַפֵּר עָוֹן וְלֹא יַשְׁחִית, וְהִרְבָּה לְהָשִׁיב אַפּוֹ, וְלֹא יָעִיר כָּל חֲמָתוֹ.⁷ כִּי אַתָּה אֲדֹנָי טוֹב וְסַלָּח, וְרַב חֶסֶד לְכָל קֹרְאֶיךָ.⁸ צִדְקָתְךָ צֶדֶק לְעוֹלָם, וְתוֹרָתְךָ אֱמֶת.⁹ תִּתֵּן אֱמֶת לְיַעֲקֹב, חֶסֶד לְאַבְרָהָם, אֲשֶׁר נִשְׁבַּעְתָּ לַאֲבֹתֵינוּ מִימֵי קֶדֶם.¹⁰ בָּרוּךְ אֲדֹנָי יוֹם יוֹם יַעֲמָס לָנוּ, הָאֵל יְשׁוּעָתֵנוּ סֶלָה.¹¹ יהוה צְבָאוֹת עִמָּנוּ, מִשְׂגָּב לָנוּ אֱלֹהֵי יַעֲקֹב סֶלָה.¹² יהוה צְבָאוֹת, אַשְׁרֵי אָדָם בֹּטֵחַ בָּךְ.¹³ יהוה הוֹשִׁיעָה, הַמֶּלֶךְ יַעֲנֵנוּ בְיוֹם קָרְאֵנוּ.¹⁴

MINCHAH

Sit up erect and recite:

שׁוֹמֵר *O Guardian of Israel, protect the remnant of Israel; let not Israel be destroyed — those who proclaim, "Hear O Israel."*

O Guardian of the unique nation, protect the remnant of the unique people; let not the unique nation be destroyed — those who proclaim the Oneness of Your Name, "HASHEM is our God, HASHEM — the One and Only!"

O Guardian of the holy nation, protect the remnant of the holy people; let not the holy nation be destroyed — those who proclaim three-fold sanctifications to the Holy One.

Become favorable through compassion and become appeased through supplications. Become favorable and appeased to the poor generation for there is no helper. Our Father, our King — be gracious with us and answer us, though we have no worthy deeds; treat us with charity and kindness, and save us.

MAARIV FOR THE CONCLUSION OF THE SABBATH

Master of Legions — the entire world is filled with the radiance of His glory."[1]

Chazzan— And a wind lifted me; and I heard behind me the sound of a great noise: "Blessed is the glory of HASHEM from His place."[2] *And a wind lifted me and I heard behind me the sound of the powerful movement of those who praised saying: "Blessed is the honor of HASHEM from the place of the abode of His Presence."*[3]

HASHEM shall reign for all eternity.[4] *HASHEM — His kingdom is established forever and ever.*[5]

HASHEM, God of Abraham, Isaac, and Israel, our forefathers, may You preserve this forever as the realization of the thoughts in Your people's heart, and may You direct their heart to You.[6] *He, the Merciful One, is forgiving of iniquity and does not destroy; frequently He withdraws His anger, not arousing His entire rage.*[7] *For You, my Lord, are good and forgiving, and abundantly kind to all who call upon You.*[8] *Your righteousness remains righteous forever, and Your Torah is truth.*[9] *Grant truth to Jacob, kindness to Abraham, as You swore to our forefathers from ancient times.*[10] *Blessed is my Lord for every single day, He burdens us with blessings, the God of our salvation, Selah.*[11] *HASHEM, Master of Legions, is with us, a stronghold for us is the God of Jacob, Selah.*[12] *HASHEM, Master of Legions, praiseworthy is the man who trusts in You.*[13] *HASHEM, save! May the King answer us on the day we call.*[14]

---

(1) Targum Yonasan. (2) Ezekiel 3:12. (3) Targum Yonasan. (4) Exodus 15:18.
(5) Targum Onkelos. (6) I Chronicles 29:18. (7) Psalms 78:38. (8) 86:5.
(9) 119:142. (10) Micah 7:20. (11) Psalms 68:20. (12) 46:8. (13) 84:13. (14) 20:10.

MINCHAH

Stand up after the words וַאֲנַחְנוּ לֹא נֵדַע, until conclusion of the paragraph.

וַאֲנַחְנוּ לֹא נֵדַע מַה נַּעֲשֶׂה,* כִּי עָלֶיךָ עֵינֵינוּ.¹ זְכֹר רַחֲמֶיךָ
יהוה וַחֲסָדֶיךָ, כִּי מֵעוֹלָם הֵמָּה.² יְהִי חַסְדְּךָ יהוה
עָלֵינוּ, כַּאֲשֶׁר יִחַלְנוּ לָךְ.*³ אַל תִּזְכָּר לָנוּ עֲוֹנוֹת רִאשׁוֹנִים,
מַהֵר יְקַדְּמוּנוּ רַחֲמֶיךָ, כִּי דַלּוֹנוּ מְאֹד.*⁴ חָנֵּנוּ יהוה חָנֵּנוּ, כִּי
רַב שָׂבַעְנוּ בוּז.⁵ כִּי הוּא יָדַע יִצְרֵנוּ, זָכוּר
כִּי עָפָר אֲנָחְנוּ.⁷ ❖ עָזְרֵנוּ אֱלֹהֵי יִשְׁעֵנוּ עַל דְּבַר כְּבוֹד שְׁמֶךָ,
וְהַצִּילֵנוּ וְכַפֵּר עַל חַטֹּאתֵינוּ לְמַעַן שְׁמֶךָ.⁸

וַאֲנַחְנוּ לֹא נֵדַע מַה נַּעֲשֶׂה — *We know not what to do.* We have prayed in every possible manner — sitting, standing, and casting ourselves down in supplication. Moses, too, prayed in these three postures. Now, we beg of God to help, for "we know not what else we can do." To allude to this thought it is customary to sit while reciting the first three words of this prayer and

then to stand (*Abudraham*).

We are like orphaned children who depend totally on their guardian. Similarly, we look to God for His help and mercy, recognizing that only He can rescue us from our plight (*Etz Yosef*). Appropriately, this verse is from the prayer of King Yehoshafat, who prayed for help against an overwhelming invasion.

MAARIV FOR THE CONCLUSION OF THE SABBATH

בָּרוּךְ הוּא אֱלֹהֵינוּ שֶׁבְּרָאָנוּ לִכְבוֹדוֹ, וְהִבְדִּילָנוּ מִן
הַתּוֹעִים, וְנָתַן לָנוּ תּוֹרַת אֱמֶת, וְחַיֵּי עוֹלָם נָטַע בְּתוֹכֵנוּ. הוּא
יִפְתַּח לִבֵּנוּ בְּתוֹרָתוֹ, וְיָשֵׂם בְּלִבֵּנוּ אַהֲבָתוֹ וְיִרְאָתוֹ וְלַעֲשׂוֹת
רְצוֹנוֹ וּלְעָבְדוֹ בְּלֵבָב שָׁלֵם, לְמַעַן לֹא נִיגַע לָרִיק, וְלֹא נֵלֵד
לַבֶּהָלָה.¹

יְהִי רָצוֹן מִלְּפָנֶיךָ, יהוה אֱלֹהֵינוּ וֵאלֹהֵי אֲבוֹתֵינוּ, שֶׁנִּשְׁמֹר
חֻקֶּיךָ בָּעוֹלָם הַזֶּה, וְנִזְכֶּה וְנִחְיֶה וְנִרְאֶה וְנִירַשׁ טוֹבָה וּבְרָכָה
לִשְׁנֵי יְמוֹת הַמָּשִׁיחַ וּלְחַיֵּי הָעוֹלָם הַבָּא. לְמַעַן יְזַמֶּרְךָ כָבוֹד
וְלֹא יִדֹּם, יהוה אֱלֹהַי לְעוֹלָם אוֹדֶךָּ.² בָּרוּךְ הַגֶּבֶר אֲשֶׁר
יִבְטַח בַּיהוה, וְהָיָה יהוה מִבְטַחוֹ.³ בִּטְחוּ בַיהוה עֲדֵי עַד, כִּי
בְּיָהּ יהוה צוּר עוֹלָמִים.⁵ ❖ וְיִבְטְחוּ בְךָ יוֹדְעֵי שְׁמֶךָ, כִּי לֹא
עָזַבְתָּ דֹרְשֶׁיךָ, יהוה.⁵ יהוה חָפֵץ לְמַעַן צִדְקוֹ, יַגְדִּיל תּוֹרָה
וְיַאְדִּיר.⁶

MINCHAH

Stand up after the words "We know not," until conclusion of the paragraph.

וַאֲנַחְנוּ *We know not what to do•* — *but our eyes are upon You.* [1] *Remember Your mercies, HASHEM, and Your kindness, for they are from the beginning of the world.* [2] *May Your kindness be upon us, HASHEM, just as we awaited You.* •[3] *Recall not against us the sins of the ancients; may Your mercies meet us swiftly, for we have become exceedingly impoverished.* •[4] *Be gracious to us, HASHEM, be gracious to us, for we are abundantly sated with scorn.* [5] *Amid rage — remember to be merciful!* [6] *For He knew our nature, He remembers that we are dust.* [7] Chazzan – *Assist us, O God of our salvation, for the sake of Your Name's glory; rescue us and atone for our sins for Your Name's sake.* [8]

---

(1) II Chronicles 20:12. (2) Psalms 25:6. (3) 33:22. (4) 79:8.
(5) 123:3 (6) Habakkuk 3:2. (7) Psalms 103:14. (8) 79:9.

כַּאֲשֶׁר יִחַלְנוּ לָךְ — *Just as we awaited You.* If we are undeserving, O God, then help us because You will thereby sanctify Your Name (Alshich).

כִּי דַלּוֹנוּ מְאֹד — *For we have become exceedingly impoverished.* A concluding plea that we have already suffered mightily and God knows that we are helpless without Him.

MAARIV FOR THE CONCLUSION OF THE SABBATH

Blessed is He, our God, Who created us for His glory, separated us from those who stray, gave us the Torah of truth and implanted eternal life within us. May He open our heart through His Torah and imbue our heart with love and awe of Him and that we may do His will and serve Him wholeheartedly, so that we do not struggle in vain nor produce for futility. [1]

May it be Your will, HASHEM, our God and the God of our forefathers, that we observe Your decrees in This World, and merit that we live and see and inherit goodness and blessing in the years of Messianic times and for the life of the World to Come. So that my soul might sing to You and not be stilled, HASHEM, my God, forever will I thank You. [2] *Blessed is the man who trusts in HASHEM, then HASHEM will be his security.* [3] *Trust in HASHEM forever, for in God, HASHEM, is the strength of the worlds.* [4] Chazzan – *Those knowing Your Name will trust in You, and You forsake not those Who seek You, HASHEM.* [5] *HASHEM desired, for the sake of its [Israel's] righteousness, that the Torah be made great and glorious.* [6]

---

(1) Cf. Isaiah 65:23. (2) Psalms 30:13. (3) Jeremiah 17:7.
(4) Isaiah 26:4. (5) Psalms 9:11. (6) Isaiah 42:21.

קדיש שלם

קַדִּישׁ שָׁלֵם. The chazzan recites

יִתְגַּדַּל וְיִתְקַדַּשׁ שְׁמֵהּ רַבָּא. (.Cong – אָמֵן) בְּעָלְמָא דִּי בְרָא
כִרְעוּתֵהּ. וְיַמְלִיךְ מַלְכוּתֵהּ, בְּחַיֵּיכוֹן וּבְיוֹמֵיכוֹן וּבְחַיֵּי דְכָל
בֵּית יִשְׂרָאֵל, בַּעֲגָלָא וּבִזְמַן קָרִיב. וְאִמְרוּ: אָמֵן.

(.Cong – אָמֵן. יְהֵא שְׁמֵהּ רַבָּא מְבָרַךְ לְעָלַם וּלְעָלְמֵי עָלְמַיָּא.)

יְהֵא שְׁמֵהּ רַבָּא מְבָרַךְ לְעָלַם וּלְעָלְמֵי עָלְמַיָּא.

יִתְבָּרַךְ וְיִשְׁתַּבַּח וְיִתְפָּאַר וְיִתְרוֹמַם וְיִתְנַשֵּׂא וְיִתְהַדָּר וְיִתְעַלֶּה
וְיִתְהַלָּל שְׁמֵהּ דְּקֻדְשָׁא בְּרִיךְ הוּא (.Cong – בְּרִיךְ הוּא) – לְעֵלָּא מִן
כָּל [From Rosh Hashanah to Yom Kippur substitute ° – לְעֵלָּא (וּ)לְעֵלָּא מִכָּל]
בִּרְכָתָא וְשִׁירָתָא תֻּשְׁבְּחָתָא וְנֶחֱמָתָא דַּאֲמִירָן בְּעָלְמָא. וְאִמְרוּ: אָמֵן.
(.Cong – אָמֵן.)

(.Cong – קַבֵּל בְּרַחֲמִים וּבְרָצוֹן אֶת תְּפִלָּתֵנוּ.)

תִּתְקַבֵּל צְלוֹתְהוֹן וּבָעוּתְהוֹן דְּכָל (בֵּית) יִשְׂרָאֵל קֳדָם אֲבוּהוֹן דִּי
בִשְׁמַיָּא. וְאִמְרוּ: אָמֵן. (.Cong – אָמֵן.)

(.Cong – יְהֵא שֵׁם יהוה מְבָרַךְ מֵעַתָּה וְעַד עוֹלָם.[1])

יְהֵא שְׁלָמָא רַבָּא מִן שְׁמַיָּא, וְחַיִּים עָלֵינוּ וְעַל כָּל יִשְׂרָאֵל. וְאִמְרוּ:
אָמֵן. (.Cong – אָמֵן.)

(.Cong – עֶזְרִי מֵעִם יהוה, עֹשֵׂה שָׁמַיִם וָאָרֶץ.[2])

Bow. Take three steps back. Bow left and say . . . עֹשֶׂה; bow right and say . . . הוּא; bow forward and say . . . וְעַל כָּל. Remain in place for a few moments, then take three steps forward.

עֹשֶׂה °שָׁלוֹם בִּמְרוֹמָיו, הוּא יַעֲשֶׂה שָׁלוֹם עָלֵינוּ, וְעַל כָּל יִשְׂרָאֵל.
וְאִמְרוּ: אָמֵן. (.Cong – אָמֵן.)

°הַשָּׁלוֹם – From Rosh Hashanah to Yom Kippur some say

AT MAARIV: Between Pesach and Shavuos the *Omer* is counted (p. 62).
On Tishah B'Av, *Eichah* and *Kinnos* are recited at this point.

Stand while reciting עָלֵינוּ.

עָלֵינוּ לְשַׁבֵּחַ לַאֲדוֹן הַכֹּל, לָתֵת גְּדֻלָּה לְיוֹצֵר בְּרֵאשִׁית,
שֶׁלֹּא עָשָׂנוּ כְּגוֹיֵי הָאֲרָצוֹת, וְלֹא שָׂמָנוּ כְּמִשְׁפְּחוֹת
הָאֲדָמָה. שֶׁלֹּא שָׂם חֶלְקֵנוּ כָּהֶם, וְגוֹרָלֵנוּ כְּכָל הֲמוֹנָם. (שֶׁהֵם
מִשְׁתַּחֲוִים לְהֶבֶל וָרִיק, וּמִתְפַּלְלִים אֶל אֵל לֹא יוֹשִׁיעַ.[3])
וַאֲנַחְנוּ כּוֹרְעִים וּמִשְׁתַּחֲוִים וּמוֹדִים, לִפְנֵי מֶלֶךְ
מַלְכֵי הַמְּלָכִים הַקָּדוֹשׁ בָּרוּךְ הוּא. שֶׁהוּא נוֹטֶה   Bow while reciting וַאֲנַחְנוּ כּוֹרְעִים וּמִשְׁתַּחֲוִים
שָׁמַיִם וְיֹסֵד אָרֶץ,[4] וּמוֹשַׁב יְקָרוֹ בַּשָּׁמַיִם מִמַּעַל, וּשְׁכִינַת עֻזּוֹ
בְּגָבְהֵי מְרוֹמִים. הוּא אֱלֹהֵינוּ, אֵין עוֹד. אֱמֶת מַלְכֵּנוּ, אֶפֶס

FULL KADDISH
The chazzan recites Full *Kaddish:*

יִתְגַּדַּל *May His great Name grow exalted and sanctified* (Cong.— Amen.) *in the world that He created as He willed. May He give reign to His kingship in your lifetimes and in your days, and in the lifetimes of the entire Family of Israel, swiftly and soon. Now respond: Amen.*

(Cong. — Amen. May His great Name be blessed forever and ever.)

May His great Name be blessed forever and ever.

Blessed, praised, glorified, exalted, extolled, mighty, upraised, and lauded be the Name of the Holy One, Blessed is He (Cong.— Blessed is He) — [From Rosh Hashanah to Yom Kippur add: exceedingly] *beyond any blessing and song, praise and consolation that are uttered in the world. Now respond: Amen.* (Cong.— Amen.)

(Cong.— Accept our prayers with mercy and favor.)

May the prayers and supplications of the entire Family of Israel be accepted before their Father Who is in Heaven. Now respond: Amen. (Cong.— Amen.)

(Cong.— Blessed be the Name of HASHEM, from this time and forever. [1])

May there be abundant peace from Heaven, and life, upon us and upon all Israel. Now respond: Amen. (Cong.— Amen.)

(Cong.— My help is from HASHEM, Maker of heaven and earth. [2])

Bow. Take three steps back. Bow left and say, *"He Who makes peace . . .";* bow right and say, *"may He . . .";* bow forward and say, *"and upon all Israel . . ."* Remain in place for a few moments, then take three steps forward.

He Who makes peace in His heights, may He make peace upon us, and upon all Israel. Now respond: Amen. (Cong.— Amen.)

> **AT MAARIV:** Between Pesach and Shavuos the *Omer* is counted (p. 62).
> On Tishah B'Av, *Eichah* and *Kinnos* are recited at this point.

Stand while reciting עָלֵינוּ, *"It is our duty . . ."*

עָלֵינוּ *It is our duty to praise the Master of all, to ascribe greatness to the Molder of primeval creation, for He has not made us like the nations of the lands and has not emplaced us like the families of the earth; for He has not assigned our portion like theirs nor our lot like all their multitudes. (For they bow to vanity and emptiness and pray to a god* Bow while reciting "But we bend our knees." *which helps not. [3]) But we bend our knees, bow, and acknowledge our thanks before the King Who reigns over kings, the Holy One, Blessed is He. He stretches out heaven and establishes earth's foundation, [4] the seat of His homage is in the heavens above and His powerful Presence is in the loftiest heights. He is our God and there is none other. True is our King, there is nothing*

(1) *Psalms* 113:2. (2) 121:2. (3) *Isaiah* 45:20. (4) 51:13.

עָלֵינוּ **/ Aleinu**

According to many early sources, this declaration of faith and dedication was composed by Joshua after he led Israel across the Jordan. During the Talmudic era it was part of the Rosh Hashanah *Mussaf* service, and at some point during medieval times it began to find its way into the daily service.

זוּלָתוֹ, כַּכָּתוּב בְּתוֹרָתוֹ: וְיָדַעְתָּ הַיּוֹם וַהֲשֵׁבֹתָ אֶל לְבָבֶךָ, כִּי יְהֹוָה
הוּא הָאֱלֹהִים בַּשָּׁמַיִם מִמַּעַל וְעַל הָאָרֶץ מִתָּחַת, אֵין עוֹד.[1]

עַל כֵּן נְקַוֶּה לְּךָ, יְהֹוָה אֱלֹהֵינוּ, לִרְאוֹת מְהֵרָה בְּתִפְאֶרֶת
עֻזֶּךָ, לְהַעֲבִיר גִּלּוּלִים מִן הָאָרֶץ, וְהָאֱלִילִים כָּרוֹת
יִכָּרֵתוּן, לְתַקֵּן עוֹלָם בְּמַלְכוּת שַׁדַּי. וְכָל בְּנֵי בָשָׂר יִקְרְאוּ בִשְׁמֶךָ,
לְהַפְנוֹת אֵלֶיךָ כָּל רִשְׁעֵי אָרֶץ. יַכִּירוּ וְיֵדְעוּ כָּל יוֹשְׁבֵי תֵבֵל, כִּי
לְךָ תִּכְרַע כָּל בֶּרֶךְ, תִּשָּׁבַע כָּל לָשׁוֹן.[2] לְפָנֶיךָ יְהֹוָה אֱלֹהֵינוּ
יִכְרְעוּ וְיִפֹּלוּ, וְלִכְבוֹד שִׁמְךָ יְקָר יִתֵּנוּ. וִיקַבְּלוּ כֻלָּם אֶת עֹל
מַלְכוּתֶךָ, וְתִמְלֹךְ עֲלֵיהֶם מְהֵרָה לְעוֹלָם וָעֶד. כִּי הַמַּלְכוּת שֶׁלְּךָ
הִיא וּלְעוֹלְמֵי עַד תִּמְלוֹךְ בְּכָבוֹד, כַּכָּתוּב בְּתוֹרָתֶךָ: יְהֹוָה יִמְלֹךְ
לְעֹלָם וָעֶד.[3] ✧ וְנֶאֱמַר: וְהָיָה יְהֹוָה לְמֶלֶךְ עַל כָּל הָאָרֶץ, בַּיּוֹם
הַהוּא יִהְיֶה יְהֹוָה אֶחָד וּשְׁמוֹ אֶחָד.[4]

אַל תִּירָא מִפַּחַד פִּתְאֹם, וּמִשֹּׁאַת רְשָׁעִים כִּי תָבֹא.[5] עֻצוּ עֵצָה וְתֻפָר,
דַּבְּרוּ דָבָר וְלֹא יָקוּם, כִּי עִמָּנוּ אֵל.[6] וְעַד זִקְנָה אֲנִי הוּא,
וְעַד שֵׂיבָה אֲנִי אֶסְבֹּל, אֲנִי עָשִׂיתִי וַאֲנִי אֶשָּׂא, וַאֲנִי אֶסְבֹּל וַאֲמַלֵּט.[7]

In the presence of a *minyan*, mourners recite קַדִּישׁ יָתוֹם the Mourner's *Kaddish*.

יִתְגַּדַּל וְיִתְקַדַּשׁ שְׁמֵהּ רַבָּא. (.Cong – אָמֵן) בְּעָלְמָא דִּי בְרָא כִרְעוּתֵהּ.
וְיַמְלִיךְ מַלְכוּתֵהּ, בְּחַיֵּיכוֹן וּבְיוֹמֵיכוֹן וּבְחַיֵּי דְכָל בֵּית יִשְׂרָאֵל,
בַּעֲגָלָא וּבִזְמַן קָרִיב. וְאִמְרוּ: אָמֵן.

(.Cong – אָמֵן. יְהֵא שְׁמֵהּ רַבָּא מְבָרַךְ לְעָלַם וּלְעָלְמֵי עָלְמַיָּא.)

יְהֵא שְׁמֵהּ רַבָּא מְבָרַךְ לְעָלַם וּלְעָלְמֵי עָלְמַיָּא.

יִתְבָּרַךְ וְיִשְׁתַּבַּח וְיִתְפָּאַר וְיִתְרוֹמַם וְיִתְנַשֵּׂא וְיִתְהַדָּר וְיִתְעַלֶּה
וְיִתְהַלָּל שְׁמֵהּ דְּקֻדְשָׁא בְּרִיךְ הוּא (.Cong – בְּרִיךְ הוּא) °לְעֵלָּא מִן
כָּל [°From Rosh Hashanah to Yom Kippur substitute לְעֵלָּא (וּ)לְעֵלָּא מִכָּל]
בִּרְכָתָא וְשִׁירָתָא תֻּשְׁבְּחָתָא וְנֶחָמָתָא דַּאֲמִירָן בְּעָלְמָא. וְאִמְרוּ:
אָמֵן. (.Cong – אָמֵן.)

יְהֵא שְׁלָמָא רַבָּא מִן שְׁמַיָּא, וְחַיִּים עָלֵינוּ וְעַל כָּל יִשְׂרָאֵל. וְאִמְרוּ: אָמֵן. (.Cong – אָמֵן.)

Bow. Take three steps back. Bow left and say . . . עֹשֶׂה; bow right and say . . . הוּא; bow forward
and say . . . עָל כָּל. Remain in place for a few moments, then take three steps forward.

עֹשֶׂה °שָׁלוֹם בִּמְרוֹמָיו, הוּא יַעֲשֶׂה שָׁלוֹם עָלֵינוּ, וְעַל כָּל יִשְׂרָאֵל.
וְאִמְרוּ: אָמֵן. (.Cong – אָמֵן.)

°הַשָּׁלוֹם – From Rosh Hashanah to Yom Kippur some say

besides Him, as it is written in His Torah: "You are to know this day and take to your heart that HASHEM is the only God — in heaven above and on the earth below — there is none other."[1]

עָל כֵּן Therefore we put our hope in You, HASHEM, our God, that we may soon see Your mighty splendor, to remove detestable idolatry from the earth, and false gods will be utterly cut off, to perfect the universe through the Almighty's sovereignty. Then all humanity will call upon Your Name, to turn all the earth's wicked toward You. All the world's inhabitants will recognize and know that to You every knee should bend, every tongue should swear.[2] Before You, HASHEM, our God, they will bend every knee and cast themselves down, and to the glory of Your Name they will render homage, and they will all accept upon themselves the yoke of Your kingship that You may reign over them soon and eternally. For the kingdom is Yours and You will reign for all eternity in glory, as it is written in Your Torah: HASHEM shall reign for all eternity.[3] Chazzan— And it is said: HASHEM will be King over all the world — on that day HASHEM will be One and His Name will be One.[4]

אַל תִּירָא Do not fear sudden terror, or the holocaust of the wicked when it comes.[5] Plan a conspiracy and it shall be annulled; speak your piece and it shall not stand, for God is with us.[6] Even till your seniority, I remain unchanged; and even till your ripe old age, I shall endure. I created you and I shall bear you; I shall endure and rescue.[7]

In the presence of a *minyan*, mourners recite the Mourner's Kaddish.
[A transliteration of this Kaddish appears on page 127.]

יִתְגַּדַּל May His great Name grow exalted and sanctified (Cong.— Amen.) in the world that He created as He willed. May He give reign to His kingship in your lifetimes and in your days, and in the lifetimes of the entire Family of Israel, swiftly and soon. Now respond: Amen.
(Cong. — Amen. May His great Name be blessed forever and ever.)
        May His great Name be blessed forever and ever.

Blessed, praised, glorified, exalted, extolled, mighty, upraised, and lauded be the Name of the Holy One, Blessed is He, (Cong.— Blessed is He) — [From Rosh Hashanah to Yom Kippur add: *exceedingly*] beyond any blessing and song, praise and consolation that are uttered in the world. Now respond: Amen. (Cong.— Amen.)

May there be abundant peace from Heaven, and life, upon us and upon all Israel. Now respond: Amen. (Cong.— Amen.)

        Bow. Take three steps back. Bow left and say, "He Who makes peace . . ."; bow right and say, "may He . . ."; bow forward and say, "and upon all Israel . . ."
        Remain in place for a few moments, then take three steps forward.

He Who makes peace in His heights, may He make peace upon us, and upon all Israel. Now respond: Amen. (Cong.— Amen.)

---

(1) *Deuteronomy* 4:39. (2) Cf. *Isaiah* 45:23. (3) *Exodus* 15:18.
(4) *Zechariah* 14:9. (5) *Proverbs* 3:25. (6) *Isaiah* 8:10. (7) 46:4.

From Rosh Chodesh Elul through Shemini Atzeres, Psalm 27 is recited after Maariv.

לְדָוִד, יהוה אוֹרִי וְיִשְׁעִי, מִמִּי אִירָא, יהוה מָעוֹז חַיַּי, מִמִּי אֶפְחָד.
בִּקְרֹב עָלַי מְרֵעִים לֶאֱכֹל אֶת בְּשָׂרִי, צָרַי וְאֹיְבַי לִי, הֵמָּה
כָשְׁלוּ וְנָפָלוּ. אִם תַּחֲנֶה עָלַי מַחֲנֶה, לֹא יִירָא לִבִּי, אִם תָּקוּם עָלַי
מִלְחָמָה, בְּזֹאת אֲנִי בוֹטֵחַ. אַחַת שָׁאַלְתִּי מֵאֵת יהוה, אוֹתָהּ אֲבַקֵּשׁ,
שִׁבְתִּי בְּבֵית יהוה כָּל יְמֵי חַיַּי, לַחֲזוֹת בְּנֹעַם יהוה, וּלְבַקֵּר בְּהֵיכָלוֹ.
כִּי יִצְפְּנֵנִי בְּסֻכֹּה בְּיוֹם רָעָה, יַסְתִּרֵנִי בְּסֵתֶר אָהֳלוֹ, בְּצוּר יְרוֹמְמֵנִי.
וְעַתָּה יָרוּם רֹאשִׁי עַל אֹיְבַי סְבִיבוֹתַי, וְאֶזְבְּחָה בְאָהֳלוֹ זִבְחֵי תְרוּעָה,
אָשִׁירָה וַאֲזַמְּרָה לַיהוה. שְׁמַע יהוה קוֹלִי אֶקְרָא, וְחָנֵּנִי וַעֲנֵנִי. לְךָ
אָמַר לִבִּי בַּקְּשׁוּ פָנָי, אֶת פָּנֶיךָ יהוה אֲבַקֵּשׁ. אַל תַּסְתֵּר פָּנֶיךָ מִמֶּנִּי,
אַל תַּט בְּאַף עַבְדֶּךָ, עֶזְרָתִי הָיִיתָ, אַל תִּטְּשֵׁנִי וְאַל תַּעַזְבֵנִי, אֱלֹהֵי
יִשְׁעִי. כִּי אָבִי וְאִמִּי עֲזָבוּנִי, וַיהוה יַאַסְפֵנִי. הוֹרֵנִי יהוה דַּרְכֶּךָ, וּנְחֵנִי
בְּאֹרַח מִישׁוֹר, לְמַעַן שׁוֹרְרָי. אַל תִּתְּנֵנִי בְּנֶפֶשׁ צָרָי, כִּי קָמוּ בִי עֵדֵי
שֶׁקֶר, וִיפֵחַ חָמָס. ❖ לוּלֵא הֶאֱמַנְתִּי לִרְאוֹת בְּטוּב יהוה בְּאֶרֶץ חַיִּים.
קַוֵּה אֶל יהוה, חֲזַק וְיַאֲמֵץ לִבֶּךָ, וְקַוֵּה אֶל יהוה.

In the presence of a minyan, mourners recite the Mourner's Kaddish (page 58).

In a house of mourning, Psalm 49 is recited after Maariv.

לַמְנַצֵּחַ לִבְנֵי קֹרַח מִזְמוֹר. שִׁמְעוּ זֹאת כָּל הָעַמִּים, הַאֲזִינוּ כָּל
יֹשְׁבֵי חָלֶד. גַּם בְּנֵי אָדָם, גַּם בְּנֵי אִישׁ, יַחַד עָשִׁיר וְאֶבְיוֹן.
פִּי יְדַבֵּר חָכְמוֹת, וְהָגוּת לִבִּי תְבוּנוֹת. אַטֶּה לְמָשָׁל אָזְנִי, אֶפְתַּח
בְּכִנּוֹר חִידָתִי. לָמָּה אִירָא בִּימֵי רָע, עֲוֹן עֲקֵבַי יְסֻבֵּנִי. הַבֹּטְחִים עַל
חֵילָם, וּבְרֹב עָשְׁרָם יִתְהַלָּלוּ. אָח לֹא פָדֹה יִפְדֶּה אִישׁ, לֹא יִתֵּן
לֵאלֹהִים כָּפְרוֹ. וְיֵקַר פִּדְיוֹן נַפְשָׁם, וְחָדַל לְעוֹלָם. וִיחִי עוֹד לָנֶצַח, לֹא
יִרְאֶה הַשָּׁחַת. כִּי יִרְאֶה חֲכָמִים יָמוּתוּ, יַחַד כְּסִיל וָבַעַר יֹאבֵדוּ, וְעָזְבוּ
לַאֲחֵרִים חֵילָם. קִרְבָּם בָּתֵּימוֹ לְעוֹלָם, מִשְׁכְּנֹתָם לְדֹר וָדֹר, קָרְאוּ
בִשְׁמוֹתָם עֲלֵי אֲדָמוֹת. וְאָדָם בִּיקָר בַּל יָלִין, נִמְשַׁל כַּבְּהֵמוֹת נִדְמוּ.
זֶה דַרְכָּם, כֵּסֶל לָמוֹ, וְאַחֲרֵיהֶם בְּפִיהֶם יִרְצוּ, סֶלָה. כַּצֹּאן לִשְׁאוֹל
שַׁתּוּ, מָוֶת יִרְעֵם, וַיִּרְדּוּ בָם יְשָׁרִים לַבֹּקֶר, וְצוּרָם לְבַלּוֹת שְׁאוֹל,
מִזְּבֻל לוֹ. אַךְ אֱלֹהִים יִפְדֶּה נַפְשִׁי מִיַּד שְׁאוֹל, כִּי יִקָּחֵנִי סֶלָה. אַל
תִּירָא כִּי יַעֲשִׁר אִישׁ, כִּי יִרְבֶּה כְּבוֹד בֵּיתוֹ. כִּי לֹא בְמוֹתוֹ יִקַּח הַכֹּל,
לֹא יֵרֵד אַחֲרָיו כְּבוֹדוֹ. כִּי נַפְשׁוֹ בְּחַיָּיו יְבָרֵךְ, וְיוֹדֻךָ כִּי תֵיטִיב לָךְ.
תָּבוֹא עַד דּוֹר אֲבוֹתָיו, עַד נֵצַח לֹא יִרְאוּ אוֹר. ❖ אָדָם בִּיקָר וְלֹא
יָבִין, נִמְשַׁל כַּבְּהֵמוֹת נִדְמוּ.

In the presence of a minyan, mourners recite the Mourner's Kaddish (page 58).

From Rosh Chodesh Elul through Shemini Atzeres, Psalm 27 is recited after Maariv.

לְדָוִד *Of David; HASHEM is my light and my salvation, whom shall I fear? HASHEM is my life's strength, whom shall I dread? When evildoers approach me to devour my flesh, my tormentors and my foes against me — it is they who stumble and fall. Though an army would besiege me, my heart would not fear; though war would arise against me, in this I trust. One thing I asked of HASHEM, that shall I seek: That I dwell in the House of HASHEM all the days of my life; to behold the sweetness of HASHEM and to contemplate in His Sanctuary. Indeed, He will hide me in His shelter on the day of evil; He will conceal me in the concealment of His Tent, He will lift me upon a rock. Now my head is raised above my enemies around me, and I will slaughter offerings in His Tent accompanied by joyous song; I will sing and make music to HASHEM. HASHEM, hear my voice when I call, be gracious toward me and answer me. In Your behalf, my heart has said, "Seek My Presence"; Your Presence, HASHEM, do I seek. Conceal not Your Presence from me, repel not Your servant in anger. You have been my Helper, abandon me not, forsake me not, O God of my salvation. Though my father and mother have forsaken me, HASHEM will gather me in. Teach me Your way, HASHEM, and lead me on the path of integrity, because of my watchful foes. Deliver me not to the wishes of my tormentors, for there have arisen against me false witnesses who breathe violence. Chazzan — Had I not trusted that I would see the goodness of HASHEM in the land of life! Hope to HASHEM, strengthen yourself and He will give you courage; and hope to HASHEM.*

In the presence of a minyan, mourners recite the Mourner's Kaddish (page 58).

In a house of mourning, Psalm 49 is recited after Maariv.

לַמְנַצֵּחַ *For the conductor, by the sons of Korah, a psalm. Hear this all you peoples, give ear all you dwellers of decaying earth; sons of Adam and sons of man alike; rich and poor together. My mouth will speak wisdom, and the meditations of my heart are insightful. I will incline my ear to the parable; with a harp I will solve my riddle. Why should I be fearful in days of evil, when the injunctions that I trod upon will surround me? Those who rely on their possessions, and they are boastful of their great wealth — yet a man cannot redeem a brother, he cannot give his ransom to God. Too costly is their soul's redemption and unattainable forever. Can one live eternally, never to see the pit? Though he sees that wise men die, that the foolish and boorish perish together and leave their possessions to others, [nevertheless,] in their imagination their houses are forever, their dwellings for generation after generation; they have proclaimed their names throughout the lands. But as for man: In glory he shall not repose, he is likened to the silenced animals. This is their way, folly is theirs, yet of their destiny their mouths speak soothingly, Selah! Like sheep, they are destined for the Lower World, death shall consume them; and the upright shall dominate them at daybreak, their form is doomed to rot in the grave, each from his dwelling. But God will redeem my soul from the hand of the Lower World, for He will take me, Selah! Fear not when a man grows rich, when he increases the glory of his house, for upon his death he will not take anything, his glory will not descend after him. Though he may bless himself in his lifetime, others will praise you if you improve yourself. It shall come to the generation of its fathers; unto eternity they shall see no light. Chazzan — Man is glorious but [if he] understands not, he is likened to the silenced animals.*

In the presence of a minyan, mourners recite the Mourner's Kaddish (page 58).

❊ ספירת העומר ❊

The *Omer* is counted from the second night of Pesach until the night before Shavuos.
In some congregations, the following Kabbalistic prayer
precedes the Counting of the *Omer*.

לְשֵׁם יִחוּד קוּדְשָׁא בְּרִיךְ הוּא וּשְׁכִינְתֵּיהּ, בִּדְחִילוּ וּרְחִימוּ, לְיַחֵד
שֵׁם יוֹ"ד הֵ"א בְּוָא"ו הֵ"א בְּיִחוּדָא שְׁלִים, בְּשֵׁם כָּל יִשְׂרָאֵל.
הִנְנִי מוּכָן וּמְזֻמָּן לְקַיֵּם מִצְוַת עֲשֵׂה שֶׁל סְפִירַת הָעוֹמֶר, כְּמוֹ שֶׁכָּתוּב
בַּתּוֹרָה: וּסְפַרְתֶּם לָכֶם מִמָּחֳרַת הַשַּׁבָּת, מִיּוֹם הֲבִיאֲכֶם אֶת עֹמֶר
הַתְּנוּפָה, שֶׁבַע שַׁבָּתוֹת תְּמִימֹת תִּהְיֶינָה. עַד מִמָּחֳרַת הַשַּׁבָּת
הַשְּׁבִיעִת תִּסְפְּרוּ חֲמִשִּׁים יוֹם, וְהִקְרַבְתֶּם מִנְחָה חֲדָשָׁה לַיהוה.[1]
וִיהִי נְעַם אֲדֹנָי אֱלֹהֵינוּ עָלֵינוּ, וּמַעֲשֵׂה יָדֵינוּ כּוֹנְנָה עָלֵינוּ, וּמַעֲשֵׂה
יָדֵינוּ כּוֹנְנֵהוּ.[2]

The *chazzan*, followed by the congregation, recites the blessing and counts.
One praying without a *minyan* should also recite the entire *Omer* service.

בָּרוּךְ אַתָּה יהוה אֱלֹהֵינוּ מֶלֶךְ הָעוֹלָם, אֲשֶׁר קִדְּשָׁנוּ
בְּמִצְוֹתָיו וְצִוָּנוּ עַל סְפִירַת הָעוֹמֶר.

INSERT THE APPROPRIATE DAY'S COUNT. SEE CHART ON PP. 66-67.

הָרַחֲמָן הוּא יַחֲזִיר לָנוּ עֲבוֹדַת בֵּית הַמִּקְדָּשׁ לִמְקוֹמָהּ,
בִּמְהֵרָה בְיָמֵינוּ. אָמֵן סֶלָה.

תהלים סז

לַמְנַצֵּחַ בִּנְגִינֹת מִזְמוֹר שִׁיר. אֱלֹהִים יְחָנֵּנוּ וִיבָרְכֵנוּ, יָאֵר
פָּנָיו אִתָּנוּ סֶלָה. לָדַעַת בָּאָרֶץ דַּרְכֶּךָ, בְּכָל
גּוֹיִם יְשׁוּעָתֶךָ. יוֹדוּךָ עַמִּים, אֱלֹהִים, יוֹדוּךָ עַמִּים כֻּלָּם.
יִשְׂמְחוּ וִירַנְּנוּ לְאֻמִּים, כִּי תִשְׁפֹּט עַמִּים מִישׁוֹר, וּלְאֻמִּים
בָּאָרֶץ תַּנְחֵם סֶלָה. יוֹדוּךָ עַמִּים, אֱלֹהִים, יוֹדוּךָ עַמִּים

---

(1) *Leviticus* 23:15-16. (2) *Psalms* 90:17.

ספירת העומר / Counting the Omer
The Torah commands that from the second day of Pesach — the day the *Omer* offering of new barley is brought in the Temple — forty-nine days are to be counted, and the festival of Shavuos celebrated on the fiftieth day. This period is

called *Sefiras HaOmer*, the Counting of the Omer. The *Sefirah* count also recalls an earlier event. During the seven weeks following the Exodus, our ancestors prepared themselves for receiving the Torah at Mount Sinai. This responsibility to prepare oneself to receive the Torah is present every year, as

⁂ COUNTING THE OMER ⁂

The *Omer* is counted from the second night of Pesach until the night before Shavuos.

In some congregations, the following Kabbalistic prayer
precedes the Counting of the *Omer*.

לְשֵׁם *For the sake of the unification of the Holy One, Blessed is He, and His Presence, in fear and love to unify the Name Yud-Kei with Vav-Kei in perfect unity, in the name of all Israel. Behold I am prepared and ready to perform the commandment of counting the Omer, as it is written in the Torah: "You are to count from the morrow of the rest day, from the day you brought the Omer-offering that is waved — they are to be seven complete weeks — until the morrow of the seventh week you are to count fifty days, and then offer a new meal-offering to HASHEM."[1] May the pleasantness of my Lord, our God, be upon us — may He establish our handiwork for us; our handiwork, may He establish.[2]*

The *chazzan*, followed by the congregation, recites the blessing and counts.
One praying without a *minyan* should also recite the entire *Omer* service.

בָּרוּךְ *Blessed are You, HASHEM, our God, King of the universe, Who has sanctified us with His commandments and has commanded us regarding the counting of the Omer.*

INSERT THE APPROPRIATE DAY'S COUNT. SEE CHART ON PP. 66-67.

הָרַחֲמָן *The Compassionate One! May He return for us the service of the Temple to its place, speedily in our days. Amen, Selah!*

Psalm 67

לַמְנַצֵּחַ *For the Conductor, upon Neginos, a psalm, a song. May God favor us and bless us, may He illuminate His countenance with us, Selah. To make known Your way on earth, among all the nations Your salvation. The peoples will acknowledge You, O God, the peoples will acknowledge You, all of them. Nations will be glad and sing for joy, because You will judge the people fairly and guide the nations on earth, Selah. The peoples will acknowledge You, O God, the peoples will acknowledge You,*

⊷§ A Summary of Laws of Sefirah

The *Omer* is counted, standing, after nightfall. Before reciting the blessing, one should be careful *not* to say, "Today is the ———th day." If he did so, for example, in response to someone who asked which day it is, he may not recite the blessing, since he has already counted that day. Where there are days and weeks, this does not apply unless he also mentioned the week. In both cases, he may recite the blessing on succeeding nights.

If one forgets to count at night, he counts during the day *without* a blessing, but may recite the blessing on succeeding nights. But if one forgot to count all day, he counts without a blessing on succeeding nights.

כֻּלָּם. אֶרֶץ נָתְנָה יְבוּלָהּ, יְבָרְכֵנוּ אֱלֹהִים אֱלֹהֵינוּ. יְבָרְכֵנוּ
אֱלֹהִים, וְיִירְאוּ אוֹתוֹ כָּל אַפְסֵי אָרֶץ.

אָנָּא בְּכֹחַ גְּדֻלַּת יְמִינְךָ תַּתִּיר צְרוּרָה.
אב״ג ית״ץ

קַבֵּל רִנַּת עַמְּךָ שַׂגְּבֵנוּ טַהֲרֵנוּ נוֹרָא.
קר״ע שט״ן

נָא גִבּוֹר דּוֹרְשֵׁי יִחוּדְךָ כְּבָבַת שָׁמְרֵם.
נג״ד יכ״ש

בָּרְכֵם טַהֲרֵם רַחֲמֵי צִדְקָתְךָ תָּמִיד גָּמְלֵם.
בט״ר צת״ג

חֲסִין קָדוֹשׁ בְּרוֹב טוּבְךָ נַהֵל עֲדָתֶךָ.
חק״ב טנ״ע

יָחִיד גֵּאֶה לְעַמְּךָ פְּנֵה זוֹכְרֵי קְדֻשָּׁתֶךָ.
יג״ל פז״ק

שַׁוְעָתֵנוּ קַבֵּל וּשְׁמַע צַעֲקָתֵנוּ יוֹדֵעַ תַּעֲלוּמוֹת.
שק״ו צי״ת

בָּרוּךְ שֵׁם כְּבוֹד מַלְכוּתוֹ לְעוֹלָם וָעֶד.

רִבּוֹנוֹ שֶׁל עוֹלָם, אַתָּה צִוִּיתָנוּ עַל יְדֵי מֹשֶׁה עַבְדְּךָ
לִסְפּוֹר סְפִירַת הָעוֹמֶר, כְּדֵי לְטַהֲרֵנוּ
מִקְּלִפּוֹתֵינוּ וּמִטֻּמְאוֹתֵינוּ, כְּמוֹ שֶׁכָּתַבְתָּ בְּתוֹרָתֶךָ: וּסְפַרְתֶּם
לָכֶם מִמָּחֳרַת הַשַּׁבָּת מִיּוֹם הֲבִיאֲכֶם אֶת עֹמֶר הַתְּנוּפָה,
שֶׁבַע שַׁבָּתוֹת תְּמִימֹת תִּהְיֶינָה. עַד מִמָּחֳרַת הַשַּׁבָּת
הַשְּׁבִיעִת תִּסְפְּרוּ חֲמִשִּׁים יוֹם.[1] כְּדֵי שֶׁיִּטַּהֲרוּ נַפְשׁוֹת עַמְּךָ
יִשְׂרָאֵל מִזֻּהֲמָתָם. וּבְכֵן יְהִי רָצוֹן מִלְּפָנֶיךָ, יהוה אֱלֹהֵינוּ
וֵאלֹהֵי אֲבוֹתֵינוּ, שֶׁבִּזְכוּת סְפִירַת הָעוֹמֶר שֶׁסָּפַרְתִּי הַיּוֹם,
יְתֻקַּן מַה שֶּׁפָּגַמְתִּי בִּסְפִירָה

(Insert the appropriate *sefirah*; see chart on 66-67.)

וְאֶטַּהֵר וְאֶתְקַדֵּשׁ בִּקְדֻשָּׁה שֶׁל מַעְלָה, וְעַל יְדֵי זֶה יֻשְׁפַּע שֶׁפַע
רַב בְּכָל הָעוֹלָמוֹת. וּלְתַקֵּן אֶת נַפְשׁוֹתֵינוּ, וְרוּחוֹתֵינוּ,
וְנִשְׁמוֹתֵינוּ, מִכָּל סִיג וּפְגָם, וּלְטַהֲרֵנוּ וּלְקַדְּשֵׁנוּ בִּקְדֻשָּׁתְךָ
הָעֶלְיוֹנָה. אָמֵן סֶלָה.

In some congregations, if a mourner is present, the Mourner's *Kaddish* (p. 58)
is recited, followed by עָלֵינוּ (p. 56). In others, עָלֵינוּ is recited immediately.

(1) *Leviticus* 23:15-16.

all of them. The earth has yielded its produce, may God, our own God, bless us. May God bless us and may all the ends of the earth fear him.

אָנָּא *We beg You! With the strength of Your right hand's greatness, untie the bundled sins. Accept the prayer of Your people; strengthen us, purify us, O Awesome One. Please, O Strong One — those who foster Your Oneness, guard them like the apple of an eye. Bless them, purify them, show them pity, may Your righteousness always recompense them. Powerful Holy One, with Your abundant goodness guide Your congregation. One and only Exalted One, turn to Your people, which proclaims Your holiness. Accept our entreaty and hear our cry, O Knower of mysteries.*

Blessed is the Name of His glorious Kingdom for all eternity.

רִבּוֹנוֹ שֶׁל עוֹלָם *Master of the universe, You commanded us through Moses, Your servant, to count the Omer Count in order to cleanse us from our encrustations of evil and from our contaminations, as You have written in Your Torah: "You are to count from the morrow of the rest day, from the day you brought the Omer-offering that is waved — they are to be seven complete weeks. Until the morrow of the seventh week you are to count fifty days,"[1] so that the souls of Your people Israel be cleansed of their contamination. Therefore, may it be Your will, HASHEM, our God and the God of our forefathers, that in the merit of the Omer Count that I have counted today, may there be corrected whatever blemish I have caused in the sefirah*

(Insert the appropriate *sefirah*; see chart on pp. 66-67.)

and may I be cleansed and sanctified with the holiness of Above, and through this may abundant bounty flow in all the worlds. And may it correct our lives, spirits, and souls from all sediment and blemish; may it cleanse us and sanctify us with Your exalted holiness. Amen, Selah!

In some congregations, if a mourner is present, the Mourner's *Kaddish* (p. 58) is recited, followed by *Aleinu* (p. 56). In others, *Aleinu* is recited immediately.

---

we relive the Exodus from bondage and materialism, and strive to be worthy of the gift of Torah. In ancient times, the *Sefirah* period was a time of rejoicing, but it is now observed as a time of semi-mourning because of several reasons: the absence of the Temple; the death of R' Akiva's 24,000 students during thirty-three days of the *Sefirah*; and a string of bloody massacres of Jewish communities during the Crusades.

SEFIRAH	COUNT	DAY
חֶסֶד שֶׁבְּחֶסֶד	הַיּוֹם יוֹם אֶחָד בָּעוֹמֶר	1
גְּבוּרָה שֶׁבְּחֶסֶד	הַיּוֹם שְׁנֵי יָמִים בָּעוֹמֶר	2
תִּפְאֶרֶת שֶׁבְּחֶסֶד	הַיּוֹם שְׁלֹשָׁה יָמִים בָּעוֹמֶר	3
נֶצַח שֶׁבְּחֶסֶד	הַיּוֹם אַרְבָּעָה יָמִים בָּעוֹמֶר	4
הוֹד שֶׁבְּחֶסֶד	הַיּוֹם חֲמִשָּׁה יָמִים בָּעוֹמֶר	5
יְסוֹד שֶׁבְּחֶסֶד	הַיּוֹם שִׁשָּׁה יָמִים בָּעוֹמֶר	6
מַלְכוּת שֶׁבְּחֶסֶד	הַיּוֹם שִׁבְעָה יָמִים, שֶׁהֵם שָׁבוּעַ אֶחָד, בָּעוֹמֶר	7
חֶסֶד שֶׁבִּגְבוּרָה	הַיּוֹם שְׁמוֹנָה יָמִים, שֶׁהֵם שָׁבוּעַ אֶחָד וְיוֹם אֶחָד, בָּעוֹמֶר	8
גְּבוּרָה שֶׁבִּגְבוּרָה	הַיּוֹם תִּשְׁעָה יָמִים, שֶׁהֵם שָׁבוּעַ אֶחָד וּשְׁנֵי יָמִים, בָּעוֹמֶר	9
תִּפְאֶרֶת שֶׁבִּגְבוּרָה	הַיּוֹם עֲשָׂרָה יָמִים, שֶׁהֵם שָׁבוּעַ אֶחָד וּשְׁלֹשָׁה יָמִים, בָּעוֹמֶר	10
נֶצַח שֶׁבִּגְבוּרָה	הַיּוֹם אַחַד עָשָׂר יוֹם, שֶׁהֵם שָׁבוּעַ אֶחָד וְאַרְבָּעָה יָמִים, בָּעוֹמֶר	11
הוֹד שֶׁבִּגְבוּרָה	הַיּוֹם שְׁנֵים עָשָׂר יוֹם, שֶׁהֵם שָׁבוּעַ אֶחָד וַחֲמִשָּׁה יָמִים, בָּעוֹמֶר	12
יְסוֹד שֶׁבִּגְבוּרָה	הַיּוֹם שְׁלֹשָׁה עָשָׂר יוֹם, שֶׁהֵם שָׁבוּעַ אֶחָד וְשִׁשָּׁה יָמִים, בָּעוֹמֶר	13
מַלְכוּת שֶׁבִּגְבוּרָה	הַיּוֹם אַרְבָּעָה עָשָׂר יוֹם, שֶׁהֵם שְׁנֵי שָׁבוּעוֹת, בָּעוֹמֶר	14
חֶסֶד שֶׁבְּתִפְאֶרֶת	הַיּוֹם חֲמִשָּׁה עָשָׂר יוֹם, שֶׁהֵם שְׁנֵי שָׁבוּעוֹת וְיוֹם אֶחָד, בָּעוֹמֶר	15
גְּבוּרָה שֶׁבְּתִפְאֶרֶת	הַיּוֹם שִׁשָּׁה עָשָׂר יוֹם, שֶׁהֵם שְׁנֵי שָׁבוּעוֹת וּשְׁנֵי יָמִים, בָּעוֹמֶר	16
תִּפְאֶרֶת שֶׁבְּתִפְאֶרֶת	הַיּוֹם שִׁבְעָה עָשָׂר יוֹם, שֶׁהֵם שְׁנֵי שָׁבוּעוֹת וּשְׁלֹשָׁה יָמִים, בָּעוֹמֶר	17
נֶצַח שֶׁבְּתִפְאֶרֶת	הַיּוֹם שְׁמוֹנָה עָשָׂר יוֹם, שֶׁהֵם שְׁנֵי שָׁבוּעוֹת וְאַרְבָּעָה יָמִים, בָּעוֹמֶר	18
הוֹד שֶׁבְּתִפְאֶרֶת	הַיּוֹם תִּשְׁעָה עָשָׂר יוֹם, שֶׁהֵם שְׁנֵי שָׁבוּעוֹת וַחֲמִשָּׁה יָמִים, בָּעוֹמֶר	19
יְסוֹד שֶׁבְּתִפְאֶרֶת	הַיּוֹם עֶשְׂרִים יוֹם, שֶׁהֵם שְׁנֵי שָׁבוּעוֹת וְשִׁשָּׁה יָמִים, בָּעוֹמֶר	20
מַלְכוּת שֶׁבְּתִפְאֶרֶת	הַיּוֹם אֶחָד וְעֶשְׂרִים יוֹם, שֶׁהֵם שְׁלֹשָׁה שָׁבוּעוֹת, בָּעוֹמֶר	21
חֶסֶד שֶׁבְּנֶצַח	הַיּוֹם שְׁנַיִם וְעֶשְׂרִים יוֹם, שֶׁהֵם שְׁלֹשָׁה שָׁבוּעוֹת וְיוֹם אֶחָד, בָּעוֹמֶר	22
גְּבוּרָה שֶׁבְּנֶצַח	הַיּוֹם שְׁלֹשָׁה וְעֶשְׂרִים יוֹם, שֶׁהֵם שְׁלֹשָׁה שָׁבוּעוֹת וּשְׁנֵי יָמִים, בָּעוֹמֶר	23
תִּפְאֶרֶת שֶׁבְּנֶצַח	הַיּוֹם אַרְבָּעָה וְעֶשְׂרִים יוֹם, שֶׁהֵם שְׁלֹשָׁה שָׁבוּעוֹת וּשְׁלֹשָׁה יָמִים, בָּעוֹמֶר	24
נֶצַח שֶׁבְּנֶצַח	הַיּוֹם חֲמִשָּׁה וְעֶשְׂרִים יוֹם, שֶׁהֵם שְׁלֹשָׁה שָׁבוּעוֹת וְאַרְבָּעָה יָמִים, בָּעוֹמֶר	25
הוֹד שֶׁבְּנֶצַח	הַיּוֹם שִׁשָּׁה וְעֶשְׂרִים יוֹם, שֶׁהֵם שְׁלֹשָׁה שָׁבוּעוֹת וַחֲמִשָּׁה יָמִים, בָּעוֹמֶר	26
יְסוֹד שֶׁבְּנֶצַח	הַיּוֹם שִׁבְעָה וְעֶשְׂרִים יוֹם, שֶׁהֵם שְׁלֹשָׁה שָׁבוּעוֹת וְשִׁשָּׁה יָמִים, בָּעוֹמֶר	27
מַלְכוּת שֶׁבְּנֶצַח	הַיּוֹם שְׁמוֹנָה וְעֶשְׂרִים יוֹם, שֶׁהֵם אַרְבָּעָה שָׁבוּעוֹת, בָּעוֹמֶר	28
חֶסֶד שֶׁבְּהוֹד	הַיּוֹם תִּשְׁעָה וְעֶשְׂרִים יוֹם, שֶׁהֵם אַרְבָּעָה שָׁבוּעוֹת וְיוֹם אֶחָד, בָּעוֹמֶר	29
גְּבוּרָה שֶׁבְּהוֹד	הַיּוֹם שְׁלֹשִׁים יוֹם, שֶׁהֵם אַרְבָּעָה שָׁבוּעוֹת וּשְׁנֵי יָמִים, בָּעוֹמֶר	30
תִּפְאֶרֶת שֶׁבְּהוֹד	הַיּוֹם אֶחָד וּשְׁלֹשִׁים יוֹם, שֶׁהֵם אַרְבָּעָה שָׁבוּעוֹת וּשְׁלֹשָׁה יָמִים, בָּעוֹמֶר	31
נֶצַח שֶׁבְּהוֹד	הַיּוֹם שְׁנַיִם וּשְׁלֹשִׁים יוֹם, שֶׁהֵם אַרְבָּעָה שָׁבוּעוֹת וְאַרְבָּעָה יָמִים, בָּעוֹמֶר	32
הוֹד שֶׁבְּהוֹד	הַיּוֹם שְׁלֹשָׁה וּשְׁלֹשִׁים יוֹם, שֶׁהֵם אַרְבָּעָה שָׁבוּעוֹת וַחֲמִשָּׁה יָמִים, בָּעוֹמֶר	33
יְסוֹד שֶׁבְּהוֹד	הַיּוֹם אַרְבָּעָה וּשְׁלֹשִׁים יוֹם, שֶׁהֵם אַרְבָּעָה שָׁבוּעוֹת וְשִׁשָּׁה יָמִים, בָּעוֹמֶר	34
מַלְכוּת שֶׁבְּהוֹד	הַיּוֹם חֲמִשָּׁה וּשְׁלֹשִׁים יוֹם, שֶׁהֵם חֲמִשָּׁה שָׁבוּעוֹת, בָּעוֹמֶר	35
חֶסֶד שֶׁבִּיסוֹד	הַיּוֹם שִׁשָּׁה וּשְׁלֹשִׁים יוֹם, שֶׁהֵם חֲמִשָּׁה שָׁבוּעוֹת וְיוֹם אֶחָד, בָּעוֹמֶר	36
גְּבוּרָה שֶׁבִּיסוֹד	הַיּוֹם שִׁבְעָה וּשְׁלֹשִׁים יוֹם, שֶׁהֵם חֲמִשָּׁה שָׁבוּעוֹת וּשְׁנֵי יָמִים, בָּעוֹמֶר	37
תִּפְאֶרֶת שֶׁבִּיסוֹד	הַיּוֹם שְׁמוֹנָה וּשְׁלֹשִׁים יוֹם, שֶׁהֵם חֲמִשָּׁה שָׁבוּעוֹת וּשְׁלֹשָׁה יָמִים, בָּעוֹמֶר	38
נֶצַח שֶׁבִּיסוֹד	הַיּוֹם תִּשְׁעָה וּשְׁלֹשִׁים יוֹם, שֶׁהֵם חֲמִשָּׁה שָׁבוּעוֹת וְאַרְבָּעָה יָמִים, בָּעוֹמֶר	39
הוֹד שֶׁבִּיסוֹד	הַיּוֹם אַרְבָּעִים יוֹם, שֶׁהֵם חֲמִשָּׁה שָׁבוּעוֹת וַחֲמִשָּׁה יָמִים, בָּעוֹמֶר	40
יְסוֹד שֶׁבִּיסוֹד	הַיּוֹם אֶחָד וְאַרְבָּעִים יוֹם, שֶׁהֵם חֲמִשָּׁה שָׁבוּעוֹת וְשִׁשָּׁה יָמִים, בָּעוֹמֶר	41
מַלְכוּת שֶׁבִּיסוֹד	הַיּוֹם שְׁנַיִם וְאַרְבָּעִים יוֹם, שֶׁהֵם שִׁשָּׁה שָׁבוּעוֹת, בָּעוֹמֶר	42
חֶסֶד שֶׁבְּמַלְכוּת	הַיּוֹם שְׁלֹשָׁה וְאַרְבָּעִים יוֹם, שֶׁהֵם שִׁשָּׁה שָׁבוּעוֹת וְיוֹם אֶחָד, בָּעוֹמֶר	43
גְּבוּרָה שֶׁבְּמַלְכוּת	הַיּוֹם אַרְבָּעָה וְאַרְבָּעִים יוֹם, שֶׁהֵם שִׁשָּׁה שָׁבוּעוֹת וּשְׁנֵי יָמִים, בָּעוֹמֶר	44
תִּפְאֶרֶת שֶׁבְּמַלְכוּת	הַיּוֹם חֲמִשָּׁה וְאַרְבָּעִים יוֹם, שֶׁהֵם שִׁשָּׁה שָׁבוּעוֹת וּשְׁלֹשָׁה יָמִים, בָּעוֹמֶר	45
נֶצַח שֶׁבְּמַלְכוּת	הַיּוֹם שִׁשָּׁה וְאַרְבָּעִים יוֹם, שֶׁהֵם שִׁשָּׁה שָׁבוּעוֹת וְאַרְבָּעָה יָמִים, בָּעוֹמֶר	46
הוֹד שֶׁבְּמַלְכוּת	הַיּוֹם שִׁבְעָה וְאַרְבָּעִים יוֹם, שֶׁהֵם שִׁשָּׁה שָׁבוּעוֹת וַחֲמִשָּׁה יָמִים, בָּעוֹמֶר	47
יְסוֹד שֶׁבְּמַלְכוּת	הַיּוֹם שְׁמוֹנָה וְאַרְבָּעִים יוֹם, שֶׁהֵם שִׁשָּׁה שָׁבוּעוֹת וְשִׁשָּׁה יָמִים, בָּעוֹמֶר	48
מַלְכוּת שֶׁבְּמַלְכוּת	הַיּוֹם תִּשְׁעָה וְאַרְבָּעִים יוֹם, שֶׁהֵם שִׁבְעָה שָׁבוּעוֹת, בָּעוֹמֶר	49

COUNTING THE OMER

DAY	COUNT
1	TODAY IS ONE DAY OF THE *OMER*.
2	TODAY IS TWO DAYS OF THE *OMER*.
3	TODAY IS THREE DAYS OF THE *OMER*.
4	TODAY IS FOUR DAYS OF THE *OMER*.
5	TODAY IS FIVE DAYS OF THE *OMER*.
6	TODAY IS SIX DAYS OF THE *OMER*.
7	TODAY IS SEVEN DAYS, WHICH ARE ONE WEEK OF THE *OMER*.
8	TODAY IS EIGHT DAYS, WHICH ARE ONE WEEK AND ONE DAY OF THE *OMER*.
9	TODAY IS NINE DAYS, WHICH ARE ONE WEEK AND TWO DAYS OF THE *OMER*.
10	TODAY IS TEN DAYS, WHICH ARE ONE WEEK AND THREE DAYS OF THE *OMER*.
11	TODAY IS ELEVEN DAYS, WHICH ARE ONE WEEK AND FOUR DAYS OF THE *OMER*.
12	TODAY IS TWELVE DAYS, WHICH ARE ONE WEEK AND FIVE DAYS OF THE *OMER*.
13	TODAY IS THIRTEEN DAYS, WHICH ARE ONE WEEK AND SIX DAYS OF THE *OMER*.
14	TODAY IS FOURTEEN DAYS, WHICH ARE TWO WEEKS OF THE *OMER*.
15	TODAY IS FIFTEEN DAYS, WHICH ARE TWO WEEKS AND ONE DAY OF THE *OMER*.
16	TODAY IS SIXTEEN DAYS, WHICH ARE TWO WEEKS AND TWO DAYS OF THE *OMER*.
17	TODAY IS SEVENTEEN DAYS, WHICH ARE TWO WEEKS AND THREE DAYS OF THE *OMER*.
18	TODAY IS EIGHTEEN DAYS, WHICH ARE TWO WEEKS AND FOUR DAYS OF THE *OMER*.
19	TODAY IS NINETEEN DAYS, WHICH ARE TWO WEEKS AND FIVE DAYS OF THE *OMER*.
20	TODAY IS TWENTY DAYS, WHICH ARE TWO WEEKS AND SIX DAYS OF THE *OMER*.
21	TODAY IS TWENTY-ONE DAYS, WHICH ARE THREE WEEK OF THE *OMER*.
22	TODAY IS TWENTY-TWO DAYS, WHICH ARE THREE WEEKS AND ONE DAY OF THE *OMER*.
23	TODAY IS TWENTY-THREE DAYS, WHICH ARE THREE WEEKS AND TWO DAYS OF THE *OMER*.
24	TODAY IS TWENTY-FOUR DAYS, WHICH ARE THREE WEEKS AND THREE DAYS OF THE *OMER*.
25	TODAY IS TWENTY-FIVE DAYS, WHICH ARE THREE WEEKS AND FOUR DAYS OF THE *OMER*.
26	TODAY IS TWENTY-SIX DAYS, WHICH ARE THREE WEEKS AND FIVE DAYS OF THE *OMER*.
27	TODAY IS TWENTY-SEVEN DAYS, WHICH ARE THREE WEEKS AND SIX DAYS OF THE *OMER*.
28	TODAY IS TWENTY-EIGHT DAYS, WHICH ARE FOUR WEEKS OF THE *OMER*.
29	TODAY IS TWENTY-NINE DAYS, WHICH ARE FOUR WEEKS AND ONE DAY OF THE *OMER*.
30	TODAY IS THIRTY DAYS, WHICH ARE FOUR WEEKS AND TWO DAYS OF THE *OMER*.
31	TODAY IS THIRTY-ONE DAYS, WHICH ARE FOUR WEEKS AND THREE DAYS OF THE *OMER*.
32	TODAY IS THIRTY-TWO DAYS, WHICH ARE FOUR WEEKS AND FOUR DAYS OF THE *OMER*.
33	TODAY IS THIRTY-THREE DAYS, WHICH ARE FOUR WEEKS AND FIVE DAYS OF THE *OMER*.
34	TODAY IS THIRTY-FOUR DAYS, WHICH ARE FOUR WEEKS AND SIX DAYS OF THE *OMER*.
35	TODAY IS THIRTY-FIVE DAYS, WHICH ARE FIVE WEEKS OF THE *OMER*.
36	TODAY IS THIRTY-SIX DAYS, WHICH ARE FIVE WEEKS AND ONE DAY OF THE *OMER*.
37	TODAY IS THIRTY-SEVEN DAYS, WHICH ARE FIVE WEEKS AND TWO DAYS OF THE *OMER*.
38	TODAY IS THIRTY-EIGHT DAYS, WHICH ARE FIVE WEEKS AND THREE DAYS OF THE *OMER*.
39	TODAY IS THIRTY-NINE DAYS, WHICH ARE FIVE WEEKS AND FOUR DAYS OF THE *OMER*.
40	TODAY IS FORTY DAYS, WHICH ARE FIVE WEEKS AND FIVE DAYS OF THE *OMER*.
41	TODAY IS FORTY-ONE DAYS, WHICH ARE FIVE WEEKS AND SIX DAYS OF THE *OMER*.
42	TODAY IS FORTY-TWO DAYS, WHICH ARE SIX WEEKS OF THE *OMER*.
43	TODAY IS FORTY-THREE DAYS, WHICH ARE SIX WEEKS AND ONE DAY OF THE *OMER*.
44	TODAY IS FORTY-FOUR DAYS, WHICH ARE SIX WEEKS AND TWO DAYS OF THE *OMER*.
45	TODAY IS FORTY-FIVE DAYS, WHICH ARE SIX WEEKS AND THREE DAYS OF THE *OMER*.
46	TODAY IS FORTY-SIX DAYS, WHICH ARE SIX WEEKS AND FOUR DAYS OF THE *OMER*.
47	TODAY IS FORTY-SEVEN DAYS, WHICH ARE SIX WEEKS AND FIVE DAYS OF THE *OMER*.
48	TODAY IS FORTY-EIGHT DAYS, WHICH ARE SIX WEEKS AND SIX DAYS OF THE *OMER*.
49	TODAY IS FORTY-NINE DAYS, WHICH ARE SEVEN WEEKS OF THE *OMER*.

קידוש לבנה

תהלים קמח:א-יג

הַלְלוּיָהּ, הַלְלוּ אֶת יהוה מִן הַשָּׁמַיִם, הַלְלוּהוּ בַּמְּרוֹמִים.
הַלְלוּהוּ כָל מַלְאָכָיו, הַלְלוּהוּ כָּל צְבָאָיו. הַלְלוּהוּ שֶׁמֶשׁ וְיָרֵחַ, הַלְלוּהוּ כָּל כּוֹכְבֵי אוֹר. הַלְלוּהוּ שְׁמֵי
הַשָּׁמַיִם, וְהַמַּיִם אֲשֶׁר מֵעַל הַשָּׁמַיִם. יְהַלְלוּ אֶת שֵׁם יהוה, כִּי
הוּא צִוָּה וְנִבְרָאוּ. וַיַּעֲמִידֵם לָעַד לְעוֹלָם, חָק נָתַן וְלֹא יַעֲבוֹר.
הֲרֵינִי מוּכָן וּמְזֻמָּן לְקַיֵּם הַמִּצְוָה לְקַדֵּשׁ הַלְּבָנָה. לְשֵׁם יִחוּד
קֻדְשָׁא בְּרִיךְ הוּא וּשְׁכִינְתֵּיהּ עַל יְדֵי הַהוּא טָמִיר וְנֶעְלָם, בְּשֵׁם
כָּל יִשְׂרָאֵל.

One should look at the moon before reciting this blessing.

בָּרוּךְ אַתָּה יהוה אֱלֹהֵינוּ מֶלֶךְ הָעוֹלָם, אֲשֶׁר בְּמַאֲמָרוֹ
בָּרָא שְׁחָקִים, וּבְרוּחַ פִּיו כָּל צְבָאָם. חֹק וּזְמַן נָתַן
לָהֶם שֶׁלֹּא יְשַׁנּוּ אֶת תַּפְקִידָם. שָׂשִׂים וּשְׂמֵחִים לַעֲשׂוֹת רְצוֹן
קוֹנָם, פּוֹעֵל אֱמֶת שֶׁפְּעֻלָּתוֹ אֱמֶת. וְלַלְּבָנָה אָמַר שֶׁתִּתְחַדֵּשׁ,
עֲטֶרֶת תִּפְאֶרֶת לַעֲמוּסֵי בָטֶן, שֶׁהֵם עֲתִידִים לְהִתְחַדֵּשׁ
כְּמוֹתָהּ, וּלְפָאֵר לְיוֹצְרָם עַל שֵׁם כְּבוֹד מַלְכוּתוֹ. בָּרוּךְ אַתָּה
יהוה, מְחַדֵּשׁ חֳדָשִׁים.

קידוש לְבָנָה / Sanctification of the Moon
The Sanctification of the Moon [*Kiddush Levanah*] should not be confused with the

קִדּוּשׁ הַחֹדֶשׁ, *Sanctification of the Month*, by which the court pronounced the appropriate day as the beginning of a Sanhedrin's

◆ Laws of Kiddush Levanah

It is preferable that *Kiddush Levanah* be recited: (a) under the open sky; (b) with a *minyan*; (c) at the departure of the Sabbath. When these optimal conditions are not feasible, they may be waived (e.g., a shut-in may recite *Kiddush Levanah* indoors if he can see the moon through a window or door; one who cannot form a *minyan*; the sky is cloudy at the departure of the Sabbath).

The earliest time for reciting *Kiddush Levanah* is seventy-two hours after the *molad* (new moon), although some authorities would delay its recitation until seven full days after the *molad*.

The latest time for reciting *Kiddush Levanah* is mid-month, i.e., fourteen days, eighteen hours and twenty-two minutes (some authorities extend this limit to fifteen full days) after the *molad*. *Kiddush Levanah* should not be recited on a Sabbath or a Festival unless it is the last remaining night before the mid-month deadline.

If one cannot recite *Kiddush Levanah* with a *minyan* he should try to do so in the presence of at least three others with whom to exchange the *Shalom Aleichem* greeting. If this, too, is not possible, one may recite *Kiddush Levanah* by himself. During Tishrei, *Kiddush Levanah* is generally postponed until after Yom Kippur; during Av, until after Tishah B'Av.

◄§ SANCTIFICATION OF THE MOON/KIDDUSH LEVANAH ◄§

Psalms 148:1-6

הַלְלוּיָהּ *Halleluyah! Praise HASHEM from the heavens; praise Him in the heights. Praise Him, all His angels; praise Him, all His legions. Praise Him, sun and moon; praise Him, all bright stars. Praise Him, the most exalted of the heavens and the waters that are above the heavens. Let them praise the Name of HASHEM, for He commanded and they were created. And He established them forever and ever, He issued a decree that will not change.*

Behold I am prepared and ready to perform the commandment to sanctify the moon. For the sake of the unification of the Holy One, Blessed is He, and His Presence, through Him Who is hidden and inscrutable — [I pray] in the name of all Israel.

One should look at the moon before reciting this blessing:

בָּרוּךְ *Blessed are You, HASHEM, our God, King of the Universe, Who with His utterance created the heavens, and with the breath of His mouth all their legion. A decree and a schedule did He give them that they not alter their assigned task. They are joyous and glad to perform the will of their Owner — the Worker of truth Whose work is truth. To the moon He said that it should renew itself as a crown of splendor for those borne [by Him] from the womb, those who are destined to renew themselves like it, and to glorify their Molder for the name of His glorious kingdom. Blessed are You, HASHEM, Who renews the months.*

new month. That proclamation was the sole province of the court and affected the calendar; the Sanctification of the Moon — not the month — has no calendrical significance.

There are two bases for this ritual. Rabbi Yochanan taught that one who blesses the new moon in its proper time is regarded like one who greets the *Shechinah* [God's Presence] (*Sanhedrin* 42a). This is because the only way we can recognize the existence of God is through His miracles and revelations to Israel. In nature it is seen through the orderly functioning of the enormously complex heavenly bodies. We may note that as science unfolds more and more of the vastness of the universe, the presence of a Creator becomes more and more obvious to one who wishes to see; indeed, to deny Him is ludicrous. This phenomenon is most apparent in the cycles of the moon, because its changes are more visible than those of any other body. Thus, when we greet the moon,

we greet its Maker and Guide (*Rabbeinu Yonah, Berachos* 4).

The second aspect of the prayer is its significance for the history of Israel. Just as the moon is reborn after a period of decline and total disappearance, so too, Israel's decline will end and its light will once again blaze to fullness. As an example, the Midrash (*Shemos Rabbah* 15) states that when Israel is worthy of God's favor it is like the waxing moon, but when it is not worthy, it is like the declining moon. In this vein, ancient Israel's rise and fall paralleled the phases of the moon. There were fifteen generations from Abraham to Solomon, during which Israel rose to the zenith of its greatness. The decline began during Solomon's reign; there were fifteen generations from then (including Solomon) to the reign of Zedekiah, when the First Temple was destroyed. This corresponds to the twenty-nine-day lunar cycle.

Because the moon is such a significant

Recite three times:

בָּרוּךְ יוֹצְרֵךְ,* בָּרוּךְ עוֹשֵׂךְ, בָּרוּךְ קוֹנֵךְ, בָּרוּךְ בּוֹרְאֵךְ.

Recite three times. Rise on the toes as if in dance:

כְּשֵׁם שֶׁאֲנִי רוֹקֵד* כְּנֶגְדֵּךְ וְאֵינִי יָכוֹל לִנְגּוֹעַ בָּךְ, כַּךְ לֹא יוּכְלוּ כָּל אוֹיְבַי לִנְגּוֹעַ בִּי לְרָעָה.

Recite three times:

תִּפֹּל עֲלֵיהֶם* אֵימָתָה וָפַחַד, בִּגְדֹל זְרוֹעֲךָ יִדְּמוּ כָּאָבֶן.¹

Recite three times:

כָּאָבֶן יִדְּמוּ זְרוֹעֲךָ בִּגְדֹל וָפַחַד אֵימָתָה עֲלֵיהֶם תִּפֹּל.

Recite three times:

דָּוִד מֶלֶךְ יִשְׂרָאֵל חַי וְקַיָּם.

Extend greetings three times:

שָׁלוֹם עֲלֵיכֶם.*

The person who was greeted responds:

עֲלֵיכֶם שָׁלוֹם.

Recite three times:

סִימָן טוֹב וּמַזָּל טוֹב יְהֵא לָנוּ וּלְכָל יִשְׂרָאֵל. אָמֵן.

קוֹל דּוֹדִי* הִנֵּה זֶה בָּא מְדַלֵּג עַל הֶהָרִים מְקַפֵּץ עַל הַגְּבָעוֹת. דּוֹמֶה דוֹדִי לִצְבִי אוֹ לְעֹפֶר הָאַיָּלִים, הִנֵּה זֶה עוֹמֵד אַחַר כָּתְלֵנוּ, מַשְׁגִּיחַ מִן הַחַלֹּנוֹת, מֵצִיץ מִן הַחֲרַכִּים.²

allusion to God as the Creator and to Israel's rebirth, *Kiddush Levanah* should be recited joyously, preferably at the conclusion of the Sabbath when people are still dressed in their finest clothes. Conversely, it is not recited on the Sabbath or a festival (except under unusual circumstances), because we do not set two different causes for joy in competition with one another (*World of Prayer*). It is also customary to defer *Kiddush Levanah* until after Tishah B'Av and Yom Kippur because the sadness of Av and the dread of the Days of Judgment are inappropriate to the joy required during *Kiddush Levanah*.

בָּרוּךְ יוֹצְרֵךְ — *Blessed is your Molder*. The initials of these four titles of God spell יַעֲקֹב, *Jacob*. Just as the moon is called הַמָּאוֹר הַקָּטֹן, *the smaller luminary* (Genesis 1:16), in relation to the sun, so Jacob was called בְּנָה הַקָּטֹן, *her younger* [lit. smaller] son (Genesis

27:15,42), because he was the younger of Rebecca's two sons. This verse alludes to *Isaiah* 43:1 (as explained by *Vayikra Rabbah* 36) which teaches that God created the universe for the sake of Jacob and his offspring (*Sh'lah*).

This verse and the following ones are repeated three times to give special emphasis to their message.

כְּשֵׁם שֶׁאֲנִי רוֹקֵד — *Just as I dance*. Often in Scripture, a prophecy is accompanied by a physical act. This has the effect of making the prophecy irreversible. Here, too, we in a symbolic way, exert ourselves to touch the moon while remaining on earth, and we pray that, in like fashion, the exertions of our enemies against us will be of no avail. Thus, we reinforce the point by a physical act (*Dover Shalom*).

תִּפֹּל עֲלֵיהֶם — *Let fall upon them*. This verse, taken from the Song at the Sea (*Exodus*

Recite three times:

Blessed is your Molder; • *blessed is your Maker; blessed is your Owner; blessed is your Creator.*

Recite three times. Rise on the toes as if in dance:

Just as I dance • *toward you but cannot touch you, so may none of my enemies be able to touch me for evil.*

Recite three times:

Let fall upon them • *fear and terror; at the greatness of Your arm, let them be still as stone.* [1]

Recite three times:

As stone let them be still, at Your arm's greatness; terror and fear, upon them let fall.

Recite three times:

David, King of Israel, • *is alive and enduring.*

Extend greetings three times:

Peace upon you. •

The person who was greeted responds:

Upon you, peace.

Recite three times:

May there be a good sign and a good fortune for us and for all Israel. Amen.

קוֹל *The voice of my beloved* • — *Behold! It came suddenly, leaping over mountains, skipping over hills. My beloved is like a gazelle or a young hart. Behold! He was standing behind our wall, observing through the windows, peering through the lattices.* [2]

(1) *Exodus* 15:16. (2) *Song of Songs* 2:8-9.

15:16), follows naturally from the previous one. Having said that our foes will be unable to harm us, we now declare that they will be terror stricken.

דְּוִד מֶלֶךְ יִשְׂרָאֵל — *David, King of Israel.* As noted above, the phases of the moon allude to the Davidic dynasty. Thus, we include this confident expression of faith that David's reign endures and will shine again. This verse was composed by Rabbi Yehudah HaNassi (Rosh Chodesh 25a).

שָׁלוֹם עֲלֵיכֶם — *Peace upon you.* This greeting is included for various reasons:

— Having greeted the *Shechinah*, we joyously wish the blessing of peace upon one another (*Levush*).

— After cursing our enemies, we make clear that we wish no ill to our brethren (*Mateh Moshe*).

— At the beginning of creation, as recorded in the Talmud (*Chullin* 60b), the sun and moon were of equal size. When the moon complained that two kings cannot

wear the same crown, i.e., it should be larger than the sun, the moon was made smaller. Nevertheless, the sun continues to shine its brilliant light upon the moon, thus providing a lesson to man not to harbor a grudge against others who have wronged him. We express this resolve by wishing peace upon our fellow Jews (*Anaf Yosef*).

קוֹל דּוֹדִי — *The voice of my beloved.* The inclusion of these two verses is based on the *Yalkut* which interprets them as an allusion to the Messiah.

When the Messiah [i.e., *my beloved*] announces the month of the redemption, Israel will protest disbelievingly that there are so many obstacles in his path. The Messiah will reply that he will hurdle all the barriers like a gazelle *leaping over mountains.* He goes on to say that God was never oblivious to our plight — though we felt abandoned, God was *standing . . . observed . . .* and *peering* to see our needs and plan for our salvation.

שִׁיר לַמַּעֲלוֹת, אֶשָּׂא עֵינַי אֶל הֶהָרִים, מֵאַיִן יָבֹא עֶזְרִי. עֶזְרִי מֵעִם יהוה, עֹשֵׂה שָׁמַיִם וָאָרֶץ. אַל יִתֵּן לַמּוֹט רַגְלֶךָ, אַל יָנוּם שֹׁמְרֶךָ. הִנֵּה לֹא יָנוּם וְלֹא יִישָׁן, שׁוֹמֵר יִשְׂרָאֵל. יהוה שֹׁמְרֶךָ, יהוה צִלְּךָ עַל יַד יְמִינֶךָ. יוֹמָם הַשֶּׁמֶשׁ לֹא יַכֶּכָּה וְיָרֵחַ בַּלָּיְלָה. יהוה יִשְׁמָרְךָ מִכָּל רָע, יִשְׁמֹר אֶת נַפְשֶׁךָ. יהוה יִשְׁמָר צֵאתְךָ וּבוֹאֶךָ, מֵעַתָּה וְעַד עוֹלָם.

הַלְלוּיָהּ, הַלְלוּ אֵל בְּקָדְשׁוֹ, הַלְלוּהוּ בִּרְקִיעַ עֻזּוֹ. הַלְלוּהוּ בִגְבוּרֹתָיו, הַלְלוּהוּ כְּרֹב גֻּדְלוֹ. הַלְלוּהוּ בְּתֵקַע שׁוֹפָר, הַלְלוּהוּ בְּנֵבֶל וְכִנּוֹר. הַלְלוּהוּ בְּתֹף וּמָחוֹל, הַלְלוּהוּ בְּמִנִּים וְעֻגָב. הַלְלוּהוּ בְצִלְצְלֵי שָׁמַע, הַלְלוּהוּ בְּצִלְצְלֵי תְרוּעָה. כֹּל הַנְּשָׁמָה תְּהַלֵּל יָהּ, הַלְלוּיָהּ.

תָּנָא דְּבֵי רַבִּי יִשְׁמָעֵאל: אִלְמָלֵי לֹא זָכוּ יִשְׂרָאֵל אֶלָּא לְהַקְבִּיל פְּנֵי אֲבִיהֶם שֶׁבַּשָּׁמַיִם פַּעַם אַחַת בַּחֹדֶשׁ, דַּיָּם. אָמַר אַבַּיֵי: הִלְכָּךְ צָרִיךְ לְמֵימְרָא מְעֻמָּד.

מִי זֹאת עֹלָה מִן הַמִּדְבָּר מִתְרַפֶּקֶת עַל דּוֹדָהּ.[1]

וִיהִי רָצוֹן מִלְּפָנֶיךָ, יהוה אֱלֹהַי וֵאלֹהֵי אֲבוֹתַי, לְמַלֹּאת פְּגִימַת הַלְּבָנָה, וְלֹא יִהְיֶה בָּהּ שׁוּם מְעוּט, וִיהִי אוֹר הַלְּבָנָה כְּאוֹר הַחַמָּה, וּכְאוֹר שִׁבְעַת יְמֵי בְרֵאשִׁית[2] כְּמוֹ שֶׁהָיְתָה קוֹדֶם מְעוּטָהּ, שֶׁנֶּאֱמַר: אֶת שְׁנֵי הַמְּאֹרֹת הַגְּדֹלִים,[3] וְיִתְקַיֶּם בָּנוּ מִקְרָא שֶׁכָּתוּב: וּבִקְשׁוּ אֶת יהוה אֱלֹהֵיהֶם, וְאֵת דָּוִד מַלְכָּם.[4] אָמֵן.

לַמְנַצֵּחַ בִּנְגִינֹת מִזְמוֹר שִׁיר. אֱלֹהִים יְחָנֵּנוּ וִיבָרְכֵנוּ, יָאֵר פָּנָיו אִתָּנוּ סֶלָה. לָדַעַת בָּאָרֶץ דַּרְכֶּךָ, בְּכָל גּוֹיִם יְשׁוּעָתֶךָ. יוֹדוּךָ עַמִּים אֱלֹהִים, יוֹדוּךָ עַמִּים כֻּלָּם. יִשְׂמְחוּ וִירַנְּנוּ לְאֻמִּים, כִּי תִשְׁפֹּט עַמִּים מִישֹׁר, וּלְאֻמִּים בָּאָרֶץ תַּנְחֵם סֶלָה. יוֹדוּךָ עַמִּים אֱלֹהִים, יוֹדוּךָ עַמִּים כֻּלָּם. אֶרֶץ נָתְנָה יְבוּלָהּ, יְבָרְכֵנוּ אֱלֹהִים אֱלֹהֵינוּ. יְבָרְכֵנוּ אֱלֹהִים, וְיִירְאוּ אֹתוֹ כָּל אַפְסֵי אָרֶץ.

In most congregations, עָלֵינוּ (page 56),
followed by the Mourner's *Kaddish*, is repeated at this point.

Psalm 121

שִׁיר *A song to the ascents. I raise my eyes to the mountains; whence*
will come my help? My help is from HASHEM, Maker of heaven and
earth. He will not allow your foot to falter; your Guardian will not slumber.
Behold, He neither slumbers nor sleeps — the Guardian of Israel. HASHEM
is your Guardian; HASHEM is your Shade at your right hand. By day the sun
will not harm you, nor the moon by night. HASHEM will protect you from
every evil; He will guard your soul. HASHEM will guard your departure and
your arrival, from this time and forever.

Psalm 150

הַלְלוּיָהּ *Halleluyah! Praise God in His Sanctuary; praise Him in the*
firmament of His power. Praise Him for His mighty acts; praise
Him as befits His abundant greatness. Praise Him with the blast of the
shofar; praise Him with lyre and harp. Praise Him with drum and dance;
praise Him with organ and flute. Praise Him with clanging cymbals; praise
him with resonant trumpets. Let all souls praise God, Halleluyah!

תָּנָא *The Academy of Rabbi Yishmael taught: Had Israel not been*
privileged to greet the countenance of their Father in Heaven except
for once a month — it would have sufficed them. Abaye said: Therefore one
must recite it while standing.

Who is this who rises from the desert clinging to her Beloved![1]

וִיהִי *May it be Your will, HASHEM, my God and the God of my forefa-*
thers, to fill the flaw of the moon that there be no diminution in it. May
the light of the moon be like the light of the sun and like the light of the seven
days of Creation,[2] as it was before it was diminished, as it is said: "The two
great luminaries."[3] And may there be fulfilled upon us the verse that is
written: "They shall seek HASHEM, their God, and David, their king."[4] Amen.

Psalm 67

לַמְנַצֵּחַ *For the Conductor, upon Neginos, a psalm, a song. May God*
favor us and bless us, may He illuminate His countenance with
us, Selah. To make known Your way on earth, among all the nations Your
salvation. The peoples will acknowledge You, O God, the peoples will
acknowledge You, all of them. Nations will be glad and sing for joy,
because You will judge the peoples fairly and guide the nations on earth,
Selah. Then peoples will acknowledge You, O God, the peoples will
acknowledge You, all of them. The earth has yielded its produce, may God,
our own God, bless us. May God bless us and may all the ends of the earth
fear Him.

In most congregations, עָלֵינוּ, Aleinu (page 56),
followed by the Mourner's Kaddish, is repeated at this point.

_____

(1) Song of Songs 8:5. (2) Cf. Isaiah 30:26. (3) Genesis 1:16. (4) Hoshea 3:5.

◈ ברכת המזון ◈

It is customary to recite Psalm 137, in memory of the Temple's destruction, before *Bircas HaMazon* on weekdays. On the Sabbath and Festivals, and on such occasions as the meals celebrating a marriage, *Bris*, or *Pidyon HaBen*, when it is improper to intrude upon the joy with memories of tragedy, Psalm 126, which describes the joy of redemption, is recited.

תהלים קלז

עַל נַהֲרוֹת בָּבֶל, שָׁם יָשַׁבְנוּ גַּם בָּכִינוּ, בְּזָכְרֵנוּ אֶת צִיּוֹן. עַל עֲרָבִים בְּתוֹכָהּ תָּלִינוּ כִּנֹּרוֹתֵינוּ. כִּי שָׁם שְׁאֵלוּנוּ שׁוֹבֵינוּ דִּבְרֵי שִׁיר וְתוֹלָלֵינוּ שִׂמְחָה, שִׁירוּ לָנוּ מִשִּׁיר צִיּוֹן. אֵיךְ נָשִׁיר אֶת שִׁיר יהוה, עַל אַדְמַת נֵכָר. אִם אֶשְׁכָּחֵךְ יְרוּשָׁלָיִם, תִּשְׁכַּח יְמִינִי. תִּדְבַּק לְשׁוֹנִי לְחִכִּי, אִם לֹא אֶזְכְּרֵכִי, אִם לֹא אַעֲלֶה אֶת יְרוּשָׁלַיִם עַל רֹאשׁ שִׂמְחָתִי. זְכֹר יהוה לִבְנֵי אֱדוֹם אֵת יוֹם יְרוּשָׁלָיִם, הָאֹמְרִים עָרוּ עָרוּ, עַד הַיְסוֹד בָּהּ. בַּת בָּבֶל הַשְּׁדוּדָה, אַשְׁרֵי שֶׁיְשַׁלֶּם לָךְ אֶת גְּמוּלֵךְ שֶׁגָּמַלְתְּ לָנוּ. אַשְׁרֵי שֶׁיֹּאחֵז וְנִפֵּץ אֶת עֹלָלַיִךְ אֶל הַסָּלַע.

תהלים קכו

שִׁיר הַמַּעֲלוֹת, בְּשׁוּב יהוה אֶת שִׁיבַת צִיּוֹן, הָיִינוּ כְּחֹלְמִים. אָז יִמָּלֵא שְׂחוֹק פִּינוּ וּלְשׁוֹנֵנוּ רִנָּה, אָז יֹאמְרוּ בַגּוֹיִם, הִגְדִּיל יהוה לַעֲשׂוֹת עִם אֵלֶּה. הִגְדִּיל יהוה לַעֲשׂוֹת עִמָּנוּ, הָיִינוּ שְׂמֵחִים. שׁוּבָה יהוה אֶת שְׁבִיתֵנוּ, כַּאֲפִיקִים בַּנֶּגֶב. הַזֹּרְעִים בְּדִמְעָה בְּרִנָּה יִקְצֹרוּ. הָלוֹךְ יֵלֵךְ וּבָכֹה נֹשֵׂא מֶשֶׁךְ הַזָּרַע, בֹּא יָבֹא בְרִנָּה, נֹשֵׂא אֲלֻמֹּתָיו.

תְּהִלַּת יהוה יְדַבֶּר פִּי, וִיבָרֵךְ כָּל בָּשָׂר שֵׁם קָדְשׁוֹ לְעוֹלָם וָעֶד.[1] וַאֲנַחְנוּ נְבָרֵךְ יָהּ, מֵעַתָּה וְעַד עוֹלָם, הַלְלוּיָהּ.[2] הוֹדוּ לַיהוה כִּי טוֹב, כִּי לְעוֹלָם חַסְדּוֹ.[3] מִי יְמַלֵּל גְּבוּרוֹת יהוה, יַשְׁמִיעַ כָּל תְּהִלָּתוֹ.[4]

הִנְנִי מוּכָן וּמְזֻמָּן לְקַיֵּם מִצְוַת עֲשֵׂה שֶׁל בִּרְכַּת הַמָּזוֹן, שֶׁנֶּאֱמַר: וְאָכַלְתָּ וְשָׂבָעְתָּ, וּבֵרַכְתָּ אֶת יהוה אֱלֹהֶיךָ, עַל הָאָרֶץ הַטֹּבָה אֲשֶׁר נָתַן לָךְ.[5]

◈ ברכת המזון / GRACE AFTER MEALS ◈

The commandment to thank God after a meal is of Scriptural origin: וְאָכַלְתָּ וְשָׂבָעְתָּ, וּבֵרַכְתָּ אֶת ה׳ אֱלֹהֶיךָ עַל הָאָרֶץ הַטֹּבָה אֲשֶׁר נָתַן לָךְ *And you shall eat and you shall be satisfied and you shall bless HASHEM, your God, for the good land that He gave you* (Deuteronomy 8:10). As the verse indicates, the Scriptural

requirement applies only when one has eaten his fill — *you shall eat and you shall be satisfied.* From earliest times, however, the Jewish people has undertaken to express its gratitude to God even after a modest meal, provided one had eaten at least as much bread as the volume of an olive [כְּזַיִת]. There are several opinions regarding the modern

◄§ GRACE AFTER MEALS §►

It is customary to recite Psalm 137, in memory of the Temple's destruction, before *Bircas HaMazon* on weekdays. On the Sabbath and Festivals, and on such occasions as the meals celebrating a marriage, *Bris*, or *Pidyon HaBen*, when it is improper to intrude upon the joy with memories of tragedy, Psalm 126, which describes the joy of redemption, is recited.

Psalm 137

עַל נַהֲרוֹת *By the rivers of Babylon, there we sat and also wept when we remembered Zion. On the willows within it we hung our lyres. For there our captors requested words of song from us, with our lyres [playing] joyous music, "Sing for us from Zion's song!" "How can we sing the song of* HASHEM *upon the alien's soil?" If I forget you, O Jerusalem, let my right hand forget its skill. Let my tongue adhere to my palate, if I fail to recall you, if I fail to elevate Jerusalem above my foremost joy. Remember,* HASHEM, *for the offspring of Edom, the day of Jerusalem; for those who say, "Destroy! Destroy! to its very foundation." O violated daughter of Babylon, praiseworthy is he who repays you in accordance with the manner that you treated us. Praiseworthy is he who will clutch and dash your infants against the rock.*

Psalm 126

שִׁיר הַמַּעֲלוֹת *A song of ascents. When* HASHEM *will return the captivity of Zion, we will be like dreamers. Then our mouth will be filled with laughter and our tongue with glad song. Then they will declare among the nations, "*HASHEM *has done greatly with these." *HASHEM *has done greatly with us, we were gladdened. O* HASHEM — *return our captivity like springs in the desert. Those who tearfully sow will reap in glad song. He who bears the measure of seeds walks along weeping, but will return in exultation, a bearer of his sheaves.*

תְּהִלַּת *May my mouth declare the praise of* HASHEM *and may all flesh bless His Holy Name forever.[1] We will bless* HASHEM *from this time and forever, Halleluyah![2] Give thanks to God for He is good, His kindness endures forever.[3] Who can express the mighty acts of* HASHEM? *Who can declare all His praise?[4]*

Behold I am prepared and ready to perform the positive commandment of Bircas HaMazon, for it is said: "And you shall eat and you shall be satisfied and you shall bless HASHEM, *your God, for the good land which He gave you."[5]*

---

(1) *Psalms* 145:21. (2) 115:18. (3) 118:1. (4) 106:2. (5) *Deuteronomy* 8:10.

---

equivalent of this Talmudic measurement; they range from one to one and four-fifths fluid ounces.

The first to compose a text for Grace After Meals was Moses, whose text is still recited as the first blessing of the Grace. Although Moses' blessing was composed in gratitude for the manna in the Wilderness, it makes no mention of the manna. It is equally noteworthy that the general commandment of Grace After Meals (cited above) was given in the context of a general exhortation to Israel that it remember the heavenly food with which God nourished it in the Wilderness. The message appears rather clear: When we thank God for giving us food, we are recognizing that there is no intrinsic difference between the manna and the livelihood one wrests from the earth through sweat and hard toil; both are gifts from heaven.

זימון

If three or more males, aged thirteen or older, participate in a meal, a leader is appointed to formally invite the others to join him in the recitation of *Bircas HaMazon*.

Leader – רַבּוֹתַי מִיר וֶועלֶען בֶּענְטְשֶׁען [רַבּוֹתַי נְבָרֵךְ].

Others – יְהִי שֵׁם יהוה מְבֹרָךְ מֵעַתָּה וְעַד עוֹלָם.[1]

If ten men join in the *zimun*, the words in parentheses are added.

Leader – יְהִי שֵׁם יהוה מְבֹרָךְ* מֵעַתָּה וְעַד עוֹלָם.[1]

בִּרְשׁוּת מָרָנָן וְרַבָּנָן וְרַבּוֹתַי, נְבָרֵךְ* (אֱלֹהֵינוּ) שֶׁאָכַלְנוּ מִשֶּׁלּוֹ.*

Others – בָּרוּךְ (אֱלֹהֵינוּ) שֶׁאָכַלְנוּ מִשֶּׁלּוֹ וּבְטוּבוֹ חָיִינוּ.

Those who have not eaten respond:

בָּרוּךְ (אֱלֹהֵינוּ) וּמְבֹרָךְ שְׁמוֹ תָּמִיד לְעוֹלָם וָעֶד.

Leader – בָּרוּךְ (אֱלֹהֵינוּ) שֶׁאָכַלְנוּ מִשֶּׁלּוֹ וּבְטוּבוֹ חָיִינוּ.

All – בָּרוּךְ הוּא וּבָרוּךְ שְׁמוֹ.

The *zimun* leader recites Grace After Meals (at least the first blessing and the conclusion of the others) aloud. Other than to respond *Amen* at the conclusion of each blessing, it is forbidden to interrupt Grace After Meals for any response other than those permitted during the *Shema*.

הברכה הראשונה – ברכת הזן

בָּרוּךְ אַתָּה יהוה אֱלֹהֵינוּ מֶלֶךְ הָעוֹלָם, הַזָּן אֶת הָעוֹלָם כֻּלּוֹ, בְּטוּבוֹ, בְּחֵן בְּחֶסֶד וּבְרַחֲמִים, הוּא נוֹתֵן לֶחֶם לְכָל בָּשָׂר, כִּי לְעוֹלָם חַסְדּוֹ.[2] וּבְטוּבוֹ הַגָּדוֹל, תָּמִיד לֹא חָסַר לָנוּ, וְאַל יֶחְסַר* לָנוּ מָזוֹן לְעוֹלָם וָעֶד. בַּעֲבוּר שְׁמוֹ הַגָּדוֹל,* כִּי הוּא אֵל זָן וּמְפַרְנֵס לַכֹּל, וּמֵטִיב* לַכֹּל, וּמֵכִין מָזוֹן לְכָל בְּרִיּוֹתָיו אֲשֶׁר בָּרָא. ❖ בָּרוּךְ אַתָּה יהוה, הַזָּן אֶת הַכֹּל. (אָמֵן – Others)

◆§ זימון / Zimun (Invitation)

The word *zimun* connotes both *invitation* and *presentation*. When two or more people eat together, one *invites* the others to respond to his praise of God; and all of them jointly are required to *present* themselves as a group to come together in praise of God (based on *Berachos* 49b).

יְהִי שֵׁם ה׳ מְבֹרָךְ — *Blessed be the Name* . . . The leader, too, repeats the blessings because it would be improper and even sacrilegious for him to ask others to bless God while he, being part of the group, refrains from joining them (*Rashba*).

נְבָרֵךְ — *Let us bless.* A commandment done by an individual cannot be compared to one

performed by a group. When three recite *Bircas HaMazon* together, they say נְבָרֵךְ, *let us bless;* ten say, נְבָרֵךְ אֱלֹהֵינוּ, *let us bless our God* . . . (*Berachos* 49b). A few who perform a commandment are inferior to a multitude performing it (*Rashi, Lev.* 26:8). When many people unite to do God's will, each individual in the group reaches a far higher level than he would have had he acted alone, no matter how meritoriously (*Chofetz Chaim*).

שֶׁאָכַלְנוּ מִשֶּׁלּוֹ — *He of Whose we have eaten.* This text is drawn from Abraham. He would invite wayfarers to his home and serve them lavishly. When they were sated and refreshed and ready to continue on their way,

ZIMUN/INVITATION

If three or more males, aged thirteen or older, participate in a meal, a leader is appointed
to formally invite the others to join him in the recitation of Grace After Meals.

Leader — *Gentlemen, let us bless.*

Others — *Blessed be the Name of HASHEM from this time and forever!*[1]

If ten men join in the *zimun*, the words in brackets are added.

Leader — *Blessed be the Name of HASHEM• from this time and forever!*[1]
*With the permission of the distinguished people present,
let us bless• [our God,] He of Whose we have eaten.*•

Others — *Blessed is [our God,] He of Whose we have eaten
and through Whose goodness we live.*

Those who have not eaten respond:
Blessed is He [our God] and blessed is His Name continuously forever.

Leader — *Blessed is [our God,] He of Whose we have eaten
and through Whose goodness we live.*

All — *Blessed is He and Blessed is His Name.*

The *zimun* leader recites Grace After Meals (at least the first blessing and the conclusion of the
others) aloud. Other than to respond *Amen* at the conclusion of each blessing, it is forbidden
to interrupt Grace After Meals for any response other than those permitted during the *Shema*.

FIRST BLESSING: FOR THE NOURISHMENT

בָּרוּךְ *Blessed are You, HASHEM, our God, King of the universe, Who
nourishes the entire world, in His goodness — with grace, with
kindness, and with mercy. He gives nourishment to all flesh, for His kindness is eternal.*[2] *And through His great goodness, we have never lacked, and
may we never lack,• nourishment, for all eternity. For the sake of His Great
Name,• because He is God Who nourishes and sustains all, and benefits•
all, and He prepares food for all of His creatures which He has created.*

Leader — *Blessed are You, HASHEM, Who nourishes all.*   (Others — Amen.)

(1) *Psalms* 113:2. (2) 136:25.

---

they would thank him. He would insist that
their thanks should go not to him, but to
God, the One from Whose bounty they had
eaten (*Iyun Tefillah*).

בִּרְכַּת הַזָּן / Blessing for the Nourishment

Bircas HaMazon comprises four blessings, of which the first three are Scripturally
ordained and the fourth was instituted by
the Sages. The first blessing was, as noted
above, composed by Moses in gratitude for
the manna with which God sustained Israel
daily in the desert (*Berachos* 48b). For that
reason it precedes נוֹדֶה, the Blessing for the
Land, even though it might seem more
logical to thank God first for the land that
produces food (*Bayis Chadash*).

תָּמִיד לֹא חָסַר ... וְאַל יֶחְסַר — *Have never*

lacked ... and may ... never lack. The
subject of the sentence is מָזוֹן, *nourishment*,
and the verse expresses the prayer that just
as food was never lacking in the desert, may
it never be lacking in the future (*Etz Yosef*).

בַּעֲבוּר שְׁמוֹ הַגָּדוֹל — *For the sake of His Great*
Name. We declare that the motive of our
request for eternally abundant food is but
for the sake of *His Great Name* so that we
may be better able to serve Him; and we
bless Him *because...*

זָן ... מְפַרְנֵס ... מֵטִיב — *Nourishes ... sustains*
... benefits. זָן, *nourishes*, refers to food;
מְפַרְנֵס, *sustains*, refers to clothing; מֵטִיב,
benefits, refers to shelter. These three
phrases enumerate the basic needs of life,
all of which are provided by God (*Etz Yosef*).

תברכה השניה – ברכת הארץ

נוֹדֶה לְךָ, יהוה אֱלֹהֵינוּ, עַל שֶׁהִנְחַלְתָּ לַאֲבוֹתֵינוּ* אֶרֶץ
חֶמְדָּה טוֹבָה וּרְחָבָה.* וְעַל שֶׁהוֹצֵאתָנוּ יהוה אֱלֹהֵינוּ
מֵאֶרֶץ מִצְרַיִם, וּפְדִיתָנוּ מִבֵּית עֲבָדִים, וְעַל בְּרִיתְךָ שֶׁחָתַמְתָּ
בִּבְשָׂרֵנוּ,* וְעַל תּוֹרָתְךָ שֶׁלִּמַּדְתָּנוּ, וְעַל חֻקֶּיךָ שֶׁהוֹדַעְתָּנוּ,
וְעַל חַיִּים חֵן וָחֶסֶד שֶׁחוֹנַנְתָּנוּ, וְעַל אֲכִילַת מָזוֹן שָׁאַתָּה זָן
וּמְפַרְנֵס אוֹתָנוּ תָּמִיד, בְּכָל יוֹם וּבְכָל עֵת וּבְכָל שָׁעָה.

On Chanukah and Purim add the following.

(וְ)עַל הַנִּסִּים, וְעַל הַפֻּרְקָן, וְעַל הַגְּבוּרוֹת, וְעַל הַתְּשׁוּעוֹת, וְעַל הַמִּלְחָמוֹת,
שֶׁעָשִׂיתָ לַאֲבוֹתֵינוּ בַּיָּמִים הָהֵם בַּזְּמַן הַזֶּה.

On Purim:	On Chanukah:
בִּימֵי מָרְדְּכַי וְאֶסְתֵּר בְּשׁוּשַׁן הַבִּירָה, כְּשֶׁעָמַד עֲלֵיהֶם הָמָן הָרָשָׁע, בִּקֵּשׁ לְהַשְׁמִיד לַהֲרֹג וּלְאַבֵּד אֶת כָּל הַיְּהוּדִים, מִנַּעַר וְעַד זָקֵן, טַף וְנָשִׁים בְּיוֹם אֶחָד, בִּשְׁלוֹשָׁה עָשָׂר לְחֹדֶשׁ שְׁנֵים עָשָׂר, הוּא חֹדֶשׁ אֲדָר, וּשְׁלָלָם לָבוֹז.[3] וְאַתָּה בְּרַחֲמֶיךָ הָרַבִּים הֵפַרְתָּ אֶת עֲצָתוֹ, וְקִלְקַלְתָּ אֶת מַחֲשַׁבְתּוֹ, וַהֲשֵׁבוֹתָ לּוֹ גְּמוּלוֹ בְּרֹאשׁוֹ, וְתָלוּ אוֹתוֹ וְאֶת בָּנָיו עַל הָעֵץ.	**בִּימֵי** מַתִּתְיָהוּ בֶּן יוֹחָנָן כֹּהֵן גָּדוֹל חַשְׁמוֹנָאִי וּבָנָיו, כְּשֶׁעָמְדָה מַלְכוּת יָוָן הָרְשָׁעָה עַל עַמְּךָ יִשְׂרָאֵל, לְהַשְׁכִּיחָם תּוֹרָתֶךָ, וּלְהַעֲבִירָם מֵחֻקֵּי רְצוֹנֶךָ, וְאַתָּה בְּרַחֲמֶיךָ הָרַבִּים, עָמַדְתָּ לָהֶם בְּעֵת צָרָתָם, רַבְתָּ אֶת רִיבָם, דַּנְתָּ אֶת דִּינָם, נָקַמְתָּ אֶת נִקְמָתָם.[1] מָסַרְתָּ גִבּוֹרִים בְּיַד חַלָּשִׁים, וְרַבִּים בְּיַד מְעַטִּים, וּטְמֵאִים בְּיַד טְהוֹרִים, וּרְשָׁעִים בְּיַד צַדִּיקִים, וְזֵדִים בְּיַד עוֹסְקֵי תוֹרָתֶךָ. וּלְךָ עָשִׂיתָ שֵׁם גָּדוֹל וְקָדוֹשׁ בְּעוֹלָמֶךָ, וּלְעַמְּךָ יִשְׂרָאֵל עָשִׂיתָ תְּשׁוּעָה גְדוֹלָה[2] וּפֻרְקָן כְּהַיּוֹם הַזֶּה. וְאַחַר כֵּן בָּאוּ בָנֶיךָ לִדְבִיר בֵּיתֶךָ, וּפִנּוּ אֶת הֵיכָלֶךָ, וְטִהֲרוּ אֶת מִקְדָּשֶׁךָ, וְהִדְלִיקוּ נֵרוֹת בְּחַצְרוֹת קָדְשֶׁךָ, וְקָבְעוּ שְׁמוֹנַת יְמֵי חֲנֻכָּה אֵלּוּ, לְהוֹדוֹת וּלְהַלֵּל לְשִׁמְךָ הַגָּדוֹל.

בְּרִכַּת הָאָרֶץ / Blessing for the Land

The second blessing was also ordained by the Torah [*Deut.* 8:10, see *Overview* to ArtScroll *Bircas HaMazon*] and formulated by Joshua (*Berachos* 48a). He saw how much Moses wanted to enter *Eretz Yisrael,* and how anxious the Patriarchs were to be buried in it. Therefore when Joshua was privileged to enter it, he composed this blessing in its honor (*Shibolei HaLeket*).

The blessing begins and ends with thanks. The expression of gratitude refers to each of the enumerated items: the Land, the Exodus, the covenant, the Torah, the statutes, life, grace, kindness, and food.

שֶׁהִנְחַלְתָּ לַאֲבוֹתֵינוּ — *You have given to our forefathers as a heritage.* Eretz Yisrael is referred to as a חֶלָה, *a heritage,* implying that it remains eternally our inheritance. Thus, the long exile means only that God denied us access to it in punishment for our sins, not that it ceased to be ours.

טוֹבָה וּרְחָבָה — *Good and spacious.* Whoever does not say that the Land is *desirable, good, and spacious* has not properly fulfilled his obligation [of *Bircas HaMazon*] (*Berachos* 48b); because, once the Torah required that the Land be mentioned, the Sages decreed that its praises, too, should be enumerated (*Talmidei R' Yonah*).

SECOND BLESSING: FOR THE LAND

נוֹדֶה *We thank You, Hashem, our God, because You have given to our forefathers as a heritage• a desirable, good and spacious• land; because You removed us, Hashem, our God, from the land of Egypt and You redeemed us from the house of bondage; for Your covenant which You sealed in our flesh;• for Your Torah which You taught us and for Your statutes which You made known to us; for life, grace, and lovingkindness which You granted us; and for the provision of food with which You nourish and sustain us constantly, in every day, in every season, and in every hour.*

On Chanukah and Purim add the following.

(וְ)עַל *(And) for the miracles, and for the salvation, and for the mighty deeds, and for the victories, and for the battles which You performed for our forefathers in those days, at this time.*

On Chanukah:

בִּימֵי *In the days of Mattisyahu, the son of Yochanan, the High Priest, the Hasmonean, and his sons — when the wicked Greek kingdom rose up against Your people Israel to make them forget Your Torah and compel them to stray from the statutes of Your Will — You in Your great mercy stood up for them in the time of their distress. You took up their grievance, judged their claim, and avenged their wrong.[1] You delivered the strong into the hands of the weak, the many into the hands of the few, the impure into the hands of the pure, the wicked into the hands of the righteous, and the wanton into the hands of the diligent students of Your Torah. For Yourself You made a great and holy Name in Your world, and for Your people Israel you worked a great victory[2] and salvation as this very day. Thereafter, Your children came to the Holy of Holies of Your House, cleansed Your Temple, purified the site of Your Holiness and kindled lights in the Courtyards of Your Sanctuary; and they established these eight days of Chanukah to express thanks and praise to Your great Name.*

On Purim:

בִּימֵי *In the days of Mordechai and Esther, in Shushan, the capital, when Haman, the wicked, rose up against them and sought to destroy, to slay, and to exterminate all the Jews, young and old, infants and women, on the same day, on the thirteenth of the twelfth month which is the month of Adar, and to plunder their possessions.[3] But You, in Your abundant mercy, nullified his counsel and frustrated his intention and caused his design to return upon his own head and they hanged him and his sons on the gallows.*

(1) Cf. *Jeremiah* 51:36. (2) Cf. *I Samuel* 19:5. (3) *Esther* 3:13.

**וְעַל בְּרִיתְךָ שֶׁחָתַמְתָּ בִּבְשָׂרֵנוּ — *(And) for Your covenant which You sealed in our flesh.* The reference is to circumcision, mention of which the Sages required in the blessing of the Land (*Berachos* 48b) because the Land

was promised to Abraham in the merit of circumcision (*Genesis* 17:7-8).

Women are not subject to the commandments of circumcision and Torah study. Nevertheless, women do say, *for Your*

◄§ If One Forgot to Recite עַל הַנִּסִּים on Chanukah and Purim.
If one realized his error before reaching the Name Hashem of the next blessing (בָּרוּךְ אַתָּה ה', *Blessed are You, Hashem* [p. 80]) he should go back to עַל הַנִּסִּים and continue from there.
If he has already recited the phrase בָּרוּךְ אַתָּה ה', *Blessed are You, Hashem,* he continues to recite *Bircas HaMazon* until reaching the series of seasonal prayers which begin הָרַחֲמָן, *The compassionate One* (p. 86), and rectifies the omission as indicated there. If the omission is not discovered until after that point, nothing need be done.

וְעַל הַכֹּל, יהוה אֱלֹהֵינוּ, אֲנַחְנוּ מוֹדִים לָךְ וּמְבָרְכִים
אוֹתָךְ, יִתְבָּרַךְ שִׁמְךָ בְּפִי כָּל חַי תָּמִיד לְעוֹלָם
וָעֶד. כַּכָּתוּב, וְאָכַלְתָּ וְשָׂבָעְתָּ, וּבֵרַכְתָּ אֶת יהוה אֱלֹהֶיךָ, עַל
הָאָרֶץ הַטֹּבָה אֲשֶׁר נָתַן לָךְ.[1] ❖ בָּרוּךְ אַתָּה יהוה, עַל הָאָרֶץ
וְעַל הַמָּזוֹן. (אָמֵן – Others)

הברכה השלישית – בנין ירושלים

רַחֵם יהוה אֱלֹהֵינוּ עַל יִשְׂרָאֵל עַמֶּךָ, וְעַל יְרוּשָׁלַיִם עִירֶךָ,
וְעַל צִיּוֹן מִשְׁכַּן כְּבוֹדֶךָ, וְעַל מַלְכוּת בֵּית דָּוִד
מְשִׁיחֶךָ,✶ וְעַל הַבַּיִת הַגָּדוֹל וְהַקָּדוֹשׁ שֶׁנִּקְרָא שִׁמְךָ עָלָיו.
אֱלֹהֵינוּ אָבִינוּ, רְעֵנוּ זוּנֵנוּ פַּרְנְסֵנוּ וְכַלְכְּלֵנוּ וְהַרְוִיחֵנוּ, וְהַרְוַח
לָנוּ יהוה אֱלֹהֵינוּ מְהֵרָה מִכָּל צָרוֹתֵינוּ. וְנָא אַל תַּצְרִיכֵנוּ,
יהוה אֱלֹהֵינוּ, לֹא לִידֵי מַתְּנַת בָּשָׂר וָדָם, וְלֹא לִידֵי הַלְוָאָתָם,
כִּי אִם לְיָדְךָ הַמְּלֵאָה הַפְּתוּחָה הַקְּדוֹשָׁה וְהָרְחָבָה, שֶׁלֹּא
נֵבוֹשׁ וְלֹא נִכָּלֵם לְעוֹלָם וָעֶד.

On the Sabbath add the following. [If forgotten, see below.]

רְצֵה וְהַחֲלִיצֵנוּ יהוה אֱלֹהֵינוּ בְּמִצְוֹתֶיךָ, וּבְמִצְוַת יוֹם הַשְּׁבִיעִי
הַשַּׁבָּת הַגָּדוֹל וְהַקָּדוֹשׁ הַזֶּה, כִּי יוֹם זֶה גָּדוֹל וְקָדוֹשׁ הוּא
לְפָנֶיךָ, לִשְׁבָּת בּוֹ וְלָנוּחַ בּוֹ בְּאַהֲבָה כְּמִצְוַת רְצוֹנֶךָ, וּבִרְצוֹנְךָ הָנִיחַ
לָנוּ יהוה אֱלֹהֵינוּ, שֶׁלֹּא תְהֵא צָרָה וְיָגוֹן וַאֲנָחָה בְּיוֹם מְנוּחָתֵנוּ,
וְהַרְאֵנוּ יהוה אֱלֹהֵינוּ בְּנֶחָמַת צִיּוֹן עִירֶךָ, וּבְבִנְיַן יְרוּשָׁלַיִם עִיר
קָדְשֶׁךָ, כִּי אַתָּה הוּא בַּעַל הַיְשׁוּעוֹת וּבַעַל הַנֶּחָמוֹת.

---

covenant which You sealed in our flesh; for
Your Torah which You taught us. Magen
Avraham explains that since women do not
require circumcision, they are considered
as equivalent to circumcised men in this
regard; and since women must study the
laws of whatever commandments are applicable to them, they have a share in the study
of Torah.

בְּנְיַן יְרוּשָׁלַיִם ❧ / **Blessing for Jerusalem**

This blessing is the final one required by
the Torah. It was composed in stages by
David and Solomon. David, who occupied
Jerusalem, referred to Israel, Your people,
and Jerusalem, Your city. Solomon, after

constructing the Temple, added, *the great
and holy House* (Berachos 48b).

Their blessing was a prayer that God
continue the tranquility of the Land. Following the destruction and exile, the blessing
was changed to embody a prayer for the
return of the Land, the Temple, and the
Davidic dynasty. Before Joshua's conquest
of the Land, the blessing took yet another
form (Tur), a request for God's mercy upon
the nation (Aruch HaShulchan).

וְעַל מַלְכוּת בֵּית דָּוִד מְשִׁיחֶךָ — (And) on the
*monarchy of the house of David, Your
anointed.* It is required that the monarchy of
David's dynasty be mentioned in this bless-

וְעַל הַכֹּל For all, HASHEM, our God, we thank You and bless You. May Your Name be blessed by the mouth of all the living, continuously for all eternity. As it is written: "And you shall eat and you shall be satisfied and you shall bless HASHEM, your God, for the good land which He gave you."[1] Leader— Blessed are You, HASHEM, for the land and for the nourishment. (Others— Amen.)

THIRD BLESSING: FOR JERUSALEM

רַחֵם Have mercy, HASHEM, our God, on Israel Your people; on Jerusalem, Your city; on Zion, the resting place of Your Glory; on the monarchy of the house of David, Your anointed;• and on the great and holy House upon which Your Name is called. Our God, our Father — tend us, nourish us, sustain us, support us, relieve us; HASHEM, our God, grant us speedy relief from all our troubles. Please, make us not needful — HASHEM, our God — of the gifts of human hands nor of their loans, but only of Your Hand that is full, open, holy, and generous, that we not feel inner shame nor be humiliated for ever and ever.

> On the Sabbath add the following. [If forgotten, see below.]
>
> **רְצֵה** May it please You, HASHEM, our God — give us rest through Your commandments and through the commandment of the seventh day, this great and holy Sabbath. For this day is great and holy before You to rest on it and be content on it in love, as ordained by Your will. May it be Your will, HASHEM, our God, that there be no distress, grief, or lament on this day of our contentment. And show us, HASHEM, our God, the consolation of Zion, Your city, and the rebuilding of Jerusalem, City of Your holiness, for You are the Master of salvations and Master of consolations.

(1) Deuteronomy 8:10.

ing; whoever has not mentioned it has not fulfilled his obligation (Berachos 49a), because it was David who sanctified Jerusa- lem (Rashi); and because the consolation for the exile will not be complete until David's kingdom is restored (Rambam).

⊷§ If One Omitted יַעֲלֶה וְיָבֹא **or** רְצֵה

a) If he realizes his omission after having recited the blessing of בּוֹנֵה, Who rebuilds, he makes up for the omission by reciting the appropriate Compensatory Blessing (p. 88).

b) If he realizes his omission after having recited the first six words of the fourth blessing, he may still switch immediately into the Compensatory Blessing since the words בָּרוּךְ אַתָּה . . . . הָעוֹלָם are identical in both blessings. (However, the Compensatory Blessing need not be recited after the third Sabbath meal if Bircas HaMazon is recited after sunset.)

c) If the omission is discovered after having recited the word הָאֵל, the Almighty, of the fourth blessing, it is too late for the Compensatory Blessing to be recited. In that case:

(i) On the Sabbath and on a Festival day, at the first two meals Bircas HaMazon must be repeated in its entirety; at the third meal, nothing need be done.

(ii) On Rosh Chodesh and on Chol HaMoed, nothing need be done except if the day fell on the Sabbath and רְצֵה, Retzei, was omitted. In that case, at the first two meals Bircas HaMazon must be repeated. But if רְצֵה was recited and יַעֲלֶה וְיָבֹא was omitted, nothing need be done.

On Rosh Chodesh, Chol HaMoed, and Festivals add. [If forgotten, see p. 81.]

אֱלֹהֵינוּ וֵאלֹהֵי אֲבוֹתֵינוּ, יַעֲלֶה, וְיָבֹא, וְיַגִּיעַ, וְיֵרָאֶה, וְיֵרָצֶה, וְיִשָּׁמַע, וְיִפָּקֵד, וְיִזָּכֵר, זִכְרוֹנֵנוּ וּפִקְדוֹנֵנוּ, וְזִכְרוֹן אֲבוֹתֵינוּ, וְזִכְרוֹן מָשִׁיחַ בֶּן דָּוִד עַבְדֶּךָ, וְזִכְרוֹן יְרוּשָׁלַיִם עִיר קָדְשֶׁךָ, וְזִכְרוֹן כָּל עַמְּךָ בֵּית יִשְׂרָאֵל לְפָנֶיךָ, לִפְלֵיטָה לְטוֹבָה לְחֵן וּלְחֶסֶד וּלְרַחֲמִים, לְחַיִּים וּלְשָׁלוֹם, בְּיוֹם

Shavuos	Pesach	Rosh Chodesh
חַג הַשָּׁבֻעוֹת הַזֶּה.	חַג הַמַּצּוֹת הַזֶּה.	רֹאשׁ הַחֹדֶשׁ הַזֶּה.

Shemini Atzeres/Simchas Torah	Succos
הַשְּׁמִינִי חַג הָעֲצֶרֶת הַזֶּה.	חַג הַסֻּכּוֹת הַזֶּה.

זָכְרֵנוּ יְהוָה אֱלֹהֵינוּ בּוֹ לְטוֹבָה, וּפָקְדֵנוּ בוֹ לִבְרָכָה, וְהוֹשִׁיעֵנוּ בוֹ לְחַיִּים. וּבִדְבַר יְשׁוּעָה וְרַחֲמִים, חוּס וְחָנֵּנוּ וְרַחֵם עָלֵינוּ וְהוֹשִׁיעֵנוּ, כִּי אֵלֶיךָ עֵינֵינוּ, כִּי אֵל (מֶלֶךְ) חַנּוּן וְרַחוּם אָתָּה.[1]

❖ **וּבְנֵה** יְרוּשָׁלַיִם עִיר הַקֹּדֶשׁ בִּמְהֵרָה בְיָמֵינוּ. בָּרוּךְ אַתָּה יְהוָה, בּוֹנֵה (בְרַחֲמָיו) יְרוּשָׁלָיִם. אָמֵן.

(אָמֵן. – Others)

[When required, the compensatory blessing (p. 88) is recited here.]

הברכה הרביעית – הַטּוֹב וְהַמֵּטִיב

בָּרוּךְ אַתָּה יְהוָה אֱלֹהֵינוּ מֶלֶךְ הָעוֹלָם, הָאֵל אָבִינוּ מַלְכֵּנוּ אַדִּירֵנוּ בּוֹרְאֵנוּ גֹּאֲלֵנוּ יוֹצְרֵנוּ, קְדוֹשֵׁנוּ קְדוֹשׁ יַעֲקֹב, רוֹעֵנוּ רוֹעֵה יִשְׂרָאֵל, הַמֶּלֶךְ הַטּוֹב וְהַמֵּטִיב לַכֹּל, שֶׁבְּכָל יוֹם וָיוֹם* הוּא הֵטִיב, הוּא מֵטִיב, הוּא יֵיטִיב לָנוּ. הוּא גְמָלָנוּ הוּא גוֹמְלֵנוּ הוּא יִגְמְלֵנוּ לָעַד, לְחֵן וּלְחֶסֶד וּלְרַחֲמִים וּלְרֶוַח הַצָּלָה וְהַצְלָחָה, בְּרָכָה וִישׁוּעָה נֶחָמָה פַּרְנָסָה וְכַלְכָּלָה ❖ וְרַחֲמִים וְחַיִּים וְשָׁלוֹם וְכָל טוֹב, וּמִכָּל טוּב לְעוֹלָם אַל יְחַסְּרֵנוּ.*

(אָמֵן. – Others)

וּבְנֵה יְרוּשָׁלַיִם ←◦ — *Rebuild Jerusalem.* This concludes the third blessing, and thus returns to the theme with which the blessings began — a plea for God's mercy on Jerusalem (*Pesachim* 104a).

הַטּוֹב וְהַמֵּטִיב ◦→ / **Blessing for God's Goodness**

The essence of this blessing is the phrase

הַטּוֹב וְהַמֵּטִיב, *Who is good and Who does good.* The court of Rabban Gamliel the Elder in Yavneh composed this blessing in gratitude to God for preserving the bodies of the victims of the Roman massacre at Betar, and for eventually allowing them to be brought to burial (*Berachos* 48b).

שֶׁבְּכָל יוֹם וָיוֹם — *For every single day.* It is

On Rosh Chodesh, Chol HaMoed, and Festivals add. [If forgotten ,see p. 81.]

אֱלֹהֵינוּ *Our God and God of our forefathers, may there rise, come, reach, be noted, be favored, be heard, be considered, and be remembered — the remembrance and consideration of ourselves; the remembrance of our forefathers; the remembrance of Messiah, son of David, Your servant; the remembrance of Jerusalem, the City of Your Holiness; and the remembrance of Your entire people the Family of Israel — before You for deliverance, for goodness, for grace, for kindness, and for compassion, for life, and for peace on this day of*

Rosh Chodesh:	Pesach:	Shavuos:
Rosh Chodesh.	*the Festival of Matzos.*	*the Shavuos Festival.*
Succos:	Shemini Atzeres/Simchas Torah:	
the Succos Festival.	*the Shemini Atzeres Festival.*	

Remember us on it, HASHEM, our God, for goodness; consider us on it for blessing; and help us on it for life. In the matter of salvation and compassion, pity, be gracious and compassionate with us and help us, for our eyes are turned to You, because You are God, the gracious and compassionate (King). [1]

וּבְנֵה Leader – *Rebuild Jerusalem, the Holy City, soon in our days. Blessed are You, HASHEM, Who rebuilds Jerusalem (in His mercy).*
Amen. (Others– Amen.)

[When required, the compensatory blessing (p. 88) is recited here.]

FOURTH BLESSING: GOD'S GOODNESS

בָּרוּךְ *Blessed are You, HASHEM, our God, King of the universe, the Almighty, our Father, our King, our Sovereign, our Creator, our Redeemer, our Maker, our Holy One, Holy One of Jacob, our Shepherd, the Shepherd of Israel, the King Who is good and Who does good for all. For every single day*• *He did good, He does good, and He will do good to us. He was bountiful with us, He is bountiful with us, and He will forever be bountiful with us — with grace and with kindness and with mercy, with relief, salvation, success, blessing, help, consolation, sustenance, support,* Leader– *mercy, life, peace, and all good; and of all good things may He never deprive us.* •
(Others– Amen.)

---

(1) Cf. *Nehemiah* 9:31.

insufficient to thank God for His graciousness to *past* generations. We must be conscious of the fact that His goodness and bounty occur constantly.

אַל יְחַסְּרֵנוּ — *May He never deprive us.* This is the conclusion of the fourth blessing. Unlike the other parts of *Bircas HaMazon*, this one does not conclude with a brief blessing summing up the theme of the section. As noted above, the essential text

of the blessing consists of only two words — הַטּוֹב וְהַמֵּטִיב, *Who is good and Who does good* — and it is therefore no different from the short blessings recited before performing a commandment or partaking of food. The addition to the text of considerable outpourings of gratitude does not alter the fact that the brief text does not call for a double blessing (*Rashi* to *Berachos* 49a).

הָרַחֲמָן הוּא יִמְלוֹךְ עָלֵינוּ לְעוֹלָם וָעֶד. הָרַחֲמָן הוּא יִתְבָּרַךְ בַּשָּׁמַיִם וּבָאָרֶץ. הָרַחֲמָן הוּא יִשְׁתַּבַּח לְדוֹר דּוֹרִים, וְיִתְפָּאַר בָּנוּ לָעַד וּלְנֵצַח נְצָחִים, וְיִתְהַדַּר בָּנוּ לָעַד וּלְעוֹלְמֵי עוֹלָמִים.* הָרַחֲמָן הוּא יְפַרְנְסֵנוּ בְּכָבוֹד. הָרַחֲמָן הוּא יִשְׁבּוֹר עֻלֵּנוּ מֵעַל צַוָּארֵנוּ, וְהוּא יוֹלִיכֵנוּ קוֹמְמִיּוּת לְאַרְצֵנוּ. הָרַחֲמָן הוּא יִשְׁלַח לָנוּ בְּרָכָה מְרֻבָּה בַּבַּיִת הַזֶּה, וְעַל שֻׁלְחָן זֶה שֶׁאָכַלְנוּ עָלָיו. הָרַחֲמָן הוּא יִשְׁלַח לָנוּ אֶת אֵלִיָּהוּ הַנָּבִיא זָכוּר לַטּוֹב,* וִיבַשֶּׂר לָנוּ בְּשׂוֹרוֹת טוֹבוֹת יְשׁוּעוֹת וְנֶחָמוֹת.

The following is a blessing that a guest inserts here for the host.

יְהִי רָצוֹן שֶׁלֹּא יֵבוֹשׁ וְלֹא יִכָּלֵם בַּעַל הַבַּיִת הַזֶּה, לֹא בָּעוֹלָם הַזֶּה וְלֹא בָּעוֹלָם הַבָּא, וְיַצְלִיחַ בְּכָל נְכָסָיו, וְיִהְיוּ נְכָסָיו מֻצְלָחִים וּקְרוֹבִים לָעִיר, וְאַל יִשְׁלוֹט שָׂטָן בְּמַעֲשֵׂה יָדָיו, וְאַל יִזְדַּקֵּק לְפָנָיו שׁוּם דְּבַר חֵטְא וְהִרְהוּר עָוֹן, מֵעַתָּה וְעַד עוֹלָם.

Guests recite the following (children at their parents' table include the applicable words in parentheses):

הָרַחֲמָן הוּא יְבָרֵךְ אֶת (אָבִי מוֹרִי) בַּעַל הַבַּיִת הַזֶּה, וְאֶת (אִמִּי מוֹרָתִי) בַּעֲלַת הַבַּיִת הַזֶּה, אוֹתָם וְאֶת בֵּיתָם וְאֶת זַרְעָם וְאֶת כָּל אֲשֶׁר לָהֶם.

At one's own table (include the applicable words in parentheses):

הָרַחֲמָן הוּא יְבָרֵךְ אוֹתִי (וְאֶת אִשְׁתִּי / וְאֶת בַּעֲלִי. וְאֶת זַרְעִי) וְאֶת כָּל אֲשֶׁר לִי.

אוֹתָנוּ וְאֶת כָּל אֲשֶׁר לָנוּ, כְּמוֹ שֶׁנִּתְבָּרְכוּ אֲבוֹתֵינוּ אַבְרָהָם יִצְחָק וְיַעֲקֹב בַּכֹּל מִכֹּל כֹּל,*[1] כֵּן יְבָרֵךְ אוֹתָנוּ כֻּלָּנוּ יַחַד בִּבְרָכָה שְׁלֵמָה. וְנֹאמַר: אָמֵן.

בַּמָּרוֹם יְלַמְּדוּ עֲלֵיהֶם* וְעָלֵינוּ* זְכוּת, שֶׁתְּהֵא לְמִשְׁמֶרֶת שָׁלוֹם. וְנִשָּׂא בְרָכָה מֵאֵת יהוה, וּצְדָקָה מֵאֱלֹהֵי יִשְׁעֵנוּ, וְנִמְצָא חֵן וְשֵׂכֶל טוֹב בְּעֵינֵי אֱלֹהִים וְאָדָם.[2]

הָרַחֲמָן — *The compassionate One!* After completing the four blessings of *Bircas HaMazon* we recite a collection of brief prayers for God's compassion.

לָנֵצַח נְצָחִים . . . לְעוֹלְמֵי עוֹלָמִים — *To the ultimate ends . . . for all eternity.* These expressions mean "forever" and are essentially synonymous. Our translation is based on R' Hirsch who renders נֵצַח from נִצָּחוֹן, triumph,

for God's plan for the future will ultimately overcome all barriers. The word עוֹלָם is related to נֶעֱלָם, *hidden,* implying that the hand of God is present in all occurrences, even though it seems to be hidden.

זָכוּר לַטּוֹב — *He is remembered for good.* The Sages use this generic term to refer to people who have rendered great and unforgettable service to the entire Jewish nation

הָרַחֲמָן *The compassionate One! May He reign over us forever. The compassionate One! May He be blessed in heaven and on earth.* The compassionate One! May He be praised throughout all generations, may He be glorified through us forever to the ultimate ends, and be honored through us forever and for all eternity.• The compassionate One! May He sustain us in honor. The compassionate One! May He break the yoke of oppression from our necks and guide us erect to our Land. The compassionate One! May He send us abundant blessing to this house and upon this table at which we have eaten. The compassionate One! May He send us Elijah, the Prophet — he is remembered for good• — to proclaim to us good tidings, salvations, and consolations.

The following is a blessing that a guest inserts here for the host.

יְהִי *May it be God's will that this host not be shamed nor humiliated in This World or in the World to Come. May he be successful in all his dealings. May his dealings be successful and conveniently close at hand. May no evil impediment reign over his handiwork, and may no semblance of sin or iniquitous thought attach itself to him from this time and forever.*

At one's own table (include the applicable words in parentheses):	Guests recite the following (children at their parents' table include the applicable words in parentheses):
The compassionate One! May He bless me (my wife/husband and my children) and all that is mine.	*The compassionate One! May He bless (my father, my teacher) the master of this house, and (my mother, my teacher) lady of this house, them, their house, their family, and all that is theirs.*

Ours and all that is ours — just as our forefathers Abraham, Isaac, and Jacob were blessed in everything, from everything, with everything.•¹ *So may He bless us all together with a perfect blessing. And let us say: Amen!*

בַּמָּרוֹם *On high, may merit be pleaded upon them• and upon us,• for a safeguard of peace.* • *May we receive a blessing from HASHEM and just kindness from the God of our salvation, and find favor and good understanding in the eyes of God and man.²*

---

(1) Cf. Genesis 24:1; 27:33; 33:11. (2) Cf. Proverbs 3:4.

(see *Berachos* 3a, *Shabbos* 13b, *Bava Basra* 21a, *Avodah Zarah* 8b). In addition to the service he rendered during his years on earth, Elijah will herald the arrival of Messiah [*Malachi* 3:23] (*Iyun Tefillah*).

בְּכֹל מִכֹּל כֹּל — *In everything, from everything, with everything.* The three expressions, each indicating that no necessary measure of goodness was lacking, are used respectively by the Torah referring to the three Patriarchs.

עֲלֵיהֶם — *Upon them,* i.e., the master and mistress of the home, or any others who were mentioned in the preceding prayer.

וְעָלֵינוּ — *And upon us,* i.e., all gathered around the table. [When one eats alone, this term refers to whatever people were previously specified and to the Jewish people in general.]

לְמִשְׁמֶרֶת שָׁלוֹם — *For a safeguard of peace,* i.e., to assure that the home will be peaceful.

If any of the following verses was omitted, Bircas HaMazon need not be repeated.

On the Sabbath add:

הָרַחֲמָן הוּא יַנְחִילֵנוּ יוֹם שֶׁכֻּלּוֹ שַׁבָּת וּמְנוּחָה לְחַיֵּי הָעוֹלָמִים.

On Rosh Chodesh add:

הָרַחֲמָן הוּא יְחַדֵּשׁ עָלֵינוּ אֶת הַחֹדֶשׁ הַזֶּה לְטוֹבָה וְלִבְרָכָה.

On Festivals add:

הָרַחֲמָן הוּא יַנְחִילֵנוּ יוֹם שֶׁכֻּלּוֹ טוֹב.

On Succos add:

הָרַחֲמָן הוּא יָקִים לָנוּ אֶת סֻכַּת דָּוִיד הַנֹּפֶלֶת.[1]

On Chanukah and Purim, if Al HaNissim was not recited in its proper place, add:

הָרַחֲמָן הוּא יַעֲשֶׂה לָנוּ נִסִּים וְנִפְלָאוֹת
כַּאֲשֶׁר עָשָׂה לַאֲבוֹתֵינוּ בַּיָּמִים הָהֵם בַּזְּמַן הַזֶּה.

Continue בִּימֵי (p. 78).

הָרַחֲמָן הוּא יְזַכֵּנוּ לִימוֹת הַמָּשִׁיחַ וּלְחַיֵּי הָעוֹלָם הַבָּא.
[מַגְדִּל* — on weekdays / מִגְדּוֹל* — on days Mussaf is recited]
יְשׁוּעוֹת מַלְכּוֹ וְעֹשֶׂה חֶסֶד לִמְשִׁיחוֹ לְדָוִד וּלְזַרְעוֹ עַד עוֹלָם.[2]
עֹשֶׂה שָׁלוֹם בִּמְרוֹמָיו,* הוּא יַעֲשֶׂה שָׁלוֹם עָלֵינוּ וְעַל כָּל
יִשְׂרָאֵל. וְאִמְרוּ, אָמֵן.

יְראוּ אֶת יהוה קְדֹשָׁיו, כִּי אֵין מַחְסוֹר לִירֵאָיו. כְּפִירִים
רָשׁוּ וְרָעֵבוּ, וְדֹרְשֵׁי יהוה לֹא יַחְסְרוּ כָל טוֹב.[3] הוֹדוּ
לַיהוה כִּי טוֹב, כִּי לְעוֹלָם חַסְדּוֹ.* פּוֹתֵחַ אֶת יָדֶךָ, וּמַשְׂבִּיעַ לְכָל
חַי רָצוֹן.[5] בָּרוּךְ הַגֶּבֶר אֲשֶׁר יִבְטַח בַּיהוה, וְהָיָה יהוה מִבְטַחוֹ.[6*]
נַעַר הָיִיתִי גַּם זָקַנְתִּי, וְלֹא רָאִיתִי צַדִּיק נֶעֱזָב, וְזַרְעוֹ מְבַקֶּשׁ
לָחֶם.[7*] יהוה עֹז לְעַמּוֹ יִתֵּן, יהוה יְבָרֵךְ אֶת עַמּוֹ בַשָּׁלוֹם.[8*]

יוֹם שֶׁכֻּלּוֹ שַׁבָּת — *The day which will be completely a Sabbath,* an allusion to the World to Come after the final redemption.

מַגְדִּל/מִגְדּוֹל — *He Who makes great/A tower.* Both of these verses were written by King David and, in the context of *Bircas HaMazon,* the word *king* refers to King Messiah. *Etz Yosef* explains that the phrase from Psalms [מִגְדּוֹל] was chosen for the less holy weekdays because it was written before David became king. The phrase from

Samuel [מַגְדִּל] was composed when David was at the peak of his greatness, and is therefore better suited to the Sabbath and festivals.

עֹשֶׂה שָׁלוֹם בִּמְרוֹמָיו — *He Who makes peace in His heights.* Even the heavenly beings require God to make peace among them, how much more so fractious man! (*Etz Yosef*).

יְראוּ אֶת ה׳ — *Fear HASHEM.* Those who fear God are content, even if they are lacking in

If any of the following verses was omitted, *Bircas HaMazon* need not be repeated.

On the Sabbath add:

The compassionate One! May He cause us to inherit the day which will be completely a Sabbath• and rest day for eternal life.

On Rosh Chodesh add:

The compassionate One! May He inaugurate this month upon us for goodness and for blessing.

On Festivals add:

The compassionate One! May He cause us to inherit the day which is completely good.

On Succos add:

The compassionate One! May He erect for us David's fallen booth. [1]

On Chanukah and Purim, if *Al HaNissim* was not recited in its proper place, add:

The compassionate One! May He perform for us miracles and wonders as He performed for our forefathers in those days, at this time.

Continue "In the days of . . ." (p. 78).

הָרַחֲמָן *The compassionate One! May He make us worthy of the days of Messiah and the life of the World to Come.*

on weekdays: *He Who makes great• the salvations of His king*

on days Mussaf is recited: *He Who is a tower• of salvations to His king and does kindness for His anointed, to David and to his descendants forever.* [2] *He Who makes peace in His heights,• may He make peace upon us and upon all Israel. Now respond: Amen!*

יְראוּ *Fear HASHEM,• you — His holy ones — for there is no deprivation for His reverent ones. Young lions may want and hunger, but those who seek HASHEM will not lack any good.* [3] *Give thanks to God for He is good; His kindness endures forever.* [4] *You open Your hand and satisfy the desire of every living thing.* [5] *Blessed is the man who trusts in HASHEM, then HASHEM will be his security.* •[6] *I was a youth and also have aged, and I have not seen a righteous man forsaken, with his children begging for bread.* •[7] *HASHEM will give might to His people; HASHEM will bless His people with peace.* •[8]

(1) Cf. *Amos* 9:11. (2) *Psalms* 18:51. (3) 34:10-11. (4) 136:1 et al. (5) 145:16. (6) *Jeremiah* 17:7. (7) *Psalms* 37:25. (8) 29:11.

material possessions. But the wicked are never satisfied; whatever they have only whets their appetite for more (*Anaf Yosef*).

אֲשֶׁר יִבְטַח בַּה׳ וְהָיָה ה׳ מִבְטַחוֹ — *Who trusts in HASHEM, then HASHEM will be his security.* God will be a fortress of trust to a man in direct proportion to the amount of trust he places in God (*Chidushei HaRim*).

צַדִּיק נֶעֱזָב וְזַרְעוֹ מְבַקֶּשׁ לָחֶם — *A righteous man forsaken, with his children begging for bread.* A righteous man may suffer misfortune, but God will surely have mercy on his children (*Radak; Malbim*). I have never seen a righteous man consider himself forsaken even if his children must beg for bread. Whatever his lot in life, he trusts that God

≤ ברכות למי ששכח ≥

See below for instances when Compensatory Blessings must be recited. In all cases, the conclusion of the blessing is recited only at the first two meals of the Sabbath and/or Festivals (except Chol HaMoed). After the appropriate blessing, continue with the fourth blessing (p. 82).

If one forgot רְצֵה on the Sabbath:

בָּרוּךְ אַתָּה יהוה אֱלֹהֵינוּ מֶלֶךְ הָעוֹלָם, אֲשֶׁר נָתַן שַׁבָּתוֹת לִמְנוּחָה לְעַמּוֹ יִשְׂרָאֵל בְּאַהֲבָה, לְאוֹת וְלִבְרִית. בָּרוּךְ אַתָּה יהוה, מְקַדֵּשׁ הַשַּׁבָּת.

If one forgot יַעֲלֶה וְיָבֹא on Rosh Chodesh:

בָּרוּךְ אַתָּה יהוה אֱלֹהֵינוּ מֶלֶךְ הָעוֹלָם, אֲשֶׁר נָתַן רָאשֵׁי חֳדָשִׁים לְעַמּוֹ יִשְׂרָאֵל לְזִכָּרוֹן.

If one forgot רְצֵה and יַעֲלֶה וְיָבֹא on Rosh Chodesh that falls on the Sabbath:

בָּרוּךְ אַתָּה יהוה אֱלֹהֵינוּ מֶלֶךְ הָעוֹלָם, אֲשֶׁר נָתַן שַׁבָּתוֹת לִמְנוּחָה לְעַמּוֹ יִשְׂרָאֵל בְּאַהֲבָה, לְאוֹת וְלִבְרִית, וְרָאשֵׁי חֳדָשִׁים לְזִכָּרוֹן. בָּרוּךְ אַתָּה יהוה, מְקַדֵּשׁ הַשַּׁבָּת וְיִשְׂרָאֵל וְרָאשֵׁי חֳדָשִׁים.

If one forgot יַעֲלֶה וְיָבֹא on a Festival:

בָּרוּךְ אַתָּה יהוה אֱלֹהֵינוּ מֶלֶךְ הָעוֹלָם, אֲשֶׁר נָתַן יָמִים טוֹבִים לְעַמּוֹ יִשְׂרָאֵל לְשָׂשׂוֹן וּלְשִׂמְחָה, אֶת יוֹם

Pesach	Shavuos	Succos	Shemini Atzeres / Simchas Torah
חַג הַמַּצּוֹת /	חַג הַשָּׁבֻעוֹת /	חַג הַסֻּכּוֹת /	הַשְּׁמִינִי חַג הָעֲצֶרֶת

הַזֶּה. בָּרוּךְ אַתָּה יהוה, מְקַדֵּשׁ יִשְׂרָאֵל וְהַזְּמַנִּים.

If one forgot רְצֵה and יַעֲלֶה וְיָבֹא on a Festival that falls on the Sabbath:

בָּרוּךְ אַתָּה יהוה אֱלֹהֵינוּ מֶלֶךְ הָעוֹלָם, אֲשֶׁר נָתַן שַׁבָּתוֹת לִמְנוּחָה לְעַמּוֹ יִשְׂרָאֵל בְּאַהֲבָה, לְאוֹת וְלִבְרִית, וְיָמִים טוֹבִים לְשָׂשׂוֹן וּלְשִׂמְחָה, אֶת יוֹם

Pesach	Shavuos	Succos	Shemini Atzeres / Simchas Torah
חַג הַמַּצּוֹת /	חַג הַשָּׁבֻעוֹת /	חַג הַסֻּכּוֹת /	הַשְּׁמִינִי חַג הָעֲצֶרֶת

הַזֶּה. בָּרוּךְ אַתָּה יהוה, מְקַדֵּשׁ הַשַּׁבָּת וְיִשְׂרָאֵל וְהַזְּמַנִּים.

If one forgot יַעֲלֶה וְיָבֹא on Chol HaMoed:

בָּרוּךְ אַתָּה יהוה אֱלֹהֵינוּ מֶלֶךְ הָעוֹלָם, אֲשֶׁר נָתַן מוֹעֲדִים לְעַמּוֹ יִשְׂרָאֵל לְשָׂשׂוֹן וּלְשִׂמְחָה, אֶת יוֹם

[חַג הַמַּצּוֹת – on Pesach / חַג הַסֻּכּוֹת – on Succos] הַזֶּה.

If one forgot רְצֵה and יַעֲלֶה וְיָבֹא on the Sabbath of Chol HaMoed:

בָּרוּךְ אַתָּה יהוה אֱלֹהֵינוּ מֶלֶךְ הָעוֹלָם, אֲשֶׁר נָתַן שַׁבָּתוֹת לִמְנוּחָה לְעַמּוֹ יִשְׂרָאֵל בְּאַהֲבָה, לְאוֹת וְלִבְרִית, וּמוֹעֲדִים לְשָׂשׂוֹן וּלְשִׂמְחָה, אֶת יוֹם [חַג הַמַּצּוֹת – on Pesach / חַג הַסֻּכּוֹת – on Succos] הַזֶּה. בָּרוּךְ אַתָּה יהוה, מְקַדֵּשׁ הַשַּׁבָּת וְיִשְׂרָאֵל וְהַזְּמַנִּים.

---

brings it upon him for a constructive and merciful purpose (*Anaf Yosef*).

The verse does not say that no righteous man would ever be reduced to poverty; were that the case, it would equate poverty with wickedness — a patent falsehood.

◄◙ COMPENSATORY BLESSINGS ◙►

See below for instances when Compensatory Blessings must be recited. In all cases, the conclusion of the blessing is recited only at the first two meals of the Sabbath and/or Festivals (except
Chol HaMoed). After the appropriate blessing, continue with the fourth blessing (p. 82).

If one forgot רְצֵה *on the Sabbath:*

בָּרוּךְ *Blessed are You, HASHEM, our God, King of the universe, Who gave*
Sabbaths for contentment to His people Israel with love, for a sign and a
covenant. Blessed are You, HASHEM, Who sanctifies the Sabbath.

If one forgot יַעֲלֶה וְיָבֹא *on Rosh Chodesh:*

בָּרוּךְ *Blessed are You, HASHEM, our God, King of the universe, Who gave New*
Moons to His people Israel as a remembrance.

If one forgot רְצֵה *and* יַעֲלֶה וְיָבֹא *on Rosh Chodesh that falls on the Sabbath:*

בָּרוּךְ *Blessed are You, HASHEM, our God, King of the universe, Who gave*
Sabbaths for contentment to His people Israel with love, for a sign and a
covenant, and New Moons for a remembrance. Blessed are You, HASHEM, Who
sanctifies the Sabbath, Israel, and New Moons.

If one forgot יַעֲלֶה וְיָבֹא *on a Festival:*

בָּרוּךְ *Blessed are You, HASHEM, our God, King of the universe, Who gave fes-*
tivals to His people Israel for happiness and gladness, this festival day of
Matzos / Shavuos / Succos / Shemini Atzeres.
Blessed are You, HASHEM, Who sanctifies Israel and the seasons.

If one forgot רְצֵה *and* יַעֲלֶה וְיָבֹא *on a Festival that falls on the Sabbath:*

בָּרוּךְ *Blessed are You, HASHEM, our God, King of the universe, Who gave*
Sabbaths for contentment to His people Israel with love, for a sign and a
covenant, and festivals for happiness and gladness, this festival day of
Matzos / Shavuos / Succos / Shemini Atzeres.
Blessed are You, HASHEM, Who sanctifies the Sabbath, Israel, and the seasons.

If one forgot יַעֲלֶה וְיָבֹא *on Chol HaMoed:*

בָּרוּךְ *Blessed are You, HASHEM, our God, King of the universe, Who gave*
appointed festivals to His people Israel for happiness and gladness, this
festival day of [Matzos /Succos].

If one forgot רְצֵה *and* יַעֲלֶה וְיָבֹא *on the Sabbath of Chol HaMoed:*

בָּרוּךְ *Blessed are You, HASHEM, our God, King of the universe, Who gave*
Sabbaths for contentment to His people Israel with love, for a sign and a
covenant, and appointed festivals for happiness and gladness, this festival day of
[Matzos / Succos]. Blessed are You, HASHEM, Who sanctifies the Sabbath, Israel,
and the (festive) seasons.

Rather the verse says that no righteous
person will be completely forsaken even if
he must beg alms for his sustenance. Since
Jews are obligated to help one another, it is
no disgrace for one to require the help of
another (R' Hirsch).

בְּשָׁלוֹם — *With peace.* Rabbi Shimon ben
Chalafta said: The Holy One, Blessed is He,
could find no container which would hold

Israel's blessings as well as peace, as it says:
"HASHEM will give might to His people,
HASHEM will bless His people with peace"
(Uktzin 3:12). The blessing of peace is so
vital that the word שָׁלוֹם, peace, concludes
the Oral Law (ibid.), the final blessing of
Shemoneh Esrei, the Priestly Blessings, and
Bircas HaMazon. It is also the essential
word in our greetings to one another.

ברכות אחרונות

מעין שלש

The following blessing is recited after partaking of: (a) grain products (other than bread or matzah) made from wheat, barley, rye, oats, or spelt; (b) grape wine or grape juice; (c) grapes, figs, pomegranates, olives, or dates. (If foods from two or three of these groups were eaten, then the insertions for each group are connected with the conjunctive ו, thus וְעַל. The order in such a case is grain, wine, fruit.)

בָּרוּךְ אַתָּה יהוה אֱלֹהֵינוּ מֶלֶךְ הָעוֹלָם, עַל

After fruits:	After wine:	After grain products:

הַמִּחְיָה וְעַל הַכַּלְכָּלָה, הַגֶּפֶן וְעַל פְּרִי הַגֶּפֶן, הָעֵץ וְעַל פְּרִי הָעֵץ, וְעַל תְּנוּבַת הַשָּׂדֶה, וְעַל אֶרֶץ חֶמְדָּה טוֹבָה וּרְחָבָה, שֶׁרָצִיתָ וְהִנְחַלְתָּ לַאֲבוֹתֵינוּ, לֶאֱכֹל מִפִּרְיָהּ וְלִשְׂבּוֹעַ מִטּוּבָהּ. רַחֵם נָא יהוה אֱלֹהֵינוּ עַל יִשְׂרָאֵל עַמֶּךָ, וְעַל יְרוּשָׁלַיִם עִירֶךָ, וְעַל צִיּוֹן מִשְׁכַּן כְּבוֹדֶךָ, וְעַל מִזְבְּחֶךָ וְעַל הֵיכָלֶךָ. וּבְנֵה יְרוּשָׁלַיִם עִיר הַקֹּדֶשׁ בִּמְהֵרָה בְיָמֵינוּ, וְהַעֲלֵנוּ לְתוֹכָהּ, וְשַׂמְּחֵנוּ בְּבִנְיָנָהּ, וְנֹאכַל מִפִּרְיָהּ, וְנִשְׂבַּע מִטּוּבָהּ, וּנְבָרֶכְךָ עָלֶיהָ בִּקְדֻשָּׁה וּבְטָהֳרָה.

On the Sabbath –	וּרְצֵה וְהַחֲלִיצֵנוּ בְּיוֹם הַשַּׁבָּת הַזֶּה.
On Rosh Chodesh –	וְזָכְרֵנוּ (לְטוֹבָה) בְּיוֹם רֹאשׁ הַחֹדֶשׁ הַזֶּה.
On Pesach –	וְשַׂמְּחֵנוּ בְּיוֹם חַג הַמַּצּוֹת הַזֶּה.
On Shavuos –	וְשַׂמְּחֵנוּ בְּיוֹם חַג הַשָּׁבֻעוֹת הַזֶּה.
On Succos –	וְשַׂמְּחֵנוּ בְּיוֹם חַג הַסֻּכּוֹת הַזֶּה.
On Shemini Atzeres / Simchas Torah –	וְשַׂמְּחֵנוּ בְּיוֹם הַשְּׁמִינִי חַג הָעֲצֶרֶת הַזֶּה.

כִּי אַתָּה יהוה טוֹב וּמֵטִיב לַכֹּל, וְנוֹדֶה לְּךָ עַל הָאָרֶץ וְעַל

After fruits:	After wine:	After grain products:
הַפֵּרוֹת.°°	פְּרִי הַגָּפֶן.	הַמִּחְיָה (וְעַל הַכַּלְכָּלָה).

בָּרוּךְ אַתָּה יהוה, עַל הָאָרֶץ וְעַל

הַפֵּרוֹת.°°	פְּרִי הַגָּפֶן.	הַמִּחְיָה (וְעַל הַכַּלְכָּלָה).

°If the wine is from *Eretz Yisrael*, substitute גַּפְנָהּ for הַגָּפֶן.
°°If the fruit grew in *Eretz Yisrael*, substitute פֵּרוֹתֶיהָ for הַפֵּרוֹת.

בורא נפשות

After eating or drinking any food to which neither *Bircas HaMazon* nor the Three-Faceted Blessing applies, such as fruits other than the above, vegetables, or beverages other than wine, recite:

בָּרוּךְ אַתָּה יהוה אֱלֹהֵינוּ מֶלֶךְ הָעוֹלָם, בּוֹרֵא נְפָשׁוֹת רַבּוֹת וְחֶסְרוֹנָן, עַל כָּל מַה שֶּׁבָּרָא(תָ) לְהַחֲיוֹת בָּהֶם נֶפֶשׁ כָּל חָי. בָּרוּךְ חֵי הָעוֹלָמִים.

◄❃ BLESSINGS AFTER OTHER FOODS ❃►

THE THREE-FACETED BLESSING

The following blessing is recited after partaking of: (a) grain products (other than bread or matzah) made from wheat, barley, rye, oats, or spelt; (b) grape wine or grape juice; (c) grapes, figs, pomegranates, olives, or dates. (If foods from two or three of these groups were eaten, then the insertions for each group are connected with the conjunctive ו, thus וְעַל. The order in such a case is grain, wine, fruit.)

בָּרוּךְ *Blessed are You, HASHEM, our God, King of the universe, for the*

After grain products:	After wine:	After fruits:
nourishment and	*vine and the*	*tree and the*
the sustenance,	*fruit of the vine,*	*fruit of the tree,*

and for the produce of the field; for the desirable, good, and spacious Land that You were pleased to give our forefathers as a heritage, to eat of its fruit and to be satisfied with its goodness. Have mercy, we beg You, HASHEM, our God, on Israel Your people; on Jerusalem, Your city; on Zion, the resting place of Your glory; on Your Altar, and on Your Temple. Rebuild Jerusalem the city of holiness, speedily in our days. Bring us up into it and gladden us in its rebuilding and let us eat from its fruit and be satisfied with its goodness and bless You upon it in holiness and purity.

On the Sabbath:	*And be pleased to let us rest on this Sabbath day.*
On Rosh Chodesh:	*And remember us (for goodness) on this day of Rosh Chodesh.*
On Pesach:	*And gladden us on this day of the festival of Matzos.*
On Shavuos:	*And gladden us on this day of the festival of Shavuos.*
On Succos:	*And gladden us on this day of the festival of Succos.*
On Shemini Atzeres and Simchas Torah:	*And gladden us on this day of the festival of Shemini Atzeres.*

For You, HASHEM, are good and do good to all and we thank You for the land and for the

After grain products:	After wine:	After fruits:
nourishment (and the sustenance).	*fruit of the vine.* °	*fruit.* ° °

Blessed are You, HASHEM, for the land and for the

| *nourishment (and the sustenance).* | *fruit of the vine.* ° | *fruit.* ° ° |

°If the wine is from *Eretz Yisrael*, substitute *"its wine."*
°°If the fruit grew in *Eretz Yisrael*, substitute *"its fruit."*

BOREI NEFASHOS

After eating or drinking any food to which neither the Grace After Meals nor the Three-Faceted Blessing applies, such as fruits other than the above, vegetables, or beverages other than wine, recite:

בָּרוּךְ *Blessed are You, HASHEM, our God, King of the universe, Who creates numerous living things with their deficiencies; for all that You have created with which to maintain the life of every being. Blessed is He, the life of the worlds.*

◈ סדר ברכות אירוסין ונישואין ◈

When the groom reaches the *chupah*, the *chazzan* sings:

בָּרוּךְ הַבָּא. מִי אַדִּיר עַל הַכֹּל, מִי בָרוּךְ עַל הַכֹּל, מִי גָדוֹל עַל הַכֹּל,
מִי דָגוּל עַל הַכֹּל, הוּא יְבָרֵךְ אֶת הֶחָתָן וְאֶת הַכַּלָּה.

As the bride approaches the *chupah*, the groom should take a step or two forward in greeting.
She then circles the groom, according to the custom, and the *chazzan* sings:

בְּרוּכָה הַבָּאָה. מִי בֶן שִׂיחַ שׁוֹשַׁן חוֹחִים, אַהֲבַת כַּלָּה מְשׂוֹשׂ
דּוֹדִים, הוּא יְבָרֵךְ אֶת הֶחָתָן וְאֶת הַכַּלָּה.

The *mesader kiddushin* holds a cup of wine and recites:

בָּרוּךְ אַתָּה יהוה אֱלֹהֵינוּ מֶלֶךְ הָעוֹלָם, בּוֹרֵא פְּרִי הַגָּפֶן.

בָּרוּךְ אַתָּה יהוה אֱלֹהֵינוּ מֶלֶךְ הָעוֹלָם, אֲשֶׁר קִדְּשָׁנוּ בְּמִצְוֹתָיו, וְצִוָּנוּ
עַל הָעֲרָיוֹת, וְאָסַר לָנוּ אֶת הָאֲרוּסוֹת, וְהִתִּיר לָנוּ אֶת הַנְּשׂוּאוֹת
לָנוּ עַל יְדֵי חֻפָּה וְקִדּוּשִׁין. בָּרוּךְ אַתָּה יהוה, מְקַדֵּשׁ עַמּוֹ יִשְׂרָאֵל עַל יְדֵי
חֻפָּה וְקִדּוּשִׁין.

Groom and bride each drink from the wine. The groom holds his ring
ready to place upon the bride's right index finger and says to her:

הֲרֵי אַתְּ מְקֻדֶּשֶׁת לִי, בְּטַבַּעַת זוֹ, כְּדַת מֹשֶׁה וְיִשְׂרָאֵל.

After the ring is placed on the bride's finger, the *kesubah* (marriage contract) is read aloud
and handed to the groom who presents it to the bride. Then a second cup of wine is poured
and seven blessings (שֶׁבַע בְּרָכוֹת) are recited aloud. First the blessing over wine is recited and
then blessings 1-6 on p. 94. The honor of reciting these seven blessings may be divided among
several people, but the first two should be recited by the same person. After the blessings,
both groom and bride drink from the wine. The groom then smashes a glass with his right
foot to symbolize that until the Temple is rebuilt our joy cannot be complete. This act
concludes the public marriage service. Then the groom and bride must spend some time
together in a completely private room.

◈ זימון לשבע ברכות ◈

When *Sheva Berachos* are recited, the leader recites the following *zimun*,
with a cup of wine in hand.

Leader — רַבּוֹתַי מִיר וֶעלֶן בֶּענְטְשֶׁען [רַבּוֹתָי נְבָרֵךְ].

Others — יְהִי שֵׁם יהוה מְבֹרָךְ מֵעַתָּה וְעַד עוֹלָם.

Leader — יְהִי שֵׁם יהוה מְבֹרָךְ מֵעַתָּה וְעַד עוֹלָם. דְּוַי הָסֵר וְגַם חָרוֹן, וְאָז אִלֵּם
בְּשִׁיר יָרוֹן, נְחֵנוּ בְּמַעְגְּלֵי צֶדֶק, שְׁעֵה בִרְכַּת בְּנֵי אַהֲרֹן. בִּרְשׁוּת מָרָנָן
וְרַבָּנָן וְרַבּוֹתַי, נְבָרֵךְ אֱלֹהֵינוּ שֶׁהַשִּׂמְחָה בִּמְעוֹנוֹ, (וְ)שֶׁאָכַלְנוּ מִשֶּׁלּוֹ.

Others — בָּרוּךְ אֱלֹהֵינוּ שֶׁהַשִּׂמְחָה בִּמְעוֹנוֹ, (וְ)שֶׁאָכַלְנוּ מִשֶּׁלּוֹ וּבְטוּבוֹ חָיִינוּ.

Leader — בָּרוּךְ אֱלֹהֵינוּ שֶׁהַשִּׂמְחָה בִּמְעוֹנוֹ, (וְ)שֶׁאָכַלְנוּ מִשֶּׁלּוֹ וּבְטוּבוֹ חָיִינוּ.

All — בָּרוּךְ הוּא וּבָרוּךְ שְׁמוֹ.

Continue with *Bircas HaMazon*, p. 76.

◄§ THE MARRIAGE SERVICE ►

When the groom reaches the *chupah*, the *chazzan* sings:

בָּרוּךְ הַבָּא *Blessed is he who has come! He Who is powerful above all, He Who is blessed above all, He Who is great above all, He Who is supreme above all — may He bless the groom and bride.*

As the bride approaches the *chupah*, the groom should take a step or two forward in greeting. She then circles the groom, according to the custom, and the *chazzan* sings:

בְּרוּכָה הַבָּאָה *Blessed is she who has come! He Who understands the speech of the rose among the thorns, the love of a bride, who is the joy of the beloved ones — may He bless the groom and bride.*

The *mesader kiddushin* holds a cup of wine and recites:

בָּרוּךְ *Blessed are You, Hashem, our God, King of the universe, Who creates the fruit of the vine.* (All — Amen.)

בָּרוּךְ *Blessed are You, Hashem, our God, King of the universe, Who has sanctified us with His commandments, and has commanded us regarding forbidden unions; Who forbade betrothed women to us, and permitted women who are married to us through canopy and consecration. Blessed are You, Hashem, Who sanctified His people Israel through canopy and consecration.* (All — Amen.)

Groom and bride each drink from the wine. The groom holds his ring ready to place upon the bride's right index finger and says to her:

Behold, you are consecrated to me by means of this ring, according to the ritual of Moses and Israel.

After the ring is placed on the bride's finger, the *kesubah* (marriage contract) is read aloud and handed to the groom who presents it to the bride. Then a second cup of wine is poured and seven blessings (שֶׁבַע בְּרָכוֹת) are recited aloud. First the blessing over wine is recited and then blessings 1-6 on p. 94. The honor of reciting these seven blessings may be divided among several people, but the first two should be recited by the same person. After the blessings, both groom and bride drink from the wine. The groom then smashes a glass with his right foot to symbolize that until the Temple is rebuilt our joy cannot be complete. This act concludes the public marriage service. Then the groom and bride must spend some time together in a completely private room.

◄§ ZIMUN FOR SHEVA BERACHOS ►

When *Sheva Berachos* are recited, the leader recites the following *zimun*, with a cup of wine in hand.

Leader — *Gentlemen, let us bless.*

Others — *Blessed be the Name of HASHEM from this time and forever!*

Leader — *Blessed be the Name of HASHEM from this time and forever!*
Banish pain and also wrath, and then the mute will exult in song. Guide us in the paths of righteousness, heed the blessing of the children of Aaron. With the permission of the distinguished people present, let us bless our God, in Whose abode is this celebration, of Whose we have eaten.

Others — *Blessed is our God, in Whose abode is this celebration, of Whose we have eaten and through Whose goodness we live.*

Leader — *Blessed is our God, in Whose abode is this celebration, of Whose we have eaten and through Whose goodness we live.*

All — *Blessed is He and Blessed is His Name.*

Continue with *Bircas HaMazon*, p. 76.

❧ שבע ברכות ❧

After *Bircas HaMazon* a second cup is poured and the following seven blessings are recited.
They may be recited by one person or divided among several people.
Whoever recites a blessing should hold the cup as he does so.

1. **בָּרוּךְ** אַתָּה יהוה אֱלֹהֵינוּ מֶלֶךְ הָעוֹלָם, שֶׁהַכֹּל בָּרָא
לִכְבוֹדוֹ. (אָמֵן – All)

2. **בָּרוּךְ** אַתָּה יהוה אֱלֹהֵינוּ מֶלֶךְ הָעוֹלָם, יוֹצֵר הָאָדָם.
(אָמֵן – All)

3. **בָּרוּךְ** אַתָּה יהוה אֱלֹהֵינוּ מֶלֶךְ הָעוֹלָם, אֲשֶׁר יָצַר אֶת
הָאָדָם בְּצַלְמוֹ, בְּצֶלֶם דְּמוּת תַּבְנִיתוֹ, וְהִתְקִין לוֹ
מִמֶּנּוּ בִּנְיַן עֲדֵי עַד. בָּרוּךְ אַתָּה יהוה, יוֹצֵר הָאָדָם.
(אָמֵן – All)

4. **שׂוֹשׂ** תָּשִׂישׂ וְתָגֵל הָעֲקָרָה, בְּקִבּוּץ בָּנֶיהָ לְתוֹכָהּ בְּשִׂמְחָה.
בָּרוּךְ אַתָּה יהוה, מְשַׂמֵּחַ צִיּוֹן בְּבָנֶיהָ. (אָמֵן – All)

5. **שַׂמֵּחַ** תְּשַׂמַּח רֵעִים הָאֲהוּבִים, כְּשַׂמֵּחֲךָ יְצִירְךָ בְּגַן עֵדֶן
מִקֶּדֶם. בָּרוּךְ אַתָּה יהוה, מְשַׂמֵּחַ חָתָן וְכַלָּה.
(אָמֵן – All)

6. **בָּרוּךְ** אַתָּה יהוה אֱלֹהֵינוּ מֶלֶךְ הָעוֹלָם, אֲשֶׁר בָּרָא שָׂשׂוֹן
וְשִׂמְחָה, חָתָן וְכַלָּה, גִּילָה רִנָּה, דִּיצָה וְחֶדְוָה,
אַהֲבָה וְאַחֲוָה, וְשָׁלוֹם וְרֵעוּת. מְהֵרָה, יהוה אֱלֹהֵינוּ, יִשָּׁמַע
בְּעָרֵי יְהוּדָה וּבְחֻצוֹת יְרוּשָׁלַיִם, קוֹל שָׂשׂוֹן וְקוֹל שִׂמְחָה, קוֹל
חָתָן וְקוֹל כַּלָּה, קוֹל מִצְהֲלוֹת חֲתָנִים מֵחֻפָּתָם, וּנְעָרִים
מִמִּשְׁתֵּה נְגִינָתָם. בָּרוּךְ אַתָּה יהוה, מְשַׂמֵּחַ חָתָן עִם הַכַּלָּה.
(אָמֵן – All)

The leader of *Bircas HaMazon* recites the seventh blessing:

7. **בָּרוּךְ** אַתָּה יהוה אֱלֹהֵינוּ מֶלֶךְ הָעוֹלָם, בּוֹרֵא פְּרִי הַגָּפֶן.
(אָמֵן – All)

The leader drinks some of the wine from his cup; then wine from the two cups is mixed
together and one cup is given to the groom and the other to the bride. It is laudable for those
present to drink a bit of wine from the כּוֹס שֶׁל בְּרָכָה, *Cup of Blessing*, since it was used in the
performance of a *mitzvah*.

◄§ SHEVA BERACHOS §►

After *Bircas HaMazon* a second cup is poured and the following seven blessings are recited.
They may be recited by one person or divided among several people.
Whoever recites a blessing should hold the cup as he does so.

1. **בָּרוּךְ** *Blessed are You, HASHEM, our God, King of the universe, Who has created everything for His glory.* (All – Amen.)

2. **בָּרוּךְ** *Blessed are You, HASHEM, our God, King of the universe, Who fashioned the Man.* (All – Amen.)

3. **בָּרוּךְ** *Blessed are You, HASHEM, our God, King of the universe, Who fashioned the Man in His image, in the image of his likeness, and prepared for him — from himself — a building for eternity. Blessed are You, HASHEM, Who fashioned the Man.* (All – Amen.)

4. **שׂוֹשׂ** *Bring intense joy and exultation to the barren one through the ingathering of her children amidst her in gladness. Blessed are You, HASHEM, Who gladdens Zion through her children.*

(All – Amen.)

5. **שַׂמֵּחַ** *Gladden the beloved companions as You gladdened Your creature in the Garden of Eden from aforetime. Blessed are You, HASHEM, Who gladdens groom and bride.* (All – Amen.)

6. **בָּרוּךְ** *Blessed are You, HASHEM, our God, King of the universe, Who created joy and gladness, groom and bride, mirth, glad song, pleasure, delight, love, brotherhood, peace, and companionship. HASHEM, our God, let there soon be heard in the cities of Judah and the streets of Jerusalem the sound of joy and the sound of gladness, the voice of the groom and the voice of the bride, the sound of the grooms' jubilance from their canopies and of youths from their song-filled feasts. Blessed are You, Who gladdens the groom with the bride.* (All – Amen.)

The leader of *Bircas HaMazon* recites the seventh blessing:

7. **בָּרוּךְ** *Blessed are You, HASHEM, our God, King of the universe, Who creates the fruit of the vine.* (All – Amen.)

The leader drinks some of the wine from his cup; then wine from the two cups is mixed together and one cup is given to the groom and the other to the bride. It is laudable for those present to drink a bit of wine from the כּוֹס שֶׁל בְּרָכָה, *Cup of Blessing,* since it was used in the performance of a *mitzvah.*

תפלת הדרך

One setting out on a journey recites the following prayer once he leaves the city limits.

יְהִי רָצוֹן מִלְּפָנֶיךָ, יהוה אֱלֹהֵינוּ וֵאלֹהֵי אֲבוֹתֵינוּ, שֶׁתּוֹלִיכֵנוּ לְשָׁלוֹם, וְתַצְעִידֵנוּ לְשָׁלוֹם, וְתַדְרִיכֵנוּ לְשָׁלוֹם, וְתַגִּיעֵנוּ לִמְחוֹז חֶפְצֵנוּ לְחַיִּים וּלְשִׂמְחָה וּלְשָׁלוֹם, [one planning to return the same day adds – וְתַחֲזִירֵנוּ לְבֵיתֵנוּ לְשָׁלוֹם,] וְתַצִּילֵנוּ מִכַּף כָּל אוֹיֵב וְאוֹרֵב וְלִסְטִים וְחַיּוֹת רָעוֹת בַּדֶּרֶךְ, וּמִכָּל מִינֵי פֻּרְעָנִיּוֹת הַמִּתְרַגְּשׁוֹת לָבוֹא לָעוֹלָם, וְתִשְׁלַח בְּרָכָה בְּ(כָל) מַעֲשֵׂה יָדֵינוּ, וְתִתְּנֵנוּ לְחֵן וּלְחֶסֶד וּלְרַחֲמִים בְּעֵינֶיךָ וּבְעֵינֵי כָל רוֹאֵינוּ, וְתִשְׁמַע קוֹל תַּחֲנוּנֵינוּ, כִּי אֵל שׁוֹמֵעַ תְּפִלָּה וְתַחֲנוּן אָתָּה. בָּרוּךְ אַתָּה יהוה, שׁוֹמֵעַ תְּפִלָּה.

Recite three times:

וְיַעֲקֹב הָלַךְ לְדַרְכּוֹ, וַיִּפְגְּעוּ בוֹ מַלְאֲכֵי אֱלֹהִים. וַיֹּאמֶר יַעֲקֹב כַּאֲשֶׁר רָאָם, מַחֲנֵה אֱלֹהִים זֶה, וַיִּקְרָא שֵׁם הַמָּקוֹם הַהוּא מַחֲנָיִם.¹

Recite three times:

הַמַּלְאָךְ הַגֹּאֵל אֹתִי מִכָּל רָע יְבָרֵךְ אֶת הַנְּעָרִים, וְיִקָּרֵא בָהֶם שְׁמִי, וְשֵׁם אֲבֹתַי אַבְרָהָם וְיִצְחָק, וְיִדְגּוּ לָרֹב בְּקֶרֶב הָאָרֶץ.²

Recite three times:

לִישׁוּעָתְךָ קִוִּיתִי יהוה.³ (קִוִּיתִי יהוה לִישׁוּעָתְךָ. יהוה לִישׁוּעָתְךָ קִוִּיתִי.)

Recite three times:

הִנֵּה אָנֹכִי שֹׁלֵחַ מַלְאָךְ לְפָנֶיךָ לִשְׁמָרְךָ בַּדָּרֶךְ, וְלַהֲבִיאֲךָ אֶל הַמָּקוֹם אֲשֶׁר הֲכִנֹתִי.⁴

Recite three times:

יהוה עֹז לְעַמּוֹ יִתֵּן, יהוה יְבָרֵךְ אֶת עַמּוֹ בַשָּׁלוֹם.⁵

תְּפִלַּת הַדֶּרֶךְ / Wayfarer's Prayer
Someone who sets out on a journey must pray that he complete it safely (*Berachos* 29b). This applies even if there is no reason to expect danger, provided that the trip will be at least one *parsah* (approx. 3 miles). The

prayer should be recited as soon as one has gone about 140 feet past the last house of his town. In the event the entire journey will be less that one *parsah*, the prayer may be recited, but the concluding blessing בָּרוּךְ אַתָּה ה׳ שׁוֹמֵעַ תְּפִלָּה, *Blessed are You, HASHEM,*

⚜ WAYFARER'S PRAYER ⚜

One setting out on a journey recites the following prayer once he leaves the city limits.

יְהִי רָצוֹן May it be Your will, HASHEM, our God and the God of our forefathers, that You lead us toward peace, emplace our footsteps toward peace, guide us toward peace, and make us reach our desired destination for life, gladness, and peace [one planning to return the same day adds: *and return us to our homes in peace*]. May You rescue us from the hand of every foe, ambush, (bandits, and evil animals) along the way, and from all manner of punishments that assemble to come to earth. May You send blessing in our every handiwork, and grant us grace, kindness, and mercy in Your eyes and in the eyes of all who see us. May You hear the sound of our supplication, because You are God Who hears prayer and supplication. Blessed are You, HASHEM, Who hears prayer.

Recite three times:

וַיַּעֲקֹב Jacob went on his way and angels of God encountered him. Jacob said when he saw them, "This is a Godly camp." So he named the place Machanayim. [1]

Recite three times:

הַמַּלְאָךְ May the angel who redeems me from all evil bless the lads, and may my name be declared upon them — and the names of my forefathers Abraham and Isaac — and may they proliferate abundantly like fish within the land. [2]

Recite three times:

לִישׁוּעָתְךָ For Your salvation I do long, Hashem. [3] I do long, HASHEM, for Your salvation. HASHEM, for Your salvation I do long.

Recite three times:

הִנֵּה Behold I send an angel before you to protect you on the way and bring you to the place that I have prepared. [4]

Recite three times:

ה' HASHEM will give might to His nation, HASHEM will bless His nation with peace. [5]

---

(1) *Genesis* 32:2-3. (2) 48:16. (3) 49:18. (4) *Exodus* 23:20. (5) *Psalms* 29:11.

Who hears prayer) should be omitted. The prayer is recited once each day, even though the journey will be interrupted by rest, work, sightseeing and so on. However, if one's journey has ended, and he subsequently decides to embark on another journey on the same day, the Wayfarer's Prayer should be recited a second time. On a journey that will last for many days, the prayer is recited once each day.

It is preferable to recite a blessing before the beginning of the prayer so that it will be preceded as well as concluded by blessings. Customarily this is done by eating something before beginning the prayer. It is also customary for one member of a group to recite the blessing aloud and for the others to fulfill their obligation by listening and responding אָמֵן, *Amen.*

Although it is preferable to interrupt one's travel and to stand while reciting the prayer, it need not be done if it is difficult.

❊ קריאת שמע על המטה ❊

רִבּוֹנוֹ שֶׁל עוֹלָם, הֲרֵינִי מוֹחֵל לְכָל מִי שֶׁהִכְעִיס וְהִקְנִיט אוֹתִי, אוֹ שֶׁחָטָא כְּנֶגְדִּי – בֵּין בְּגוּפִי, בֵּין בְּמָמוֹנִי, בֵּין בִּכְבוֹדִי, בֵּין בְּכָל אֲשֶׁר לִי; בֵּין בְּאוֹנֶס, בֵּין בְּרָצוֹן, בֵּין בְּשׁוֹגֵג, בֵּין בְּמֵזִיד, בֵּין בְּדִבּוּר, בֵּין בְּמַעֲשֶׂה, בֵּין בְּמַחֲשָׁבָה, בֵּין בְּהַרְהוּר; בֵּין בְּגִלְגּוּל זֶה, בֵּין בְּגִלְגּוּל אַחֵר – לְכָל בַּר יִשְׂרָאֵל, וְלֹא יֵעָנֵשׁ שׁוּם אָדָם בִּסְבָתִי. יְהִי רָצוֹן מִלְּפָנֶיךָ, יְהוָה אֱלֹהַי וֵאלֹהֵי אֲבוֹתַי, שֶׁלֹּא אֶחֱטָא עוֹד, וּמַה שֶּׁחָטָאתִי לְפָנֶיךָ מְחוֹק בְּרַחֲמֶיךָ הָרַבִּים, אֲבָל לֹא עַל יְדֵי יִסּוּרִים וָחֳלָיִים רָעִים. יִהְיוּ לְרָצוֹן אִמְרֵי פִי וְהֶגְיוֹן לִבִּי לְפָנֶיךָ, יְהוָה צוּרִי וְגֹאֲלִי.[1]

בִּרְכַּת הַמַּפִּיל

בָּרוּךְ אַתָּה יְהוָה אֱלֹהֵינוּ מֶלֶךְ הָעוֹלָם, הַמַּפִּיל חֶבְלֵי שֵׁנָה עַל עֵינָי, וּתְנוּמָה עַל עַפְעַפָּי. וִיהִי רָצוֹן מִלְּפָנֶיךָ, יְהוָה אֱלֹהַי וֵאלֹהֵי אֲבוֹתַי, שֶׁתַּשְׁכִּיבֵנִי לְשָׁלוֹם וְתַעֲמִידֵנִי לְשָׁלוֹם. וְאַל יְבַהֲלוּנִי רַעְיוֹנַי, וַחֲלוֹמוֹת רָעִים, וְהִרְהוּרִים רָעִים. וּתְהֵא מִטָּתִי שְׁלֵמָה לְפָנֶיךָ. וְהָאֵר עֵינַי פֶּן אִישַׁן הַמָּוֶת.[2] כִּי אַתָּה הַמֵּאִיר לְאִישׁוֹן בַּת עָיִן. בָּרוּךְ אַתָּה יְהוָה, הַמֵּאִיר לָעוֹלָם כֻּלּוֹ בִּכְבוֹדוֹ.

אֵל מֶלֶךְ נֶאֱמָן.

Recite the first verse aloud, with the right hand covering the eyes,
and concentrate intensely upon accepting God's absolute sovereignty.

שְׁמַע ׀ יִשְׂרָאֵל, יְהוָה ׀ אֱלֹהֵינוּ, יְהוָה ׀ אֶחָד:[3]

— In an undertone — בָּרוּךְ שֵׁם כְּבוֹד מַלְכוּתוֹ לְעוֹלָם וָעֶד.

דברים ו:ד-ט

וְאָהַבְתָּ אֵת ׀ יְהוָה ׀ אֱלֹהֶיךָ, בְּכָל-לְבָבְךָ, וּבְכָל-נַפְשְׁךָ, וּבְכָל-מְאֹדֶךָ: וְהָיוּ הַדְּבָרִים הָאֵלֶּה, אֲשֶׁר אָנֹכִי מְצַוְּךָ הַיּוֹם, עַל-לְבָבֶךָ: וְשִׁנַּנְתָּם לְבָנֶיךָ, וְדִבַּרְתָּ בָּם, בְּשִׁבְתְּךָ בְּבֵיתֶךָ, וּבְלֶכְתְּךָ בַדֶּרֶךְ, וּבְשָׁכְבְּךָ וּבְקוּמֶךָ: וּקְשַׁרְתָּם לְאוֹת ׀ עַל-יָדֶךָ, וְהָיוּ לְטֹטָפֹת בֵּין ׀ עֵינֶיךָ: וּכְתַבְתָּם ׀ עַל-מְזֻזוֹת בֵּיתֶךָ, וּבִשְׁעָרֶיךָ:

וִיהִי נֹעַם אֲדֹנָי אֱלֹהֵינוּ עָלֵינוּ, וּמַעֲשֵׂה יָדֵינוּ כּוֹנְנָה עָלֵינוּ, וּמַעֲשֵׂה יָדֵינוּ כּוֹנְנֵהוּ.[4]

⋖ THE BEDTIME SHEMA ⋗

רִבּוֹנוֹ שֶׁל עוֹלָם *Master of the universe, I hereby forgive anyone who angered or antagonized me or who sinned against me — whether against my body, my property, my honor or against anything of mine; whether he did so accidentally, willfully, carelessly, or purposely; whether through speech, deed, thought, or notion; whether in this transmigration or another transmigration — I forgive every Jew. May no man be punished because of me. May it be Your will, Hashem, my God and the God of my forefathers, that I may sin no more. Whatever sins I have done before You, may You blot out in Your abundant mercies, but not through suffering or bad illnesses. May the expressions of my mouth and the thoughts of my heart find favor before You, Hashem, my Rock and my Redeemer.* [1]

HAMAPIL

בָּרוּךְ *Blessed are You, HASHEM, our God, King of the universe, who casts the bonds of sleep upon my eyes and slumber upon my eyelids. May it be Your will, Hashem, my God and the God of my forefathers, that You lay me down to sleep in peace and raise me erect in peace. May my ideas, bad dreams, and bad notions not confound me; may my offspring be perfect before You, and may You illuminate my eyes lest I die in sleep,* [2] *for it is You Who illuminates the pupil of the eye. Blessed are You, Hashem, Who illuminates the entire world with His glory.*

God, trustworthy King.

Recite the first verse aloud, with the right hand covering the eyes, and concentrate intensely upon accepting God's absolute sovereignty.

Hear, O Israel: HASHEM is our God, HASHEM, the One and Only. [3]

In an undertone: Blessed is the Name of His glorious kingdom for all eternity.

Deuteronomy 6:5-9

וְאָהַבְתָּ *You shall love HASHEM, your God, with all your heart, with all your soul and with all your resources. Let these matters that I command you today be upon your heart. Teach them thoroughly to your children and speak of them while you sit in your home, while you walk on the way, when you retire and when you arise. Bind them as a sign upon your arm and let them be tefillin between your eyes. And write them on the doorposts of your house and upon your gates.*

וִיהִי נֹעַם *May the pleasantness of my Lord, our God, be upon us — may He establish our handiwork for us; our handiwork may He establish.* [4]

---

(1) *Psalms* 19:15. (2) Cf. 13:4. (3) *Deuteronomy* 6:4. (4) *Psalms* 90:17.

יֹשֵׁב בְּסֵתֶר עֶלְיוֹן, בְּצֵל שַׁדַּי יִתְלוֹנָן. אֹמַר לַיהוה, מַחְסִי
וּמְצוּדָתִי, אֱלֹהַי אֶבְטַח בּוֹ. כִּי הוּא יַצִּילְךָ מִפַּח יָקוּשׁ,
מִדֶּבֶר הַוּוֹת. בְּאֶבְרָתוֹ יָסֶךְ לָךְ, וְתַחַת כְּנָפָיו תֶּחְסֶה, צִנָּה
וְסֹחֵרָה אֲמִתּוֹ. לֹא תִירָא מִפַּחַד לָיְלָה, מֵחֵץ יָעוּף יוֹמָם.
מִדֶּבֶר בָּאֹפֶל יַהֲלֹךְ, מִקֶּטֶב יָשׁוּד צָהֳרָיִם. יִפֹּל מִצִּדְּךָ אֶלֶף,
וּרְבָבָה מִימִינֶךָ, אֵלֶיךָ לֹא יִגָּשׁ. רַק בְּעֵינֶיךָ תַבִּיט, וְשִׁלֻּמַת
רְשָׁעִים תִּרְאֶה. כִּי אַתָּה יהוה מַחְסִי, עֶלְיוֹן שַׂמְתָּ מְעוֹנֶךָ. לֹא
תְאֻנֶּה אֵלֶיךָ רָעָה, וְנֶגַע לֹא יִקְרַב בְּאָהֳלֶךָ. כִּי מַלְאָכָיו יְצַוֶּה
לָּךְ, לִשְׁמָרְךָ בְּכָל דְּרָכֶיךָ. עַל כַּפַּיִם יִשָּׂאוּנְךָ, פֶּן תִּגֹּף בָּאֶבֶן
רַגְלֶךָ. עַל שַׁחַל וָפֶתֶן תִּדְרֹךְ, תִּרְמֹס כְּפִיר וְתַנִּין. כִּי בִי חָשַׁק
וַאֲפַלְּטֵהוּ, אֲשַׂגְּבֵהוּ, כִּי יָדַע שְׁמִי. יִקְרָאֵנִי וְאֶעֱנֵהוּ, עִמּוֹ אָנֹכִי
בְצָרָה, אֲחַלְּצֵהוּ וַאֲכַבְּדֵהוּ. אֹרֶךְ יָמִים אַשְׂבִּיעֵהוּ, וְאַרְאֵהוּ
בִּישׁוּעָתִי. אֹרֶךְ יָמִים אַשְׂבִּיעֵהוּ, וְאַרְאֵהוּ בִּישׁוּעָתִי.

יהוה, מָה רַבּוּ צָרָי, רַבִּים קָמִים עָלָי. רַבִּים אֹמְרִים לְנַפְשִׁי,
אֵין יְשׁוּעָתָה לּוֹ בֵאלֹהִים סֶלָה. וְאַתָּה יהוה מָגֵן
בַּעֲדִי, כְּבוֹדִי וּמֵרִים רֹאשִׁי. קוֹלִי אֶל יהוה אֶקְרָא, וַיַּעֲנֵנִי מֵהַר
קָדְשׁוֹ סֶלָה. אֲנִי שָׁכַבְתִּי וָאִישָׁנָה, הֱקִיצוֹתִי, כִּי יהוה יִסְמְכֵנִי.
לֹא אִירָא מֵרִבְבוֹת עָם, אֲשֶׁר סָבִיב שָׁתוּ עָלָי. קוּמָה יהוה,
הוֹשִׁיעֵנִי אֱלֹהַי, כִּי הִכִּיתָ אֶת כָּל אֹיְבַי לֶחִי, שִׁנֵּי רְשָׁעִים
שִׁבַּרְתָּ. לַיהוה הַיְשׁוּעָה, עַל עַמְּךָ בִרְכָתֶךָ סֶּלָה.

הַשְׁכִּיבֵנוּ יהוה אֱלֹהֵינוּ לְשָׁלוֹם, וְהַעֲמִידֵנוּ מַלְכֵּנוּ לְחַיִּים.
וּפְרֹשׂ עָלֵינוּ סֻכַּת שְׁלוֹמֶךָ. וְתַקְּנֵנוּ בְּעֵצָה טוֹבָה
מִלְּפָנֶיךָ. וְהוֹשִׁיעֵנוּ לְמַעַן שְׁמֶךָ. וְהָגֵן בַּעֲדֵנוּ, וְהָסֵר מֵעָלֵינוּ
אוֹיֵב דֶּבֶר וְחֶרֶב וְרָעָב וְיָגוֹן. וְהָסֵר שָׂטָן מִלְּפָנֵינוּ וּמֵאַחֲרֵינוּ.
וּבְצֵל כְּנָפֶיךָ תַּסְתִּירֵנוּ.[1] כִּי אֵל שׁוֹמְרֵנוּ וּמַצִּילֵנוּ אָתָּה, כִּי אֵל
מֶלֶךְ חַנּוּן וְרַחוּם אָתָּה.[2] וּשְׁמוֹר צֵאתֵנוּ וּבוֹאֵנוּ לְחַיִּים
וּלְשָׁלוֹם, מֵעַתָּה וְעַד עוֹלָם.[3]

Psalm 91

יֹשֵׁב *Whoever sits in the refuge of the Most High, he shall dwell in the shadow of the Almighty. I will say of HASHEM, "He is my refuge and my fortress, my God, I will trust in Him." For He will deliver you from the ensnaring trap, from devastating pestilence. With His pinion He will cover you, and beneath His wings you will be protected; shield and armor is His truth. You shall not fear the terror of night; nor the arrow that flies by day; nor the pestilence that walks in gloom; nor the destroyer who lays waste at noon. Let a thousand encamp at your side and a myriad at your right hand, but to you they shall not approach. You will merely peer with your eyes and you will see the retribution of the wicked. Because [you said,] "You, HASHEM, are my refuge," you have made the Most High your dwelling place. No evil will befall you, nor will any plague come near your tent. He will charge His angels for you, to protect you in all your ways. On your palms they will carry you, lest you strike your foot against a stone. Upon the lion and the viper you will tread; you will trample the young lion and the serpent. For he has yearned for Me and I will deliver him; I will elevate him because he knows My Name. He will call upon Me and I will answer him, I am with him in distress, I will release him and I will honor him. With long life will I satisfy him, and I will show him My salvation. With long life will I satisfy him, and I will show him My salvation.*

Psalm 3:2-9

ה' *HASHEM, how many are my tormentors! The great rise up against me! The great say of my soul, "There is no salvation for him from God — Selah!" But You HASHEM are a shield for me, for my soul, and the One Who raises my head. With my voice I call out to HASHEM, and He answers me from His holy mountain — Selah. I lay down and slept, yet I awoke, for HASHEM supports me. I fear not the myriad people deployed against me from every side. Rise up, HASHEM; save me, my God; for You struck all of my enemies on the cheek, You broke the teeth of the wicked. Salvation is HASHEM's, upon Your people is Your blessing — Selah.*

הַשְׁכִּיבֵנוּ *Lay us down to sleep, HASHEM, our God, in peace, raise us erect, our King, to life; and spread over us the shelter of Your peace. Set us aright with good counsel from before Your Presence, and save us for Your Name's sake. Shield us, remove from us foe, plague, sword, famine, and woe; and remove spiritual impediment from before us and behind us, and in the shadow of Your wings shelter us*[1] *— for God Who protects and rescues us are You; for God, the Gracious and Compassionate King, are You.*[2] *Safeguard our going and coming — for life and for peace — from now to eternity.*[3]

---

(1) Cf. *Psalms* 17:8. (2) Cf. *Nechemiah* 9:31. (3) Cf. *Psalms* 121:8.

בָּרוּךְ יהוה בַּיּוֹם, בָּרוּךְ יהוה בַּלַּיְלָה, בָּרוּךְ יהוה בְּשָׁכְבֵנוּ, בָּרוּךְ יהוה בְּקוּמֵנוּ. כִּי בְיָדְךָ נַפְשׁוֹת הַחַיִּים וְהַמֵּתִים. אֲשֶׁר בְּיָדוֹ נֶפֶשׁ כָּל חָי, וְרוּחַ כָּל בְּשַׂר אִישׁ.[1] בְּיָדְךָ אַפְקִיד רוּחִי, פָּדִיתָה אוֹתִי, יהוה אֵל אֱמֶת.[2] אֱלֹהֵינוּ שֶׁבַּשָּׁמַיִם, יַחֵד שִׁמְךָ וְקַיֵּם מַלְכוּתְךָ תָּמִיד, וּמְלוֹךְ עָלֵינוּ לְעוֹלָם וָעֶד.

יִרְאוּ עֵינֵינוּ וְיִשְׂמַח לִבֵּנוּ וְתָגֵל נַפְשֵׁנוּ בִּישׁוּעָתְךָ בֶּאֱמֶת, בֶּאֱמֹר לְצִיּוֹן מָלַךְ אֱלֹהָיִךְ.[3] יהוה מֶלֶךְ,[4] יהוה מָלָךְ,[5] יהוה יִמְלוֹךְ לְעֹלָם וָעֶד.[6] כִּי הַמַּלְכוּת שֶׁלְּךָ הִיא, וּלְעוֹלְמֵי עַד תִּמְלוֹךְ בְּכָבוֹד, כִּי אֵין לָנוּ מֶלֶךְ אֶלָּא אַתָּה.

הַמַּלְאָךְ הַגֹּאֵל אֹתִי מִכָּל רָע יְבָרֵךְ אֶת הַנְּעָרִים, וְיִקָּרֵא בָהֶם שְׁמִי, וְשֵׁם אֲבֹתַי אַבְרָהָם וְיִצְחָק וְיִדְגּוּ לָרֹב בְּקֶרֶב הָאָרֶץ.[7]

וַיֹּאמֶר, אִם שָׁמוֹעַ תִּשְׁמַע לְקוֹל יהוה אֱלֹהֶיךָ, וְהַיָּשָׁר בְּעֵינָיו תַּעֲשֶׂה, וְהַאֲזַנְתָּ לְמִצְוֹתָיו, וְשָׁמַרְתָּ כָּל חֻקָּיו, כָּל הַמַּחֲלָה אֲשֶׁר שַׂמְתִּי בְמִצְרַיִם לֹא אָשִׂים עָלֶיךָ, כִּי אֲנִי יהוה רֹפְאֶךָ.[8]

וַיֹּאמֶר יהוה אֶל הַשָּׂטָן, יִגְעַר יהוה בְּךָ הַשָּׂטָן, וְיִגְעַר יהוה בְּךָ הַבֹּחֵר בִּירוּשָׁלָיִם, הֲלוֹא זֶה אוּד מֻצָּל מֵאֵשׁ.[9]

הִנֵּה מִטָּתוֹ שֶׁלִּשְׁלֹמֹה, שִׁשִּׁים גִּבֹּרִים סָבִיב לָהּ, מִגִּבֹּרֵי יִשְׂרָאֵל. כֻּלָּם אֲחֻזֵי חֶרֶב, מְלֻמְּדֵי מִלְחָמָה, אִישׁ חַרְבּוֹ עַל יְרֵכוֹ מִפַּחַד בַּלֵּילוֹת.[10]

Recite three times:

יְבָרֶכְךָ יהוה, וְיִשְׁמְרֶךָ. יָאֵר יהוה פָּנָיו אֵלֶיךָ, וִיחֻנֶּךָּ. יִשָּׂא יהוה פָּנָיו אֵלֶיךָ, וְיָשֵׂם לְךָ שָׁלוֹם.[11]

Recite three times:

הִנֵּה לֹא יָנוּם וְלֹא יִישָׁן, שׁוֹמֵר יִשְׂרָאֵל.[12]

בָּרוּךְ Blessed is HASHEM by day; blessed is HASHEM by night; blessed is HASHEM when we retire; blessed is HASHEM when we arise. For in Your hand are the souls of the living and the dead. He in Whose hand is the soul of all the living and the spirit of every human being. [1] In Your hand I shall entrust my spirit, You redeemed me, HASHEM, God of truth. [2] Our God, Who is in heaven, bring unity to Your Name; establish Your kingdom forever and reign over us for all eternity.

יִרְאוּ May our eyes see, our heart rejoice and our soul exult in Your salvation in truth, when Zion is told, "Your God has reigned!"[3] HASHEM reigns, [4] HASHEM has reigned, [5] HASHEM will reign for all eternity. [6] For the kingdom is Yours and You will reign for all eternity in glory, for we have no King but You.

הַמַּלְאָךְ May the angel who redeems me from all evil bless the lads, and may my name be declared upon them — and the names of my forefathers Abraham and Isaac — and may they proliferate abundantly like fish within the land. [7]

וַיֹּאמֶר He said: "If you diligently heed the voice of HASHEM, your God, and do what is proper in His eyes, and you listen closely to His commandments and observe His decrees — the entire malady that I inflicted upon Egypt I will not inflict upon you, for I am HASHEM your Healer."[8]

וַיֹּאמֶר HASHEM said to the Satan, "HASHEM shall denounce you, O Satan, and HASHEM, Who selects Jerusalem, shall denounce you again. This is indeed a firebrand rescued from flames."[9]

הִנֵּה Behold! The couch of Shlomo! Sixty mighty ones round about it, of the mighty ones of Israel. All gripping the sword, learned in warfare, each with his sword on his thigh, from fear in the nights. [10]

Recite three times:

יְבָרֶכְךָ May HASHEM bless you and safeguard you. May HASHEM illuminate His countenance for you and be gracious to you: May HASHEM turn His face toward you and establish peace for you. [11]

Recite three times:

הִנֵּה Behold, the Guardian of Israel neither slumbers nor sleeps. [12]

---

(1) Job 12:10. (2) Psalms 31:6. (3) Cf. Isaiah 52:7. (4) Psalms 10:16.
(5) 93:1 et al. (6) Exodus 15:18. (7) Genesis 48:16. (8) Exodus 15:26.
(9) Zechariah 3:2. (10) Song of Songs 3:7-8. (11) Numbers 6:24-26. (12) Psalms 121:4.

Recite three times:

לִישׁוּעָתְךָ קִוִּיתִי יהוה.[1] קִוִּיתִי יהוה לִישׁוּעָתְךָ. יהוה לִישׁוּעָתְךָ קִוִּיתִי.

Recite three times:

בְּשֵׁם יהוה אֱלֹהֵי יִשְׂרָאֵל, מִימִינִי מִיכָאֵל, וּמִשְּׂמֹאלִי גַבְרִיאֵל, וּמִלְּפָנַי אוּרִיאֵל, וּמֵאֲחוֹרַי רְפָאֵל, וְעַל רֹאשִׁי שְׁכִינַת אֵל.

תהלים קכח

שִׁיר הַמַּעֲלוֹת, אַשְׁרֵי כָּל יְרֵא יהוה, הַהֹלֵךְ בִּדְרָכָיו. יְגִיעַ כַּפֶּיךָ כִּי תֹאכֵל, אַשְׁרֶיךָ וְטוֹב לָךְ. אֶשְׁתְּךָ כְּגֶפֶן פֹּרִיָּה בְּיַרְכְּתֵי בֵיתֶךָ, בָּנֶיךָ כִּשְׁתִלֵי זֵיתִים סָבִיב לְשֻׁלְחָנֶךָ. הִנֵּה כִי כֵן יְבֹרַךְ גָּבֶר, יְרֵא יהוה. יְבָרֶכְךָ יהוה מִצִּיּוֹן, וּרְאֵה בְּטוּב יְרוּשָׁלָיִם כֹּל יְמֵי חַיֶּיךָ. וּרְאֵה בָנִים לְבָנֶיךָ, שָׁלוֹם עַל יִשְׂרָאֵל.

Recite three times:

רִגְזוּ וְאַל תֶּחֱטָאוּ, אִמְרוּ בִלְבַבְכֶם עַל מִשְׁכַּבְכֶם, וְדֹמּוּ סֶלָה.[2]

אֲדוֹן עוֹלָם אֲשֶׁר מָלַךְ, בְּטֶרֶם כָּל יְצִיר נִבְרָא.
לְעֵת נַעֲשָׂה בְחֶפְצוֹ כֹּל, אֲזַי מֶלֶךְ שְׁמוֹ נִקְרָא.
וְאַחֲרֵי כִּכְלוֹת הַכֹּל, לְבַדּוֹ יִמְלוֹךְ נוֹרָא.
וְהוּא הָיָה וְהוּא הֹוֶה, וְהוּא יִהְיֶה בְּתִפְאָרָה.
וְהוּא אֶחָד וְאֵין שֵׁנִי, לְהַמְשִׁיל לוֹ לְהַחְבִּירָה.
בְּלִי רֵאשִׁית בְּלִי תַכְלִית, וְלוֹ הָעֹז וְהַמִּשְׂרָה.
וְהוּא אֵלִי וְחַי גֹּאֲלִי, וְצוּר חֶבְלִי בְּעֵת צָרָה.
וְהוּא נִסִּי וּמָנוֹס לִי, מְנָת כּוֹסִי בְּיוֹם אֶקְרָא.
בְּיָדוֹ אַפְקִיד רוּחִי, בְּעֵת אִישָׁן וְאָעִירָה.
וְעִם רוּחִי גְּוִיָּתִי, יהוה לִי וְלֹא אִירָא.

---

(1) *Genesis* 49:18. (2) *Psalms* 4:5.

Recite three times:

לִישׁוּעָתְךָ *For Your salvation do I long, HASHEM.* [1] *I do long, HASHEM,*
for your salvation. HASHEM, for Your salvation do I long.

Recite three times:

בְּשֵׁם *In the Name of HASHEM, God of Israel: may Michael be at my right,*
Gabriel at my left, Uriel before me, and Raphael behind me; and
above my head the Presence of God.

Psalm 128

שִׁיר הַמַּעֲלוֹת *A song of ascents. Praiseworthy is each person who*
fears HASHEM, who walks in His paths. When you eat
the labor of your hands, you are praiseworthy, and it is well with you.
Your wife shall be like a fruitful vine in the inner chambers of your
home; your children shall be like olive shoots surrounding your table.
Behold! For so is blessed the man who fears HASHEM. May HASHEM bless
you from Zion, and may you gaze upon the goodness of Jerusalem, all
the days of your life. And may you see children born to children, peace
upon Israel.

Recite three times:

רִגְזוּ *Tremble and sin not. Reflect in your hearts while on your beds,*
and be utterly silent. Selah. [2]

אֲדוֹן עוֹלָם *Master of the universe, Who reigned*
before any form was created,
At the time when His will brought all into being —
then as "King" was His Name proclaimed.
After all has ceased to be,
He, the Awesome One, will reign alone.
It is He Who was, He Who is,
and He Who shall remain, in splendor.
He is One — there is no second
to compare to Him, to declare as His equal.
Without beginning, without conclusion —
His is the power and dominion.
He is my God, my living Redeemer,
Rock of my pain in time of distress.
He is my banner, a refuge for me,
the portion in my cup on the day I call.
Into His hand I shall entrust my spirit
when I go to sleep — and I shall awaken!
With my spirit shall my body remain.
HASHEM is with me, I shall not fear.

אבינו מלכנו

From Rosh Hashanah to Yom Kippur and on fast days, most congregations recite אָבִינוּ מַלְכֵּנוּ
after *Shemoneh Esrei* (except on those days on which *Tachanun* is omitted). See p. 126.

The doors of the Ark are kept open while אָבִינוּ מַלְכֵּנוּ is recited.

[As the Ark is opened, some say the words: פְּתַח שַׁעֲרֵי שָׁמַיִם לִתְפִלָּתֵנוּ.]

אָבִינוּ מַלְכֵּנוּ, חָטָאנוּ לְפָנֶיךָ.

אָבִינוּ מַלְכֵּנוּ, אֵין לָנוּ מֶלֶךְ אֶלָּא אָתָּה.

אָבִינוּ מַלְכֵּנוּ, עֲשֵׂה עִמָּנוּ לְמַעַן שְׁמֶךָ.

אָבִינוּ מַלְכֵּנוּ, בָּרֵךְ [On fast days] — [From Rosh Hashanah to Yom Kippur — חַדֵּשׁ]
עָלֵינוּ שָׁנָה טוֹבָה.

אָבִינוּ מַלְכֵּנוּ, בַּטֵּל מֵעָלֵינוּ כָּל גְּזֵרוֹת קָשׁוֹת.

אָבִינוּ מַלְכֵּנוּ, בַּטֵּל מַחְשְׁבוֹת שׂוֹנְאֵינוּ.

אָבִינוּ מַלְכֵּנוּ, הָפֵר עֲצַת אוֹיְבֵינוּ.

אָבִינוּ מַלְכֵּנוּ, כַּלֵּה כָּל צַר וּמַשְׂטִין מֵעָלֵינוּ.

אָבִינוּ מַלְכֵּנוּ, סְתוֹם פִּיּוֹת מַשְׂטִינֵנוּ וּמְקַטְרִיגֵנוּ.

אָבִינוּ מַלְכֵּנוּ, כַּלֵּה דֶּבֶר וְחֶרֶב וְרָעָב וּשְׁבִי וּמַשְׁחִית
וְעָוֹן וּשְׁמַד מִבְּנֵי בְרִיתֶךָ.

אָבִינוּ מַלְכֵּנוּ, מְנַע מַגֵּפָה מִנַּחֲלָתֶךָ.

אָבִינוּ מַלְכֵּנוּ, סְלַח וּמְחַל לְכָל עֲוֹנוֹתֵינוּ.

אָבִינוּ מַלְכֵּנוּ, מְחֵה וְהַעֲבֵר פְּשָׁעֵינוּ וְחַטֹּאתֵינוּ מִנֶּגֶד עֵינֶיךָ.

אָבִינוּ מַלְכֵּנוּ, מְחוֹק בְּרַחֲמֶיךָ הָרַבִּים כָּל שִׁטְרֵי חוֹבוֹתֵינוּ.

Each of the next nine verses is recited by *chazzan*, then congregation.

אָבִינוּ מַלְכֵּנוּ, הַחֲזִירֵנוּ בִּתְשׁוּבָה שְׁלֵמָה לְפָנֶיךָ.

אָבִינוּ מַלְכֵּנוּ, שְׁלַח רְפוּאָה שְׁלֵמָה לְחוֹלֵי עַמֶּךָ.

אָבִינוּ מַלְכֵּנוּ, קְרַע רוֹעַ גְּזַר דִּינֵנוּ.

אָבִינוּ מַלְכֵּנוּ, זָכְרֵנוּ בְּזִכָּרוֹן טוֹב לְפָנֶיךָ.

From Rosh Hashanah to Yom Kippur:	On fast days:
אָבִינוּ מַלְכֵּנוּ, כָּתְבֵנוּ בְּסֵפֶר חַיִּים טוֹבִים.	אָבִינוּ מַלְכֵּנוּ, זָכְרֵנוּ לְחַיִּים טוֹבִים.
אָבִינוּ מַלְכֵּנוּ, כָּתְבֵנוּ בְּסֵפֶר גְּאֻלָּה וִישׁוּעָה.	אָבִינוּ מַלְכֵּנוּ, זָכְרֵנוּ לִגְאֻלָּה וִישׁוּעָה.
אָבִינוּ מַלְכֵּנוּ, כָּתְבֵנוּ בְּסֵפֶר פַּרְנָסָה וְכַלְכָּלָה.	אָבִינוּ מַלְכֵּנוּ, זָכְרֵנוּ לְפַרְנָסָה וְכַלְכָּלָה.

﴾ AVINU MALKEINU ﴿

From Rosh Hashanah to Yom Kippur and on fast days, most congregations recite *Avinu Malkeinu* after *Shemoneh Esrei* (except on those days on which *Tachanun* is omitted). See p. 126.

The doors of the Ark are kept open while *Avinu Malkeinu* is recited. [As the Ark is opened, some say the words: *"Open the gates of heaven to our prayer."*]

אָבִינוּ מַלְכֵּנוּ *Our Father, our King, we have sinned before You.*

Our Father, our King, we have no King but You.

Our Father, our King, deal [kindly] with us for Your Name's sake.

Our Father, our King, On fast days — *bless us with a good year.*

From Rosh Hashanah to Yom Kippur — *inaugurate upon us a good year.*

Our Father, our King, nullify all harsh decrees upon us.

Our Father, our King, nullify the thoughts of those who hate us.

Our Father, our King, thwart the counsel of our enemies.

Our Father, our King, exterminate every foe and adversary from upon us.

Our Father, our King, seal the mouths of our adversaries and accusers.

Our Father, our King, exterminate pestilence, sword, famine, captivity, destruction, iniquity, and eradication from the members of Your covenant.

Our Father, our King, withhold the plague from Your heritage.

Our Father, our King, forgive and pardon all our iniquities.

Our Father, our King, wipe away and remove our willful sins and errors from Your sight.

Our Father, our King, erase through Your abundant compassion all records of our guilt.

Each of the next nine verses is recited by chazzan, then congregation.

Our Father, our King, return us to You in perfect repentance.

Our Father, our King, send complete recovery to the sick of Your people.

Our Father, our King, tear up the evil decree of our verdict.

Our Father, our King, recall us with a favorable memory before you.

On fast days:	From Rosh Hashanah to Yom Kippur:
Our Father, our King, remember us for good life.	*Our Father, our King, inscribe us in the book of good life.*
Our Father, our King, remember us for redemption and salvation.	*Our Father, our King, inscribe us in the book of redemption and salvation.*
Our Father, our King, remember us for sustenance and support.	*Our Father, our King, inscribe us in the book of sustenance and support.*

On fast days:	From Rosh Hashanah to Yom Kippur:
אָבִינוּ מַלְכֵּנוּ, זָכְרֵנוּ לְזָכֻיּוֹת.	אָבִינוּ מַלְכֵּנוּ, כָּתְבֵנוּ בְּסֵפֶר זְכֻיּוֹת.
אָבִינוּ מַלְכֵּנוּ, זָכְרֵנוּ לִסְלִיחָה וּמְחִילָה.	אָבִינוּ מַלְכֵּנוּ, כָּתְבֵנוּ בְּסֵפֶר סְלִיחָה וּמְחִילָה.

End of responsive reading. All continue:

אָבִינוּ מַלְכֵּנוּ, הַצְמַח לָנוּ יְשׁוּעָה בְּקָרוֹב.

אָבִינוּ מַלְכֵּנוּ, הָרֵם קֶרֶן יִשְׂרָאֵל עַמֶּךָ.

אָבִינוּ מַלְכֵּנוּ, הָרֵם קֶרֶן מְשִׁיחֶךָ.

אָבִינוּ מַלְכֵּנוּ, מַלֵּא יָדֵינוּ מִבִּרְכוֹתֶיךָ.

אָבִינוּ מַלְכֵּנוּ, מַלֵּא אֲסָמֵינוּ שָׂבָע.

אָבִינוּ מַלְכֵּנוּ, שְׁמַע קוֹלֵנוּ, חוּס וְרַחֵם עָלֵינוּ.

אָבִינוּ מַלְכֵּנוּ, קַבֵּל בְּרַחֲמִים וּבְרָצוֹן אֶת תְּפִלָּתֵנוּ.

אָבִינוּ מַלְכֵּנוּ, פְּתַח שַׁעֲרֵי שָׁמַיִם לִתְפִלָּתֵנוּ.

אָבִינוּ מַלְכֵּנוּ, זָכוֹר כִּי עָפָר אֲנָחְנוּ.

אָבִינוּ מַלְכֵּנוּ, נָא אַל תְּשִׁיבֵנוּ רֵיקָם מִלְּפָנֶיךָ.

אָבִינוּ מַלְכֵּנוּ, תְּהֵא הַשָּׁעָה הַזֹּאת שְׁעַת רַחֲמִים
וְעֵת רָצוֹן מִלְּפָנֶיךָ.

אָבִינוּ מַלְכֵּנוּ, חֲמוֹל עָלֵינוּ וְעַל עוֹלָלֵינוּ וְטַפֵּנוּ.

אָבִינוּ מַלְכֵּנוּ, עֲשֵׂה לְמַעַן הֲרוּגִים עַל שֵׁם קָדְשֶׁךָ.

אָבִינוּ מַלְכֵּנוּ, עֲשֵׂה לְמַעַן טְבוּחִים עַל יִחוּדֶךָ.

אָבִינוּ מַלְכֵּנוּ, עֲשֵׂה לְמַעַן בָּאֵי בָאֵשׁ וּבַמַּיִם עַל קִדּוּשׁ שְׁמֶךָ.

אָבִינוּ מַלְכֵּנוּ, נְקוֹם לְעֵינֵינוּ נִקְמַת דַּם עֲבָדֶיךָ הַשָּׁפוּךְ.

אָבִינוּ מַלְכֵּנוּ, עֲשֵׂה לְמַעַנְךָ אִם לֹא לְמַעֲנֵנוּ.

אָבִינוּ מַלְכֵּנוּ, עֲשֵׂה לְמַעַנְךָ וְהוֹשִׁיעֵנוּ.

אָבִינוּ מַלְכֵּנוּ, עֲשֵׂה לְמַעַן רַחֲמֶיךָ הָרַבִּים.

אָבִינוּ מַלְכֵּנוּ, עֲשֵׂה לְמַעַן שִׁמְךָ הַגָּדוֹל הַגִּבּוֹר וְהַנּוֹרָא,
שֶׁנִּקְרָא עָלֵינוּ.

❖ אָבִינוּ מַלְכֵּנוּ, חָנֵּנוּ וַעֲנֵנוּ, כִּי אֵין בָּנוּ מַעֲשִׂים,
עֲשֵׂה עִמָּנוּ צְדָקָה וָחֶסֶד וְהוֹשִׁיעֵנוּ.

THE ARK IS CLOSED.

On fast days:

Our Father, our King,
remember us for
merits.
Our Father, our King,
remember us for
forgiveness and pardon.

From Rosh Hashanah to Yom Kippur:

Our Father, our King,
inscribe us in the book of
merits.
Our Father, our King,
inscribe us in the book of
forgiveness and pardon.

End of responsive reading. All continue:

Our Father, our King, make salvation sprout for us soon.

Our Father, our King, raise high the pride of Israel, Your people.

Our Father, our King, raise high the pride of Your anointed.

Our Father, our King, fill our hands from Your blessings.

Our Father, our King, fill our storehouses with abundance.

Our Father, our King, hear our voice, pity and be compassionate to us.

Our Father, our King, accept — with compassion and favor — our prayer.

Our Father, our King, open the gates of heaven to our prayer.

Our Father, our King, remember that we are but dust.

Our Father, our King, please do not turn us from You empty-handed.

Our Father, our King, may this moment be a moment
of compassion and a time of favor before You.

Our Father, our King, take pity upon us,
and upon our children and our infants.

Our Father, our King, act for the sake of those who were murdered
for Your Holy Name.

Our Father, our King, act for the sake of those who were slaughtered
for Your Oneness.

Our Father, our King, act for the sake of those who went into fire and water
for the sanctification of Your Name.

Our Father, our King, avenge before our eyes
the spilled blood of Your servants.

Our Father, our King, act for Your sake if not for our sake.

Our Father, our King, act for Your sake and save us.

Our Father, our King, act for the sake of
Your abundant compassion.

Our Father, our King, act for the sake of Your great, mighty,
and awesome Name that is proclaimed upon us.

Chazzan — Our Father, our King, be gracious with us
and answer us, though we have no worthy deeds;
treat us with charity and kindness, and save us.

THE ARK IS CLOSED.

❧ קריאת התורה לתענית ציבור ❧
הוצאת ספר תורה

From the moment the Ark is opened until the Torah is returned to it, one must conduct himself with the utmost respect, and avoid *unnecessary* conversation. It is commendable to kiss the Torah as it is carried to the *bimah* and back to the Ark.

THE ARK IS OPENED
All rise. Before the Torah is removed the congregation recites:

וַיְהִי בִּנְסֹעַ הָאָרֹן וַיֹּאמֶר מֹשֶׁה, קוּמָה יהוה וְיָפֻצוּ אֹיְבֶיךָ, וְיָנֻסוּ מְשַׂנְאֶיךָ מִפָּנֶיךָ.[1] כִּי מִצִּיּוֹן תֵּצֵא תוֹרָה, וּדְבַר יהוה מִירוּשָׁלָיִם.[2] בָּרוּךְ שֶׁנָּתַן תּוֹרָה לְעַמּוֹ יִשְׂרָאֵל בִּקְדֻשָּׁתוֹ.

בְּרִיךְ שְׁמֵהּ דְּמָרֵא עָלְמָא, בְּרִיךְ כִּתְרָךְ וְאַתְרָךְ. יְהֵא רְעוּתָךְ עִם עַמָּךְ יִשְׂרָאֵל לְעָלַם, וּפֻרְקַן יְמִינָךְ אַחֲזֵי לְעַמָּךְ בְּבֵית מַקְדְּשָׁךְ, וּלְאַמְטוּיֵי לָנָא מִטּוּב נְהוֹרָךְ, וּלְקַבֵּל צְלוֹתָנָא בְּרַחֲמִין. יְהֵא רַעֲוָא קֳדָמָךְ, דְּתוֹרִיךְ לָן חַיִּין בְּטִיבוּתָא, וְלֶהֱוֵי אֲנָא פְּקִידָא בְּגוֹ צַדִּיקַיָּא, לְמִרְחַם עָלַי וּלְמִנְטַר יָתִי וְיַת כָּל דִּי לִי וְדִי לְעַמָּךְ יִשְׂרָאֵל. אַנְתְּ הוּא זָן לְכֹלָּא, וּמְפַרְנֵס לְכֹלָּא, אַנְתְּ הוּא שַׁלִּיט עַל כֹּלָּא. אַנְתְּ הוּא דְּשַׁלִּיט עַל מַלְכַיָּא, וּמַלְכוּתָא דִּילָךְ הִיא. אֲנָא עַבְדָּא דְקֻדְשָׁא בְּרִיךְ הוּא, דְּסָגִידְנָא קַמֵּהּ וּמִקַּמָּא דִּיקַר אוֹרַיְתֵהּ בְּכָל עִדָּן וְעִדָּן. לָא עַל אֱנָשׁ רָחִיצְנָא, וְלָא עַל בַּר אֱלָהִין סָמִיכְנָא, אֶלָּא בֶּאֱלָהָא דִשְׁמַיָּא, דְּהוּא אֱלָהָא קְשׁוֹט, וְאוֹרַיְתֵהּ קְשׁוֹט, וּנְבִיאוֹהִי קְשׁוֹט, וּמַסְגֵּא לְמֶעְבַּד טַבְוָן וּקְשׁוֹט. בֵּהּ אֲנָא רָחִיץ, וְלִשְׁמֵהּ קַדִּישָׁא יַקִּירָא אֲנָא אֵמַר תֻּשְׁבְּחָן. יְהֵא רַעֲוָא קֳדָמָךְ, דְּתִפְתַּח לִבָּאִי בְּאוֹרַיְתָא, וְתַשְׁלִים מִשְׁאֲלִין דְּלִבָּאי, וְלִבָּא דְכָל עַמָּךְ יִשְׂרָאֵל, לְטַב וּלְחַיִּין וְלִשְׁלָם. (אָמֵן.)

The *chazzan* accepts the Torah in his right arm.
He turns to the Ark and raises the Torah slightly as he bows and recites:

גַּדְּלוּ לַיהוה אִתִּי וּנְרוֹמְמָה שְׁמוֹ יַחְדָּו.[3]

Congregation responds:

לְךָ יהוה הַגְּדֻלָּה וְהַגְּבוּרָה וְהַתִּפְאֶרֶת וְהַנֵּצַח וְהַהוֹד, כִּי כֹל בַּשָּׁמַיִם וּבָאָרֶץ, לְךָ יהוה הַמַּמְלָכָה וְהַמִּתְנַשֵּׂא לְכֹל לְרֹאשׁ.[4] רוֹמְמוּ יהוה אֱלֹהֵינוּ, וְהִשְׁתַּחֲווּ לַהֲדֹם רַגְלָיו, קָדוֹשׁ הוּא. רוֹמְמוּ יהוה אֱלֹהֵינוּ, וְהִשְׁתַּחֲווּ לְהַר קָדְשׁוֹ, כִּי קָדוֹשׁ יהוה אֱלֹהֵינוּ.[5]

אַב הָרַחֲמִים, הוּא יְרַחֵם עַם עֲמוּסִים, וְיִזְכֹּר בְּרִית אֵיתָנִים, וְיַצִּיל נַפְשׁוֹתֵינוּ מִן הַשָּׁעוֹת הָרָעוֹת, וְיִגְעַר בְּיֵצֶר הָרָע מִן הַנְּשׂוּאִים, וְיָחֹן אוֹתָנוּ לִפְלֵיטַת עוֹלָמִים, וִימַלֵּא מִשְׁאֲלוֹתֵינוּ בְּמִדָּה טוֹבָה יְשׁוּעָה וְרַחֲמִים.

◄§ TORAH READING FOR FAST DAYS ◄⊱

REMOVAL OF THE TORAH FROM THE ARK

From the moment the Ark is opened until the Torah is returned to it, one must conduct himself with the utmost respect, and avoid unnecessary conversation. It is commendable to kiss the Torah as it is carried to the *bimah* and back to the Ark.

THE ARK IS OPENED

All rise. Before the Torah is removed the congregation recites:

וַיְהִי בִּנְסֹעַ *When the Ark would travel, Moses would say, "Arise, HASHEM, and let Your foes be scattered, let those who hate You flee from You."*[1] *For from Zion the Torah will come forth and the word of HASHEM from Jerusalem.*[2] *Blessed is He Who gave the Torah to His people Israel in His holiness.*

בְּרִיךְ *Blessed is the Name of the Master of the universe, blessed is Your crown and Your place. May Your favor remain with Your people Israel forever; may You display the salvation of Your right hand to Your people in Your Holy Temple, to benefit us with the goodness of Your luminescence and to accept our prayers with mercy. May it be Your will that You extend our lives with goodness and that I be numbered among the righteous; that You have mercy on me and protect me, all that is mine and that is Your people Israel's. It is You Who nourishes all and sustains all; You control everything. It is You Who controls kings, and kingship is Yours. I am a servant of the Holy One, Blessed is He, and I prostrate myself before Him and before the glory of His Torah at all times. Not in any man do I put trust, nor on any angel do I rely — only on the God of heaven Who is the God of truth, Whose Torah is truth and Whose prophets are true and Who acts liberally with kindness and truth. In Him do I trust, and to His glorious and holy Name do I declare praises. May it be Your will that You open my heart to the Torah and that You fulfill the wishes of my heart and the heart of Your entire people Israel for good, for life, and for peace. (Amen.)*

The chazzan accepts the Torah in his right arm.

He turns to the Ark and raises the Torah slightly as he bows and recites:

Declare the greatness of HASHEM with me, and let us exalt His Name together.[3]

Congregation responds:

לְךָ *Yours, HASHEM, is the greatness, the strength, the splendor, the triumph, and the glory; even everything in heaven and earth; Yours, HASHEM, is the kingdom, and the sovereignty over every leader.*[4] *Exalt HASHEM, our God, and bow at His footstool; He is Holy! Exalt HASHEM, our God, and bow to His holy mountain; for holy is HASHEM, our God.*[5]

אַב *May the Father of compassion have mercy on the people that is borne by Him, and may He remember the covenant of the spiritually mighty. May He rescue our souls from the bad times, and upbraid the Evil Inclination to leave those borne by Him, graciously make us an eternal remnant, and fulfill our requests in good measure, for salvation and mercy.*

---

(1) *Numbers* 10:35. (2) *Isaiah* 2:3. (3) *Psalms* 34:4.
(4) *I Chronicles* 29:11. (5) *Psalms* 99:5,9.

The *gabbai* uses the following formula to call a *Kohen* to the Torah:

וְתִגָּלֶה וְתֵרָאֶה מַלְכוּתוֹ עָלֵינוּ בִּזְמַן קָרוֹב, וְיָחֹן פְּלֵיטָתֵנוּ וּפְלֵיטַת עַמּוֹ בֵּית יִשְׂרָאֵל לְחֵן וּלְחֶסֶד וּלְרַחֲמִים וּלְרָצוֹן. וְנֹאמַר: אָמֵן. הַכֹּל הָבוּ גֹדֶל לֵאלֹהֵינוּ וּתְנוּ כָבוֹד לַתּוֹרָה. כֹּהֵן° קְרָב, יַעֲמֹד (name) בֶּן (father's name) הַכֹּהֵן.

°If no *Kohen* is present, the *gabbai* says:

„אֵין כָּאן כֹּהֵן, יַעֲמֹד (name) בֶּן (father's name) (לֵוִי) יִשְׂרָאֵל בִּמְקוֹם כֹּהֵן."

בָּרוּךְ שֶׁנָּתַן תּוֹרָה לְעַמּוֹ יִשְׂרָאֵל בִּקְדֻשָּׁתוֹ. (תּוֹרַת יהוה תְּמִימָה מְשִׁיבַת נָפֶשׁ, עֵדוּת יהוה נֶאֱמָנָה מַחְכִּימַת פֶּתִי. פִּקּוּדֵי יהוה יְשָׁרִים מְשַׂמְּחֵי לֵב, מִצְוַת יהוה בָּרָה מְאִירַת עֵינָיִם.[1] יהוה עֹז לְעַמּוֹ יִתֵּן, יהוה יְבָרֵךְ אֶת עַמּוֹ בַשָּׁלוֹם.[2] הָאֵל תָּמִים דַּרְכּוֹ, אִמְרַת יהוה צְרוּפָה, מָגֵן הוּא לְכֹל הַחוֹסִים בּוֹ.[3])

Congregation, then *gabbai*:

וְאַתֶּם הַדְּבֵקִים בַּיהוה אֱלֹהֵיכֶם, חַיִּים כֻּלְּכֶם הַיּוֹם.[4]

בִּרְכוֹת הַתּוֹרָה

The reader shows the *oleh* (person called to the Torah) the place in the Torah. The *oleh* touches the Torah with a corner of his *tallis*, or the belt or mantle of the Torah, and kisses it. He then begins the blessing, bowing at בָּרְכוּ, and straightening up at 'ה.

בָּרְכוּ אֶת יהוה הַמְבֹרָךְ.

Congregation, followed by *oleh*, responds, bowing at בָּרוּךְ, and straightening up at 'ה.

בָּרוּךְ יהוה הַמְבֹרָךְ לְעוֹלָם וָעֶד.

Oleh continues:

בָּרוּךְ אַתָּה יהוה אֱלֹהֵינוּ מֶלֶךְ הָעוֹלָם, אֲשֶׁר בָּחַר בָּנוּ מִכָּל הָעַמִּים, וְנָתַן לָנוּ אֶת תּוֹרָתוֹ. בָּרוּךְ אַתָּה יהוה, נוֹתֵן הַתּוֹרָה.
(אָמֵן. — Cong.)

After his Torah portion has been read, the *oleh* recites:

בָּרוּךְ אַתָּה יהוה אֱלֹהֵינוּ מֶלֶךְ הָעוֹלָם, אֲשֶׁר נָתַן לָנוּ תּוֹרַת אֱמֶת, וְחַיֵּי עוֹלָם נָטַע בְּתוֹכֵנוּ. בָּרוּךְ אַתָּה יהוה, נוֹתֵן הַתּוֹרָה.
(אָמֵן. — Cong.)

קְרִיאַת הַתּוֹרָה

Upon reaching the words in bold type, the reader pauses.
The congregation recites these verses, which are then repeated by the reader.

שמות לב:יא-יד, לד:א-י

כח – וַיְחַל מֹשֶׁה אֶת־פְּנֵי יהוה אֱלֹהָיו וַיֹּאמֶר לָמָה יהוה יֶחֱרֶה אַפְּךָ בְּעַמֶּךָ אֲשֶׁר הוֹצֵאתָ מֵאֶרֶץ מִצְרַיִם בְּכֹחַ גָּדוֹל וּבְיָד חֲזָקָה: לָמָּה יֹאמְרוּ מִצְרַיִם לֵאמֹר בְּרָעָה הוֹצִיאָם לַהֲרֹג אֹתָם בֶּהָרִים וּלְכַלֹּתָם מֵעַל פְּנֵי הָאֲדָמָה שׁוּב מֵחֲרוֹן אַפֶּךָ וְהִנָּחֵם עַל־הָרָעָה לְעַמֶּךָ: וְזָכֹר

The *gabbai* uses the following formula to call a *Kohen* to the Torah:

וְתִגָּלֶה *And may His Kingship over us be revealed and become visible soon,*
*and may He be gracious to our remnant and the remnant of His people
the Family of Israel, for graciousness, kindness, mercy, and favor. And let us respond, Amen. All of you ascribe greatness to our God and give honor to the Torah.
Kohen,* ° *approach. Stand* (name) *son of* (father's name) *the Kohen.*

°If no *Kohen* is present, the *gabbai* says:
"There is no Kohen present, stand (name) *son of* (father's name)
an Israelite (Levite) in place of the Kohen."

---

*Blessed is He Who gave the Torah to His people Israel in His holiness. (The Torah of
HASHEM is perfect, restoring the soul; the testimony of HASHEM is trustworthy, making the
simple one wise. The orders of HASHEM are upright, gladdening the heart; the command
of HASHEM is clear, enlightening the eyes.* [1] *HASHEM will give might to His people; HASHEM
will bless His people with peace.* [2] *The God Whose way is perfect, the promise of HASHEM
is flawless, He is a shield for all who take refuge in Him.* [3])

Congregation, then *gabbai*:

You who cling to HASHEM, your God,
you are all alive today. [4]

BLESSINGS OF THE TORAH

The reader shows the *oleh* (person called to the Torah) the place in the Torah. The *oleh*
touches the Torah with a corner of his *tallis*, or the belt or mantle of the Torah, and kisses
it. He then begins the blessing, bowing at *"Bless,"* and straightening up at *"HASHEM."*

Bless HASHEM, the blessed One.

Congregation, followed by *oleh*, responds, bowing at *"Blessed,"*
and straightening up at *"HASHEM."*
Blessed is HASHEM, the blessed One, for all eternity.

Oleh continues:

בָּרוּךְ *Blessed are You, HASHEM, our God, King of the universe, Who selected
us from all the peoples and gave us His Torah. Blessed are You, HASHEM,
Giver of the Torah.* (Cong.— Amen.)

After his Torah portion has been read, the *oleh* recites:

בָּרוּךְ *Blessed are You, HASHEM, our God, King of the universe, Who gave us
the Torah of truth and implanted eternal life within us. Blessed are You,
HASHEM, Giver of the Torah.* (Cong.— Amen.)

READING OF THE TORAH

Upon reaching the words in bold type, the reader pauses.
The congregation recites these verses, which are then repeated by the reader.

Exodus 32:11-14; 34:1-10

Kohen — *Moses pleaded before HASHEM, his God, and said, "Why, HASHEM,
should Your anger flare up against Your people, whom You have taken out of
the land of Egypt, with great power and a strong hand? Why should Egypt say
the following: 'With evil intent did He take them out, to kill them in the mountains
and to annihilate them from the face of the earth'? **Relent from Your flaring
anger and reconsider regarding the evil against Your people.** Remember*

---

(1) *Psalms* 19:8-9. (2) 29:11. (3) 18:31. (4) *Deuteronomy* 4:4.

לְאַבְרָהָם לְיִצְחָק וּלְיִשְׂרָאֵל עֲבָדֶיךָ אֲשֶׁר נִשְׁבַּעְתָּ לָהֶם בָּךְ וַתְּדַבֵּר
אֲלֵהֶם אַרְבֶּה אֶת־זַרְעֲכֶם כְּכוֹכְבֵי הַשָּׁמָיִם וְכָל־הָאָרֶץ הַזֹּאת אֲשֶׁר
אָמַרְתִּי אֶתֵּן לְזַרְעֲכֶם וְנָחֲלוּ לְעֹלָם: וַיִּנָּחֶם יְהוָה עַל־הָרָעָה אֲשֶׁר דִּבֶּר
לַעֲשׂוֹת לְעַמּוֹ:

לוי - וַיֹּאמֶר יְהוָה אֶל־מֹשֶׁה פְּסָל־לְךָ שְׁנֵי־לֻחֹת אֲבָנִים כָּרִאשֹׁנִים
וְכָתַבְתִּי עַל־הַלֻּחֹת אֶת־הַדְּבָרִים אֲשֶׁר הָיוּ עַל־הַלֻּחֹת הָרִאשֹׁנִים
אֲשֶׁר שִׁבַּרְתָּ: וֶהְיֵה נָכוֹן לַבֹּקֶר וְעָלִיתָ בַבֹּקֶר אֶל־הַר סִינַי וְנִצַּבְתָּ לִי שָׁם
עַל־רֹאשׁ הָהָר: וְאִישׁ לֹא־יַעֲלֶה עִמָּךְ וְגַם־אִישׁ אַל־יֵרָא בְּכָל־הָהָר
גַּם־הַצֹּאן וְהַבָּקָר אַל־יִרְעוּ אֶל־מוּל הָהָר הַהוּא:

מפטיר - וַיִּפְסֹל שְׁנֵי־לֻחֹת אֲבָנִים כָּרִאשֹׁנִים וַיַּשְׁכֵּם מֹשֶׁה בַבֹּקֶר וַיַּעַל
אֶל־הַר סִינַי כַּאֲשֶׁר צִוָּה יְהוָה אֹתוֹ וַיִּקַּח בְּיָדוֹ שְׁנֵי לֻחֹת אֲבָנִים:
וַיֵּרֶד יְהוָה בֶּעָנָן וַיִּתְיַצֵּב עִמּוֹ שָׁם וַיִּקְרָא בְשֵׁם יְהוָה: וַיַּעֲבֹר יְהוָה |
עַל־פָּנָיו וַיִּקְרָא יְהוָה | יְהוָה אֵל רַחוּם וְחַנּוּן אֶרֶךְ אַפַּיִם וְרַב־חֶסֶד
וֶאֱמֶת: נֹצֵר חֶסֶד לָאֲלָפִים נֹשֵׂא עָוֹן וָפֶשַׁע וְחַטָּאָה וְנַקֵּה לֹא יְנַקֶּה
פֹּקֵד | עֲוֹן אָבוֹת עַל־בָּנִים וְעַל־בְּנֵי בָנִים עַל־שִׁלֵּשִׁים וְעַל־רִבֵּעִים:
וַיְמַהֵר מֹשֶׁה וַיִּקֹּד אַרְצָה וַיִּשְׁתָּחוּ: וַיֹּאמֶר אִם־נָא מָצָאתִי חֵן בְּעֵינֶיךָ
אֲדֹנָי יֵלֶךְ־נָא אֲדֹנָי בְּקִרְבֵּנוּ כִּי עַם־קְשֵׁה־עֹרֶף הוּא וְסָלַחְתָּ לַעֲוֹנֵנוּ
וּלְחַטָּאתֵנוּ וּנְחַלְתָּנוּ: וַיֹּאמֶר הִנֵּה אָנֹכִי כֹּרֵת בְּרִית נֶגֶד כָּל־עַמְּךָ
אֶעֱשֶׂה נִפְלָאֹת אֲשֶׁר לֹא־נִבְרְאוּ בְכָל־הָאָרֶץ וּבְכָל־הַגּוֹיִם וְרָאָה כָל־
הָעָם אֲשֶׁר־אַתָּה בְקִרְבּוֹ אֶת־מַעֲשֵׂה יְהוָה כִּי־נוֹרָא הוּא אֲשֶׁר אֲנִי
עֹשֶׂה עִמָּךְ:

הגבהה וגלילה

The Torah is raised for all to see.
Each person looks at the Torah and recites aloud:

וְזֹאת הַתּוֹרָה אֲשֶׁר שָׂם מֹשֶׁה לִפְנֵי בְּנֵי יִשְׂרָאֵל,¹
עַל פִּי יְהוָה בְּיַד מֹשֶׁה.²

Some add:

עֵץ חַיִּים הִיא לַמַּחֲזִיקִים בָּהּ, וְתֹמְכֶיהָ מְאֻשָּׁר.³ דְּרָכֶיהָ דַרְכֵי נֹעַם,
וְכָל נְתִיבוֹתֶיהָ שָׁלוֹם.⁴ אֹרֶךְ יָמִים בִּימִינָהּ, בִּשְׂמֹאלָהּ עֹשֶׁר
וְכָבוֹד.⁵ יְהוָה חָפֵץ לְמַעַן צִדְקוֹ, יַגְדִּיל תּוֹרָה וְיַאְדִּיר.⁶

for the sake of Abraham, Isaac, and Israel, Your servants, to whom You swore by Yourself, and You told them, 'I shall increase your offspring like the stars of heaven, and this entire land of which I spoke, I shall give to your offspring and it shall be their heritage forever.'" HASHEM reconsidered regarding the evil that He declared He would do to His people.

Levi — HASHEM said to Moses, "Carve for yourself two stone Tablets like the first ones, and I shall inscribe on the Tablets the words that were on the first Tablets, which you shattered. Be prepared in the morning; ascend Mount Sinai in the morning and stand by Me there on the mountaintop. No man may ascend with you nor may anyone be seen on the entire mountain. Even the flock and the cattle may not graze facing that mountain."

Maftir — So he carved out two stone Tablets like the first ones. Moses arose early in the morning and ascended to Mount Sinai, as HASHEM had commanded him, and he took two stone Tablets in his hand. HASHEM descended in a cloud and stood with him there, and He called out with the Name HASHEM. HASHEM passed before him and proclaimed: HASHEM, HASHEM, God, Compassionate and Gracious, Slow to Anger, and Abundant in Kindness and Truth; Preserver of Kindness for thousands of generations, Forgiver of Iniquity, Willful Sin, and Error, and Who Cleanses — but does not cleanse completely, recalling the iniquity of parents upon children and grandchildren, to the third and fourth generations. Moses hastened to bow his head toward the ground and prostrate himself. He said, "If I have now found favor in Your eyes, my Lord, let my Lord go among us — for it is a stiff-necked people, and You shall forgive our iniquity and error, and make us Your heritage." He said, "Behold! I seal a covenant: Before your entire people I shall make distinctions such as have never been created in the entire world and among all the nations; and the entire people among whom you are will see the work of HASHEM — which is awesome — that I am about to do with you."

HAGBAHAH AND GELILAH

The Torah is raised for all to see.
Each person looks at the Torah and recites aloud:

This is the Torah that Moses placed before the Children of Israel,[1] upon the command of HASHEM, through Moses' hand.[2]

Some add:

עֵץ *It is a tree of life for those who grasp it, and its supporters are praiseworthy.[3] Its ways are ways of pleasantness and all its paths are peace.[4] Lengthy days are at its right; at its left are wealth and honor.[5] HASHEM desired, for the sake of its [Israel's] righteousness, that the Torah be made great and glorious.[6]*

---

(1) Deuteronomy 4:44. (2) Numbers 9:23.
(3) Proverbs 3:18. (4) 3:17. (5) 3:16. (6) Isaiah 42:21.

ברכה קודם ההפטרה

After the Torah Scroll has been wound, tied and covered,
the *oleh* for *Maftir* recites the blessing before the *Haftarah*.

בָּרוּךְ אַתָּה יהוה אֱלֹהֵינוּ מֶלֶךְ הָעוֹלָם, אֲשֶׁר בָּחַר בִּנְבִיאִים טוֹבִים, וְרָצָה בְדִבְרֵיהֶם הַנֶּאֱמָרִים בֶּאֱמֶת, בָּרוּךְ אַתָּה יהוה, הַבּוֹחֵר בַּתּוֹרָה וּבְמֹשֶׁה עַבְדּוֹ, וּבְיִשְׂרָאֵל עַמּוֹ, וּבִנְבִיאֵי הָאֱמֶת וָצֶדֶק: (אָמֵן.– Cong.)

ישעיה נה:ו–נו:ח

דִּרְשׁוּ יהוה בְּהִמָּצְאוֹ קְרָאֻהוּ בִּהְיוֹתוֹ קָרוֹב: יַעֲזֹב רָשָׁע דַּרְכּוֹ וְאִישׁ אָוֶן מַחְשְׁבֹתָיו וְיָשֹׁב אֶל־יהוה וִירַחֲמֵהוּ וְאֶל־אֱלֹהֵינוּ כִּי־יַרְבֶּה לִסְלוֹחַ: כִּי לֹא מַחְשְׁבוֹתַי מַחְשְׁבוֹתֵיכֶם וְלֹא דַרְכֵיכֶם דְּרָכָי נְאֻם יהוה: כִּי־גָבְהוּ שָׁמַיִם מֵאָרֶץ כֵּן גָּבְהוּ דְרָכַי מִדַּרְכֵיכֶם וּמַחְשְׁבֹתַי מִמַּחְשְׁבֹתֵיכֶם: כִּי כַּאֲשֶׁר יֵרֵד הַגֶּשֶׁם וְהַשֶּׁלֶג מִן־הַשָּׁמַיִם וְשָׁמָּה לֹא יָשׁוּב כִּי אִם־הִרְוָה אֶת־הָאָרֶץ וְהוֹלִידָהּ וְהִצְמִיחָהּ וְנָתַן זֶרַע לַזֹּרֵעַ וְלֶחֶם לָאֹכֵל: כֵּן יִהְיֶה דְבָרִי אֲשֶׁר יֵצֵא מִפִּי לֹא־יָשׁוּב אֵלַי רֵיקָם כִּי אִם־עָשָׂה אֶת־אֲשֶׁר חָפַצְתִּי וְהִצְלִיחַ אֲשֶׁר שְׁלַחְתִּיו: כִּי־בְשִׂמְחָה תֵצֵאוּ וּבְשָׁלוֹם תּוּבָלוּן הֶהָרִים וְהַגְּבָעוֹת יִפְצְחוּ לִפְנֵיכֶם רִנָּה וְכָל־עֲצֵי הַשָּׂדֶה יִמְחֲאוּ־כָף: תַּחַת הַנַּעֲצוּץ יַעֲלֶה בְרוֹשׁ וְתַחַת הַסִּרְפַּד יַעֲלֶה הֲדַס וְהָיָה לַיהוה לְשֵׁם לְאוֹת עוֹלָם לֹא יִכָּרֵת: כֹּה אָמַר יהוה שִׁמְרוּ מִשְׁפָּט וַעֲשׂוּ צְדָקָה כִּי־קְרוֹבָה יְשׁוּעָתִי לָבוֹא וְצִדְקָתִי לְהִגָּלוֹת: אַשְׁרֵי אֱנוֹשׁ יַעֲשֶׂה־זֹּאת וּבֶן־אָדָם יַחֲזִיק בָּהּ שֹׁמֵר שַׁבָּת מֵחַלְּלוֹ וְשֹׁמֵר יָדוֹ מֵעֲשׂוֹת כָּל־רָע: וְאַל־יֹאמַר בֶּן־הַנֵּכָר הַנִּלְוָה אֶל־יהוה לֵאמֹר הַבְדֵּל יַבְדִּילַנִי יהוה מֵעַל עַמּוֹ וְאַל־יֹאמַר הַסָּרִיס הֵן אֲנִי עֵץ יָבֵשׁ: כִּי־כֹה ׀ אָמַר יהוה לַסָּרִיסִים אֲשֶׁר יִשְׁמְרוּ אֶת־שַׁבְּתוֹתַי וּבָחֲרוּ בַּאֲשֶׁר חָפָצְתִּי וּמַחֲזִיקִים בִּבְרִיתִי: וְנָתַתִּי לָהֶם בְּבֵיתִי וּבְחוֹמֹתַי יָד וָשֵׁם טוֹב מִבָּנִים וּמִבָּנוֹת שֵׁם עוֹלָם אֶתֶּן־לוֹ אֲשֶׁר לֹא יִכָּרֵת: וּבְנֵי הַנֵּכָר הַנִּלְוִים עַל־יהוה לְשָׁרְתוֹ וּלְאַהֲבָה אֶת־שֵׁם יהוה לִהְיוֹת לוֹ לַעֲבָדִים כָּל־שֹׁמֵר שַׁבָּת מֵחַלְּלוֹ וּמַחֲזִיקִים בִּבְרִיתִי: וַהֲבִיאוֹתִים אֶל־הַר קָדְשִׁי וְשִׂמַּחְתִּים בְּבֵית תְּפִלָּתִי עוֹלֹתֵיהֶם וְזִבְחֵיהֶם לְרָצוֹן עַל־מִזְבְּחִי כִּי בֵיתִי בֵּית־תְּפִלָּה יִקָּרֵא לְכָל־הָעַמִּים: נְאֻם אֲדֹנָי יֱהֹוִה מְקַבֵּץ נִדְחֵי יִשְׂרָאֵל עוֹד אֲקַבֵּץ עָלָיו לְנִקְבָּצָיו:

BLESSING BEFORE THE HAFTARAH

After the Torah Scroll has been wound, tied and covered,
the *oleh* for *Maftir* recites the blessing before the *Haftarah*.

בָּרוּךְ *Blessed are You, HASHEM, our God, King of the universe, Who has chosen good prophets and was pleased with their words that were uttered with truth. Blessed are You, HASHEM, Who chooses the Torah; Moses, His servant; Israel, His people; and the prophets of truth and righteousness.*

(Cong.— *Amen.*)

Isaiah 55:6-56:8

דִּרְשׁוּ *Seek HASHEM when He can be found; call upon Him when He is near. Let the wicked one forsake his way and the iniquitous man his thoughts; let him return to HASHEM and He will show him mercy; to our God, for He is abundantly forgiving. For My thoughts are not your thoughts and your ways are not My ways — the word of HASHEM. As high as the heavens over the earth, so are My ways higher than your ways, and My thoughts than your thoughts. For just as the rain and snow descend from heaven and will not return there, rather it waters the earth and causes it to produce and sprout, and gives seed to the sower and food to the eater, so shall be My word that emanates from My mouth, it will not return to Me unfulfilled unless it will have accomplished what I desired and brought success where I sent it. For in gladness shall you go out and in peace shall you arrive, the mountains and hills will break out in glad song before you, and all the trees of the field will clap hands. In place of the thornbush, a cypress will rise; and in place of the nettle, a myrtle will rise. This will be a monument to HASHEM, an eternal sign never to be cut down.*

Thus said HASHEM: Observe justice and perform righteousness, for My salvation is soon to come and My righteousness to be revealed. Praiseworthy is the man who does this and the person who grasps it tightly: who guards the Sabbath against desecrating it and guards his hand against doing any evil.

Let not the foreigner, who has joined himself to HASHEM, speak, saying, "HASHEM will utterly separate me from His people"; and let not the barren one say, "Behold I am a shriveled tree." For thus said HASHEM to the barren ones who observe My Sabbaths and choose what I desire, and grasp My covenant tightly: In My house and within My walls I will give them a place of honor and renown, which is better than sons and daughters; eternal renown will I give them, which will never be terminated. And the foreigners who join themselves to HASHEM to serve Him and to love the Name of HASHEM to become servants unto Him, all who guard the Sabbath against desecration, and grasp My covenant tightly — I will bring them to My holy mountain, and I will gladden them in My house of prayer; their elevation-offerings and their feast-offerings will find favor on My Altar, for My House will be called a house of prayer for all the peoples. The word of my Lord, HASHEM/ELOHIM, Who gathers in the dispersed of Israel: I shall gather to him even more than those already gathered to him.

After the *Haftarah* is read, the *oleh* recites the following blessings:

בָּרוּךְ אַתָּה יהוה אֱלֹהֵינוּ מֶלֶךְ הָעוֹלָם, צוּר כָּל הָעוֹלָמִים, צַדִּיק בְּכָל הַדּוֹרוֹת, הָאֵל הַנֶּאֱמָן הָאוֹמֵר וְעֹשֶׂה, הַמְדַבֵּר וּמְקַיֵּם, שֶׁכָּל דְּבָרָיו אֱמֶת וָצֶדֶק. נֶאֱמָן אַתָּה הוּא יהוה אֱלֹהֵינוּ, וְנֶאֱמָנִים דְּבָרֶיךָ, וְדָבָר אֶחָד מִדְּבָרֶיךָ אָחוֹר לֹא יָשׁוּב רֵיקָם, כִּי אֵל מֶלֶךְ נֶאֱמָן (וְרַחֲמָן) אָתָּה. בָּרוּךְ אַתָּה יהוה, הָאֵל הַנֶּאֱמָן בְּכָל דְּבָרָיו. (.אָמֵן–Cong.)

רַחֵם עַל צִיּוֹן כִּי הִיא בֵּית חַיֵּינוּ, וְלַעֲלוּבַת נֶפֶשׁ תּוֹשִׁיעַ בִּמְהֵרָה בְיָמֵינוּ. בָּרוּךְ אַתָּה יהוה, מְשַׂמֵּחַ צִיּוֹן בְּבָנֶיהָ. (.אָמֵן–Cong.)

שַׂמְּחֵנוּ יהוה אֱלֹהֵינוּ בְּאֵלִיָּהוּ הַנָּבִיא עַבְדֶּךָ, וּבְמַלְכוּת בֵּית דָּוִד מְשִׁיחֶךָ, בִּמְהֵרָה יָבֹא וְיָגֵל לִבֵּנוּ, עַל כִּסְאוֹ לֹא יֵשֶׁב זָר וְלֹא יִנְחֲלוּ עוֹד אֲחֵרִים אֶת כְּבוֹדוֹ, כִּי בְשֵׁם קָדְשְׁךָ נִשְׁבַּעְתָּ לּוֹ, שֶׁלֹּא יִכְבֶּה נֵרוֹ לְעוֹלָם וָעֶד. בָּרוּךְ אַתָּה יהוה, מָגֵן דָּוִד. (.אָמֵן–Cong.)

Chazzan takes the Torah in his right arm and recites:

יְהַלְלוּ אֶת שֵׁם יהוה, כִּי נִשְׂגָּב שְׁמוֹ לְבַדּוֹ –

Congregation responds:

– הוֹדוֹ עַל אֶרֶץ וְשָׁמָיִם. וַיָּרֶם קֶרֶן לְעַמּוֹ, תְּהִלָּה לְכָל חֲסִידָיו, לִבְנֵי יִשְׂרָאֵל עַם קְרֹבוֹ, הַלְלוּיָהּ.[1]

As the Torah is carried to the Ark, congregation recites Psalm 24.

לְדָוִד מִזְמוֹר, לַיהוה הָאָרֶץ וּמְלוֹאָהּ, תֵּבֵל וְיֹשְׁבֵי בָהּ. כִּי הוּא עַל יַמִּים יְסָדָהּ, וְעַל נְהָרוֹת יְכוֹנְנֶהָ. מִי יַעֲלֶה בְהַר יהוה, וּמִי יָקוּם בִּמְקוֹם קָדְשׁוֹ. נְקִי כַפַּיִם וּבַר לֵבָב, אֲשֶׁר לֹא נָשָׂא לַשָּׁוְא נַפְשִׁי וְלֹא נִשְׁבַּע לְמִרְמָה. יִשָּׂא בְרָכָה מֵאֵת יהוה, וּצְדָקָה מֵאֱלֹהֵי יִשְׁעוֹ. זֶה דּוֹר דֹּרְשָׁיו, מְבַקְשֵׁי פָנֶיךָ, יַעֲקֹב, סֶלָה. שְׂאוּ שְׁעָרִים רָאשֵׁיכֶם, וְהִנָּשְׂאוּ פִּתְחֵי עוֹלָם, וְיָבוֹא מֶלֶךְ הַכָּבוֹד. מִי זֶה מֶלֶךְ הַכָּבוֹד, יהוה עִזּוּז וְגִבּוֹר, יהוה גִּבּוֹר מִלְחָמָה. שְׂאוּ שְׁעָרִים רָאשֵׁיכֶם, וּשְׂאוּ פִּתְחֵי עוֹלָם, וְיָבֹא מֶלֶךְ הַכָּבוֹד. מִי הוּא זֶה מֶלֶךְ הַכָּבוֹד, יהוה צְבָאוֹת הוּא מֶלֶךְ הַכָּבוֹד, סֶלָה.

As the Torah is placed into the Ark, the congregation recites:

וּבְנֻחֹה יֹאמַר, שׁוּבָה יהוה רִבְבוֹת אַלְפֵי יִשְׂרָאֵל.[2] קוּמָה יהוה לִמְנוּחָתֶךָ, אַתָּה וַאֲרוֹן עֻזֶּךָ. כֹּהֲנֶיךָ יִלְבְּשׁוּ צֶדֶק, וַחֲסִידֶיךָ יְרַנֵּנוּ. בַּעֲבוּר דָּוִד עַבְדֶּךָ אַל תָּשֵׁב פְּנֵי מְשִׁיחֶךָ.[3] כִּי לֶקַח טוֹב נָתַתִּי לָכֶם, תּוֹרָתִי אַל תַּעֲזֹבוּ.[4] עֵץ חַיִּים הִיא לַמַּחֲזִיקִים בָּהּ, וְתֹמְכֶיהָ מְאֻשָּׁר.[5] דְּרָכֶיהָ דַרְכֵי נֹעַם, וְכָל נְתִיבֹתֶיהָ שָׁלוֹם.[6] הֲשִׁיבֵנוּ יהוה אֵלֶיךָ וְנָשׁוּבָה, חַדֵּשׁ יָמֵינוּ כְּקֶדֶם.[7]

(1) *Psalms* 148:13-14. (2) *Numbers* 10:36. (3) *Psalms* 132:8-10.
(4) *Proverbs* 4:2. (5) 3:18. (6) 3:17. (7) *Lamentations* 5:21.

After the *Haftarah* is read, the *oleh* recites the following blessings:

בָּרוּךְ *Blessed are You, HASHEM, our God, King of the universe, Rock of all eternities, Righteous in all generations, the trustworthy God, Who says and does, Who speaks and fulfills, all of Whose words are true and righteous. Trustworthy are You HASHEM, our God, and trustworthy are Your words, not one of Your words is turned back to its origin unfulfilled, for You are God, trustworthy (and compassionate) King. Blessed are You, HASHEM, the God Who is trustworthy in all His words.*
(Cong. — Amen.)

רַחֵם *Have mercy on Zion for it is the source of our life; to the one who is deeply humiliated bring salvation speedily, in our days. Blessed are You, HASHEM, Who gladdens Zion through her children.*
(Cong. — Amen.)

שַׂמְּחֵנוּ *Gladden us, HASHEM, our God, with Elijah the prophet Your servant, and with the kingdom of the House of David, Your anointed, may he come speedily and cause our heart to exult. On his throne let no stranger sit nor let others continue to inherit his honor, for by Your holy Name You swore to him that his lamp will not be extinguished forever and ever. Blessed are You, HASHEM, Shield of David.*
(Cong. — Amen.)

Chazzan takes the Torah in his right arm and recites:
Let them praise the Name of HASHEM,
for His Name alone will have been exalted —
Congregation responds:
— His glory is above earth and heaven. And He will have exalted the pride of His people, causing praise for all His devout ones, for the Children of Israel, His intimate people. Halleluyah![1]

As the Torah is carried to the Ark, congregation recites Psalm 24.
לְדָוִד *Of David a psalm. HASHEM's is the earth and its fullness, the inhabited land and those who dwell in it. For He founded it upon seas, and established it upon rivers. Who may ascend the mountain of HASHEM, and who may stand in the place of His sanctity? One with clean hands and pure heart, who has not sworn in vain by My soul and has not sworn deceitfully. He will receive a blessing from HASHEM and just kindness from the God of his salvation. This is the generation of those who seek Him, those who strive for Your Presence — Jacob, Selah. Raise up your heads, O gates, and be uplifted, you everlasting entrances, so that the King of Glory may enter. Who is this King of Glory? — HASHEM, the mighty and strong, HASHEM, the strong in battle. Raise up your heads, O gates, and raise up, you everlasting entrances, so that the King of Glory may enter. Who then is the King of Glory? HASHEM, Master of Legions, He is the King of Glory. Selah!*

As the Torah is placed into the Ark, the congregation recites:
וּבְנֻחֹה *And when it rested he would say, "Return, HASHEM, to the myriad thousands of Israel."*[2] *Arise, HASHEM, to Your resting place, You and the Ark of Your strength. Let Your priests be clothed in righteousness, and Your devout ones will sing joyously. For the sake of David, Your servant, turn not away the face of Your anointed.*[3] *For I have given you a good teaching, do not forsake My Torah.*[4] *Chazzan— It is a tree of life for those who grasp it, and its supporters are praiseworthy.*[5] *Its ways are ways of pleasantness and all its paths are peace.*[6] *Bring us back to You, HASHEM, and we shall return, renew our days as of old.*[7]

◄§ VERSES FOR PEOPLE'S NAMES / פסוקים לשמות אנשים §►

Kitzur Shelah teaches that it is a source of merit to recite a Scriptural verse symbolizing one's name before יִהְיוּ לְרָצוֹן at the end of *Shemoneh Esrei*. The verse should either contain the person's name, or else begin and end with the first and last letters of the name.

Following is a selection of first and last letters of names, with appropriate verses:

א...א אָנָּא יהוה הוֹשִׁיעָה נָּא, אָנָּא יהוה הַצְלִיחָה נָּא.[1]

א...ה אַשְׁרֵי מַשְׂכִּיל אֶל דָּל, בְּיוֹם רָעָה יְמַלְּטֵהוּ יהוה.[2]

א...ו אַשְׁרֵי שֶׁאֵל יַעֲקֹב בְּעֶזְרוֹ, שִׂבְרוֹ עַל יהוה אֱלֹהָיו.[3]

א...י אָמַרְתָּ לַיהוה, אֲדֹנָי אָתָּה, טוֹבָתִי בַּל עָלֶיךָ.[5]

א...ה אָמַרְתָּ הַאֲזִינָה יהוה, בִּינָה הֲגִיגִי.[4]

א...ל אֶרֶץ רָעָשָׁה, אַף שָׁמַיִם נָטְפוּ מִפְּנֵי אֱלֹהִים, זֶה סִינַי, מִפְּנֵי אֱלֹהִים אֱלֹהֵי יִשְׂרָאֵל.[6]

א...ם אַתָּה הוּא יהוה הָאֱלֹהִים, אֲשֶׁר בָּחַרְתָּ בְּאַבְרָם, וְהוֹצֵאתוֹ מֵאוּר כַּשְׂדִּים, וְשַׂמְתָּ שְּׁמוֹ אַבְרָהָם.[7]

א...ן אֵלֶיךָ יהוה אֶקְרָא, וְאֶל אֲדֹנָי אֶתְחַנָּן.[8]

א...ע אָמַר כֻּלּוֹ בַּל אָמוּט, לְדֹר וָדֹר אֲשֶׁר לֹא בְרָע.[9]

א...ר אֵלֶּה בָרֶכֶב וְאֵלֶּה בַסּוּסִים, וַאֲנַחְנוּ בְּשֵׁם יהוה אֱלֹהֵינוּ נַזְכִּיר.[10]

ב...ה בְּרִיתִי הָיְתָה אִתּוֹ הַחַיִּים וְהַשָּׁלוֹם, וָאֶתְּנֵם לוֹ מוֹרָא וַיִּירָאֵנִי, וּמִפְּנֵי שְׁמִי נִחַת הוּא.[11]

ב...ה בַּעֲבוּר יִשְׁמְרוּ חֻקָּיו, וְתוֹרֹתָיו יִנְצֹרוּ, הַלְלוּיָהּ.[12]

ב...ז בְּיוֹם קְרָאתִי וַתַּעֲנֵנִי, תַּרְהִבֵנִי בְנַפְשִׁי עֹז.[13]

ב...ך בָּרוּךְ אַתָּה יהוה, לַמְּדֵנִי חֻקֶּיךָ.[14]

ב...ל בְּמַקְהֵלוֹת בָּרְכוּ אֱלֹהִים, אֲדֹנָי מִמְּקוֹר יִשְׂרָאֵל.[15]

ב...ן בָּרוּךְ יהוה אֱלֹהֵי יִשְׂרָאֵל מֵהָעוֹלָם וְעַד הָעֹלָם, אָמֵן וְאָמֵן.[16]

ב...ע בְּחֶסֶד וֶאֱמֶת יְכֻפַּר עָוֹן, וּבְיִרְאַת יהוה סוּר מֵרָע.[17]

ג...ה גּוֹל עַל יהוה דַּרְכֶּךָ, וּבְטַח עָלָיו וְהוּא יַעֲשֶׂה.[18]

ג...ל גַּם אֲנִי אוֹדְךָ בִכְלִי נֶבֶל אֲמִתְּךָ, אֱלֹהָי, אֲזַמְּרָה לְךָ בְכִנּוֹר, קְדוֹשׁ יִשְׂרָאֵל.[19]

ג...ן גַּם בְּנֵי אָדָם גַּם בְּנֵי אִישׁ, יַחַד עָשִׁיר וְאֶבְיוֹן.[20]

ד...א דִּרְשׁוּ יהוה בְּהִמָּצְאוֹ, קְרָאֻהוּ בִּהְיוֹתוֹ קָרוֹב.[21]

ד...ד דִּרְשׁוּ יהוה וְעֻזּוֹ, בַּקְּשׁוּ פָנָיו תָּמִיד.[22]

ד...ה דְּאָגָה בְלֶב אִישׁ יַשְׁחֶנָּה, וְדָבָר טוֹב יְשַׂמְּחֶנָּה.[23]

ד...ל דָּן יָדִין עַמּוֹ, כְּאַחַד שִׁבְטֵי יִשְׂרָאֵל.[24]

ה...א הַצּוּר תָּמִים פָּעֳלוֹ, כִּי כָל דְּרָכָיו מִשְׁפָּט, אֵל אֱמוּנָה וְאֵין עָוֶל, צַדִּיק וְיָשָׁר הוּא.[25]

ה...ה הַסְתֵּר פָּנֶיךָ מֵחֲטָאָי, וְכָל עֲוֹנֹתַי מְחֵה.[26]

ה...ל הַקְשִׁיבָה לְקוֹל שַׁוְעִי מַלְכִּי וֵאלֹהָי, כִּי אֵלֶיךָ אֶתְפַּלָּל.[27]

ז...ב זֵכֶר צַדִּיק לִבְרָכָה, וְשֵׁם רְשָׁעִים יִרְקָב.[28]

ז...ה זֹאת מְנוּחָתִי עֲדֵי עַד, פֹּה אֵשֵׁב כִּי אִוִּתִיהָ.[29]

ז...ו זָרַחְתִּי יָמִים מִקֶּדֶם, הִגִּיתִי בְכָל פָּעֳלֶךָ, בְּמַעֲשֵׂה יָדֶיךָ אֲשׂוֹחֵחַ.[30]

ז...ן זְבוּלֻן לְחוֹף יַמִּים יִשְׁכֹּן, וְהוּא לְחוֹף אֳנִיֹּת, וְיַרְכָתוֹ עַל צִידֹן.[31]

ח...ה חָגְרָה בְעוֹז מָתְנֶיהָ, וַתְּאַמֵּץ זְרוֹעֹתֶיהָ.[32]

---

(1) *Psalms* 118:25. (2) 41:2. (3) 146:5. (4) 5:2. (5) 16:2. (6) 68:9. (7) *Nehemiah* 9:7. (8) *Psalms* 30:9. (9) 10:6. (10) 20:8. (11) *Malachi* 2:5. (12) *Psalms* 105:45. (13) 138:3. (14) 119:12. (15) 68:27. (16) 41:14. (17) *Proverbs* 16:6. (18) *Psalms* 37:5. (19) 71:22. (20) 49:3. (21) *Isaiah* 55:6. (22) *Psalms* 105:4. (23) *Proverbs* 12:25. (24) *Genesis* 49:16. (25) *Deuteronomy* 32:4. (26) *Psalms* 51:11. (27) 5:3. (28) *Proverbs* 10:7. (29) *Psalms* 132:14. (30) 143:5. (31) *Genesis* 49:13. (32) *Proverbs* 31:17.

ח...ך חֲצוֹת לַיְלָה אָקוּם לְהוֹדוֹת לָךְ, עַל מִשְׁפְּטֵי צִדְקֶךָ.[1]

ח...ל חָדְלוּ פְרָזוֹן בְּיִשְׂרָאֵל חָדֵלּוּ, עַד שַׁקַּמְתִּי דְּבוֹרָה, שַׁקַּמְתִּי אֵם בְּיִשְׂרָאֵל.[2]

ח...ם חֹנֶה מַלְאַךְ יְהוָה סָבִיב לִירֵאָיו, וַיְחַלְּצֵם.[3]

ט...ב טוֹב נַחֲלוֹת בְּנֵי בָנִים, וְצָפוּן לַצַּדִּיק חֵיל חוֹטֵא.[4]

ט...ה טָמְנוּ גֵאִים פַּח לִי וַחֲבָלִים, פָּרְשׂוּ רֶשֶׁת לְיַד מַעְגָּל, מֹקְשִׁים שָׁתוּ לִי סֶלָה.[5]

י...א יִשְׂרָאֵל בְּטַח בַּיהוָה, עֶזְרָם וּמָגִנָּם הוּא.[6]

י...ע יַעַנְךָ יְהוָה בְּיוֹם צָרָה, יְשַׂגֶּבְךָ שֵׁם אֱלֹהֵי יַעֲקֹב.[7]

י...ד יָסַד אֶרֶץ עַל מְכוֹנֶיהָ, בַּל תִּמּוֹט עוֹלָם וָעֶד.[8]

י...ה יְהוָה, הַצִּילָה נַפְשִׁי מִשְּׂפַת שֶׁקֶר, מִלָּשׁוֹן רְמִיָּה.[9]

י...י יְהוָה לִי בְּעֹזְרָי, וַאֲנִי אֶרְאֶה בְשֹׂנְאָי.[10]

י...ל יְמִין יְהוָה רוֹמֵמָה, יְמִין יְהוָה עֹשָׂה חָיִל.[11]

י...מ יַעְלְזוּ חֲסִידִים בְּכָבוֹד, יְרַנְּנוּ עַל מִשְׁכְּבוֹתָם.[12]

י...ן יֵשֵׁם נְהָרוֹת לְמִדְבָּר, וּמֹצָאֵי מַיִם לְצִמָּאוֹן.[13]

י...ע יָחֹס עַל דַּל וְאֶבְיוֹן, וְנַפְשׁוֹת אֶבְיוֹנִים יוֹשִׁיעַ.[14]

י...ף יִגְמֹר בַּעֲדִי, יְהוָה חַסְדְּךָ לְעוֹלָם, מַעֲשֵׂי יָדֶיךָ אַל תֶּרֶף.[15]

י...ק יְבָרְכֵנוּ אֱלֹהִים, וְיִירְאוּ אוֹתוֹ כָּל אַפְסֵי אָרֶץ.[16]

י...ק יוֹצִיאֵם מֵחֹשֶׁךְ וְצַלְמָוֶת, וּמוֹסְרוֹתֵיהֶם יְנַתֵּק.[17]

י...ר יְהוָה שִׁמְךָ לְעוֹלָם, יְהוָה זִכְרְךָ לְדֹר וָדֹר.[18]

י...ה יְהוָה שֹׁמֵר אֶת גֵּרִים, יָתוֹם וְאַלְמָנָה יְעוֹדֵד, וְדֶרֶךְ רְשָׁעִים יְעַוֵּת.[19]

כ...ב כִּי לֹא יִטֹּשׁ יְהוָה עַמּוֹ, וְנַחֲלָתוֹ לֹא יַעֲזֹב.[20]

כ...ל כִּי מֶלֶךְ כָּל הָאָרֶץ אֱלֹהִים, זַמְּרוּ מַשְׂכִּיל.[21]

ל...א לֹא תִהְיֶה מְשַׁכֵּלָה וַעֲקָרָה בְּאַרְצֶךָ, אֶת מִסְפַּר יָמֶיךָ אֲמַלֵּא.[22]

ל...ה לְדָוִד, בָּרוּךְ יְהוָה צוּרִי, הַמְלַמֵּד יָדַי לַקְרָב, אֶצְבְּעוֹתַי לַמִּלְחָמָה.[23]

ל...ה לוּלֵי תוֹרָתְךָ שַׁעֲשֻׁעָי, אָז אָבַדְתִּי בְעָנְיִי.[24]

ל...ח לַמְנַצֵּחַ עַל שֹׁשַׁנִּים לִבְנֵי קֹרַח, מַשְׂכִּיל שִׁיר יְדִידֹת.[25]

מ...א מִי כָמֹכָה בָּאֵלִם יְהוָה, מִי כָּמֹכָה נֶאְדָּר בַּקֹּדֶשׁ, נוֹרָא תְהִלֹּת עֹשֵׂה פֶלֶא.[26]

מ...ח מַחְשְׁבוֹת בְּעֵצָה תִכּוֹן, וּבְתַחְבֻּלוֹת עֲשֵׂה מִלְחָמָה.[27]

מ...ה מַה דּוֹדֵךְ מִדּוֹד הַיָּפָה בַּנָּשִׁים, מַה דּוֹדֵךְ מִדּוֹד שֶׁכָּכָה הִשְׁבַּעְתָּנוּ.[28]

מ...י מָה אָהַבְתִּי תוֹרָתֶךָ, כָּל הַיּוֹם הִיא שִׂיחָתִי.[29]

מ...ל מַה טֹּבוּ אֹהָלֶיךָ יַעֲקֹב, מִשְׁכְּנֹתֶיךָ יִשְׂרָאֵל.[30]

מ...א מְאוֹר עֵינַיִם יְשַׂמַּח לֵב, שְׁמוּעָה טוֹבָה תְּדַשֶּׁן עָצֶם.[31]

מ...י מִי זֶה הָאִישׁ יְרֵא יְהוָה, יוֹרֶנּוּ בְּדֶרֶךְ יִבְחָר.[32]

נ...א נַפְשֵׁנוּ חִכְּתָה לַיהוָה, עֶזְרֵנוּ וּמָגִנֵּנוּ הוּא.[33]

נ...ה נָחַלְתִּי עֵדְוֹתֶיךָ לְעוֹלָם, כִּי שְׂשׂוֹן לִבִּי הֵמָּה.[34]

נ...י נִדְבוֹת פִּי רְצֵה נָא יְהוָה, וּמִשְׁפָּטֶיךָ לַמְּדֵנִי.[35]

נ...ל נֶחְשַׁבְתִּי עִם יוֹרְדֵי בוֹר, הָיִיתִי כְּגֶבֶר אֵין אֱיָל.[36]

נ...ם נַחֲמוּ נַחֲמוּ עַמִּי, יֹאמַר אֱלֹהֵיכֶם.[37]

נ...ן נֵר יְהוָה נִשְׁמַת אָדָם, חֹפֵשׂ כָּל חַדְרֵי בָטֶן.[38]

---

(1) Psalms 119:62. (2) Judges 5:7. (3) Psalms 34:8. (4) Proverbs 13:22. (5) Psalms 140:6. (6) 115:9. (7) 20:2. (8) 104:5. (9) 120:2. (10) 118:7. (11) 118:16. (12) 149:5. (13) 72:13. (14) 72:13. (15) 138:8. (16) 67:8. (17) 107:14. (18) 135:13. (19) 146:9. (20) 94:14. (21) 47:8. (22) Exodus 23:26. (23) Psalms 144:1. (24) 119:92. (25) 45:1. (26) Exodus 15:11. (27) Proverbs 20:18. (28) Song of Songs 5:9. (29) Psalms 119:97. (30) Numbers 24:5. (31) Proverbs 15:30. (32) Psalms 25:12. (33) 33:20. (34) 119:111. (35) 119:108. (36) 88:5. (37) Isaiah 40:1. (38) Proverbs 20:27.

ס...ה סְבּוּ צִיּוֹן וְהַקִּיפוּהָ, סִפְרוּ מִגְדָּלֶיהָ.[1]

ס...י סְעַפִּים שָׂנֵאתִי, וְתוֹרָתְךָ אָהָבְתִּי.[2]

ע...א עַתָּה אָקוּם, יֹאמַר יהוה, עַתָּה אֵרוֹמָם, עַתָּה אֶנָּשֵׂא.[3]

ע...ב עַד אֶמְצָא מָקוֹם לַיהוה, מִשְׁכָּנוֹת לַאֲבִיר יַעֲקֹב.[4]

ע...ז עָזִּי וְזִמְרָת יָהּ, וַיְהִי לִי לִישׁוּעָה.[5]

ע...ל עַל דַּעְתְּךָ כִּי לֹא אֶרְשָׁע, וְאֵין מִיָּדְךָ מַצִּיל.[6]

ע...ר עֶרֶב עַבְדְּךָ לְטוֹב, אַל יַעַשְׁקֻנִי זֵדִים.[7]

ע...ר עֹשֶׂה גְדֹלוֹת וְאֵין חֵקֶר, נִפְלָאוֹת עַד אֵין מִסְפָּר.[8]

פ...ה פִּתְחוּ לִי שַׁעֲרֵי צֶדֶק, אָבֹא בָם אוֹדֶה יָהּ.[9]

פ...ל פֶּן יִטְרֹף כְּאַרְיֵה נַפְשִׁי, פֹּרֵק וְאֵין מַצִּיל.[10]

פ...ס פֶּלֶס וּמֹאזְנֵי מִשְׁפָּט לַיהוה, מַעֲשֵׂהוּ כָּל אַבְנֵי כִיס.[11]

פ...נ פְּנֵה אֵלַי וְחָנֵּנִי, כִּי יָחִיד וְעָנִי אָנִי.[12]

צ...ה צֶדֶק בְּמִשְׁפָּט תֹּפֹּרֵנִי, וְשָׁבֵיהָ בִּצְדָקָה.[13]

צ...ח צִיּוֹן יִשְׁאֲלוּ דֶרֶךְ הֵנָּה פְנֵיהֶם, בֹּאוּ וְנִלְווּ אֶל יהוה, בְּרִית עוֹלָם לֹא תִשָּׁכֵחַ.[14]

צ...י צַר וּמָצוֹק מְצָאוּנִי, מִצְוֹתֶיךָ שַׁעֲשֻׁעָי.[15]

צ...ל צַהֲלִי וָרֹנִּי יוֹשֶׁבֶת צִיּוֹן, כִּי גָדוֹל בְּקִרְבֵּךְ קְדוֹשׁ יִשְׂרָאֵל.[16]

ק...א קָרַבְתָּ בְּיוֹם אֶקְרָאֶךָּ, אָמַרְתָּ אַל תִּירָא.[17]

ק...ל קָמָתִי אֲנִי לִפְתֹּחַ לְדוֹדִי, וְיָדַי נָטְפוּ מוֹר, וְאֶצְבְּעֹתַי מוֹר עֹבֵר עַל כַּפּוֹת הַמַּנְעוּל.[18]

ק...נ קוֹלִי אֶל יהוה אֶזְעָק, קוֹלִי אֶל יהוה אֶתְחַנָּן.[19]

ק...ת קָרוֹב אַתָּה יהוה, וְכָל מִצְוֹתֶיךָ אֱמֶת.[20]

ר...ו רְזוּ וְאֶל תֶּחֱטָאוּ, אִמְרוּ בִלְבַבְכֶם עַל מִשְׁכַּבְכֶם, וְדֹמּוּ סֶלָה.[21]

ר...ל רְאוּ עַתָּה כִּי אֲנִי אֲנִי הוּא, וְאֵין אֱלֹהִים עִמָּדִי, אֲנִי אָמִית וַאֲחַיֶּה, מָחַצְתִּי וַאֲנִי אֶרְפָּא, וְאֵין מִיָּדִי מַצִּיל.[22]

ר...נ רְאֵה זֶה מָצָאתִי, אָמְרָה קֹהֶלֶת, אַחַת לְאַחַת לִמְצֹא חֶשְׁבּוֹן.[23]

ר...ן רָאוּךָ מַּיִם אֱלֹהִים, רָאוּךָ מַּיִם יָחִילוּ, אַף יִרְגְּזוּ תְהֹמוֹת.[24]

ש...א שַׂמֵּחַ נֶפֶשׁ עַבְדֶּךָ, כִּי אֵלֶיךָ אֲדֹנָי נַפְשִׁי אֶשָּׂא.[25]

ש...ה שְׂאוּ יְדֵכֶם קֹדֶשׁ, וּבָרְכוּ אֶת יהוה.[26]

ש...ח שְׁמַע יהוה תְּחִנָּתִי, יהוה תְּפִלָּתִי יִקָּח.[27]

ש...י שָׂנֵאתִי הַשֹּׁמְרִים הַבְלֵי שָׁוְא, וַאֲנִי אֶל יהוה בָּטָחְתִּי.[28]

ש...ל שָׁלוֹם רָב לְאֹהֲבֵי תוֹרָתֶךָ, וְאֵין לָמוֹ מִכְשׁוֹל.[29]

ש...מ שְׁמָר תָּם וּרְאֵה יָשָׁר, כִּי אַחֲרִית לְאִישׁ שָׁלוֹם.[30]

ש...נ שִׁיתוּ לִבְּכֶם לְחֵילָה, פַּסְּגוּ אַרְמְנוֹתֶיהָ, לְמַעַן תְּסַפְּרוּ לְדוֹר אַחֲרוֹן.[31]

ש...ר שְׂפַת אֱמֶת תִּכּוֹן לָעַד, וְעַד אַרְגִּיעָה לְשׁוֹן שָׁקֶר.[32]

ת...ה תְּנוּ עֹז לֵאלֹהִים, עַל יִשְׂרָאֵל גַּאֲוָתוֹ, וְעֻזּוֹ בַּשְּׁחָקִים.[36]

ת...ה הִנֵּה בָּרְכוּ אֶת יהוה כָּל עַבְדֵי יהוה, הָעֹמְדִים בְּבֵית יהוה בַּלֵּילוֹת.[33]

ת...ע תַּעֲרֹךְ לְפָנַי שֻׁלְחָן נֶגֶד צֹרְרָי, דִּשַּׁנְתָּ בַשֶּׁמֶן רֹאשִׁי, כּוֹסִי רְוָיָה.[34]

ת...י תּוֹצִיאֵנִי מֵרֶשֶׁת זוּ טָמְנוּ לִי, כִּי אַתָּה מָעוּזִּי.[35]

(1) Psalms 48:13. (2) 119:113. (3) Isaiah 33:10. (4) Psalms 132:5. (5) 118:14. (6) Job 10:7.
(7) Psalms 119:122. (8) Job 5:9. (9) Psalms 118:19. (10) 7:3. (11) Proverbs 16:11. (12) Psalms 80:10.
(13) Isaiah 1:27. (14) Jeremiah 50:5. (15) Psalms 119:143. (16) Isaiah 12:6. (17) Lamentations 3:57.
(18) Song of Songs 5:5. (19) Psalms 142:2. (20) 119:151. (21) 4:5. (22) Deuteronomy 32:39.
(23) Ecclesiastes 7:27. (24) Psalms 77:7. (25) 86:4. (26) 134:2. (27) 6:10. (28) 31:7. (29) 119:165.
(30) 37:37. (31) 48:14. (32) Proverbs 12:19. (33) Psalms 134:1. (34) 23:5. (35) 31:5. (36) 68:35.

The Laws of *Shemoneh Esrei*

A Brief Summary

◆§ General Laws

1. Before beginning *Shemoneh Esrei*, one takes three steps backward, then three steps forward.

2. One should recite *Shemoneh Esrei* standing erect, with the feet together, and without leaning on anything. One should make every possible effort to concentrate fully on his prayer and its meaning, and to bear in mind that he is standing before God.

3. No interruption is permitted during *Shemoneh Esrei*. If one is in the midst of his silent *Shemoneh Esrei* prayer and hears the congregation reciting *Kedushah*, *Borchu*, or *Yehei Sh'mei Rabbah*, he should listen and concentrate, but not join in the recitation.

◆§ The Four Bows

4. At four points during *Shemoneh Esrei*, one should bow: (a) at the beginning of the first blessing, בָּרוּךְ אַתָּה; (b) at its end, [בָּרוּךְ אַתָּה ה' מָגֵן אַבְרָהָם]; (c) at the beginning of the blessing of thanksgiving, מוֹדִים אֲנַחְנוּ לָךְ; and (d) at the end of that blessing בָּרוּךְ אַתָּה [...ה' הַטּוֹב]. With the exception of מוֹדִים, bend the knees at בָּרוּךְ, bow forward at אַתָּה. It is sufficient to bow so that the face comes to chest level. In any case, an excessively deep bow, until below the waist, for example, is frowned upon as ostentatious. One should bow quickly as an expression of submission, but straighten up slowly, first the head and then the body. Some straighten up *while* reciting HASHEM; some *before* saying HASHEM. In the case of מוֹדִים, the

knees are not bent. Instead bow forward at מוֹדִים and straighten up at HASHEM, slowly and head first.

◆§ Additions During Ten Days of Repentance

5. During the Ten Days of Repentance between Rosh Hashanah and Yom Kippur, four brief supplications are inserted in *Shemoneh Esrei*: זָכְרֵנוּ, מִי כָמוֹךָ, וּכְתוֹב, בְּסֵפֶר חַיִּים. In case one forgot any of them, the rule is as follows: If one remembers the omission before having said the next בָּרוּךְ אַתָּה ה' (the key word is HASHEM), he goes back to the supplication and continues from there. Otherwise, the supplication is omitted. See §13 below.

6. During the same ten-day period, two of the standard blessings are amended, but their laws are different. In the third blessing, הָאֵל הַקָּדוֹשׁ is changed to הַמֶּלֶךְ הַקָּדוֹשׁ. In case one forgot to recite this version, he must *repeat* the *Shemoneh Esrei* from the beginning. If, however, one said הָאֵל הַקָּדוֹשׁ, but realized the mistake almost immediately [that is, the elapsed time is not more than it takes to say the three-word greeting, שָׁלוֹם עָלֶיךָ רַבִּי], he says the words הַמֶּלֶךְ הַקָּדוֹשׁ.

The other amended blessing is מֶלֶךְ אֹהֵב צְדָקָה וּמִשְׁפָּט, which is changed to הַמֶּלֶךְ הַמִּשְׁפָּט. If one recited the standard blessing but realized the mistake immediately, he recites the correct formula, as above. But if he remembered after that brief interval, he should simply continue the *Shemoneh Esrei*, since even the standard blessing describes God as מֶלֶךְ. If one mistakenly says ei-

ther of these Ten-Days blessings during the rest of the year, he need not repeat the blessing.

⇥ Prayers for Rain

7. From *Mussaf* of Shemini Atzeres until *Mussaf* of the first day of Pesach, the phrase מַשִּׁיב הָרוּחַ וּמוֹרִיד הַגֶּשֶׁם is added to the second blessing. If one forgot this phrase, but remembered the oversight before starting אַתָּה נֶאֱמָן, he inserts the omitted phrase at whichever place he recalls the oversight. If he remembers after starting נֶאֱמָן but before saying *HASHEM*, he recites the omitted phrase and begins again from נֶאֱמָן. If he had already said *HASHEM*, he must complete the blessing and say the phrase מַשִּׁיב הָרוּחַ וּמוֹרִיד הַגֶּשֶׁם before starting אַתָּה קָדוֹשׁ. If one remembered thereafter, he must recite *Shemoneh Esrei* again.

If, however, one said only מוֹרִיד הַגֶּשֶׁם (omitting מַשִּׁיב הָרוּחַ) — or if one prayed according to *Nusach Sefard* and said מוֹרִיד הַטַּל — the *Shemoneh Esrei* need not be repeated.

If one cannot remember whether or not he said the proper phrase, we proceed on the following assumption: If one has been reciting the current version for ninety *Amidah* prayers, he has undoubtedly prayed correctly; if less than ninety times, he probably recited the outdated version, from force of habit.

If one recited מוֹרִיד הַגֶּשֶׁם during the wrong months — if he has not yet completed the blessing, he starts again from אַתָּה גִּבּוֹר; if he has completed the blessing, he must recite *Shemoneh Esrei* again.

8. In the blessing בָּרֵךְ עָלֵינוּ, a prayer for rain and dew (וְתֵן טַל וּמָטָר) is added as follows: in *Eretz Yisrael*, it is recited from 7 Cheshvan until Pesach; in all

other countries, it is begun at *Maariv* of December 4 [December 5 in the year before a civil leap year]. In case one forgot to add it, but remembered before saying the following בָּרוּךְ אַתָּה ה', he recites it at that point and continues. If he remembers later, he may recite it during the blessing שְׁמַע קוֹלֵנוּ, in which general prayers may be inserted. The proper place for the insertion is before כִּי אַתָּה שׁוֹמֵעַ. If one remembered after beginning רְצֵה but before stepping out of *Shemoneh Esrei*, he must return to the beginning of בָּרֵךְ עָלֵינוּ. Otherwise he must repeat *Shemoneh Esrei*.

During the rest of the year, if one erroneously recited טַל וּמָטָר, one must return to בָּרֵךְ עָלֵינוּ. If he finished *Shemoneh Esrei*, he must repeat it.

If one cannot remember whether or not he said the proper phrase, we proceed on the assumption that if thirty days have gone by, he has said the proper text (even though בָּרֵךְ עָלֵינוּ is recited less than 90 times during 30 days).

⇥ Fast Days

9. On fast days, public or personal, the prayer עֲנֵנוּ is recited by individuals as part of שְׁמַע קוֹלֵנוּ. If one forgot it, he may recite it as the end of אֱלֹהַי נְצוֹר, just before יִהְיוּ לְרָצוֹן, which signifies the end of *Shemoneh Esrei*. If one forgot even then, he does not repeat *Shemoneh Esrei*. See §13 below.

If at least seven members of the *minyan* are fasting, the *chazzan* recites עֲנֵנוּ (with the addition of a concluding blessing) before beginning רְפָאֵנוּ. If he forgets and begins רְפָאֵנוּ, he should interrupt, say עֲנֵנוּ, and then begin רְפָאֵנוּ again. If, however, he has already completed רְפָאֵנוּ, or if less than seven members of the *minyan* are fasting, he should recite עֲנֵנוּ in שְׁמַע קוֹלֵנוּ, omitting

the special blessing at its conclusion.

10. שִׂים שָׁלוֹם is substituted for שָׁלוֹם רָב on fast days. If one recited שָׁלוֹם רָב on a fast day, or שִׂים שָׁלוֹם on a non-fast day, he need not repeat *Shemoneh Esrei*.

Before reciting שִׂים שָׁלוֹם in his repetition of *Shemoneh Esrei* on fast days, the *chazzan* recites בִּרְכַּת כֹּהֲנִים. If he omitted this paragraph, he need not repeat *Shemoneh Esrei*.

⋅§ Rosh Chodesh and Festivals

11. On Rosh Chodesh and Chol HaMoed, יַעֲלֶה וְיָבֹא is recited as part of רְצֵה. If one omitted it, but remembered before starting מוֹדִים, he recites it *then*, and goes on to מוֹדִים. If he remembers after starting מוֹדִים, but before stepping out of *Shemoneh Esrei*, he starts again from רְצֵה. Otherwise he must repeat *Shemoneh Esrei*. See §13 below.

However, if one forgot יַעֲלֶה וְיָבֹא during the *Maariv* of Rosh Chodesh, *Shemoneh Esrei* need not be repeated, nor does one go back to מוֹדִים if he has begun מוֹדִים. But at the *Maariv* of Chol HaMoed, the laws of the previous paragraph apply.

⋅§ Chanukah and Purim

12. If one forgot to recite עַל הַנִּסִּים, as long as he has not recited בָּרוּךְ אַתָּה ה׳ of the next blessing, he recites עַל הַנִּסִּים and continues from there. But if he has recited ה׳, he goes on, omitting עַל הַנִּסִּים. He may recite it, however, just before stepping out of *Shemoneh Esrei*, after יִהְיוּ לְרָצוֹן אִמְרֵי פִי. See §13 below.

⋅§ Wrong Prayer Added

13. If one added any of the special prayers on a day for which it was not intended, must he repeat *Shemoneh Esrei*? The general rule is that if a falsehood is implicit in his words he must go back to the beginning of that blessing. Examples of such falsehoods are the recitation of יַעֲלֶה וְיָבֹא or the fast-day prayer on ordinary days, or the mention of Pesach in יַעֲלֶה וְיָבֹא on a day other than Pesach. For the purpose of this law, the first three blessings and the last three blessings are considered to be single units. Thus, such an error before הָאֵל הַקָּדוֹשׁ requires one to begin *Shemoneh Esrei* anew, and an error in the last three blessings requires one to go back to רְצֵה. If no falsehood is implicit in his words [e.g., he said הַמֶּלֶךְ הַקָּדוֹשׁ instead of הָאֵל הַקָּדוֹשׁ], he simply continues the proper order of his prayers.

⋅§ Prayer With a *Minyan* of Ten

14. One should try his utmost to pray in the synagogue together with the congregation, for the Almighty does not reject the prayer of the many. Contrary to the popular misconception that it is sufficient to respond to בָּרְכוּ and קְדוּשָׁה, the main objective of prayer with a *minyan* is to recite *Shemoneh Esrei* with a *minyan*. Therefore one must arrive at the synagogue early enough so that he can keep up with the congregation.

15. A *minyan* (quorum of ten adult males) must be present during *Borchu*, the *chazzan's* repetition of *Shemoneh Esrei* and *Kaddish*. Therefore, it is a grave sin to leave the synagogue during any of these recitations if one's presence is necessary to complete the *minyan*, as it is stated: *And those who forsake Hashem will be destroyed* (Isaiah 1:28).

16. Nonetheless, if any of these recita-

tions began with a *minyan,* but some individuals left and a *minyan* is no longer present, the recitation may continue if at least six individuals remain.

17. Thus, if the *chazzan* began his repetition of the *Shemoneh Esrei* in the presence of a *minyan,* he may conclude it — including *Kedushah* and the *Kaddish* following the repetition — even if a *minyan* is no longer present.

18. At *Maariv,* the *chazzan* may recite the Half-*Kaddish* preceding *Shemoneh Esrei* if a *minyan* was present for the recital of *Borchu.* The Full *Kaddish* may be recited after *Shemoneh Esrei* if a *minyan* was present at the beginning of *Shemoneh Esrei.*

◆§ Tachanun

19. *Tachanun* is omitted:

(a) in a house of mourning during the *shivah* period.

(b) In the presence of a bridegroom, from the day of his wedding until after the *Sheva Berachos* week (if both bride and groom have been previously married, their period of celebration extends for only three days).

(c) In the synagogue where a circumcision will take place later that day, or in the presence of a primary participant (i.e., the father, the *mohel* or the *sandak*) in a circumcision that will take place later that day.

(d) On the Sabbath; festivals (including Chol HaMoed); Rosh Chodesh; the entire month of Nissan; Lag B'Omer; from Rosh Chodesh Sivan until the day after *Shavuos* (some congregations do not resume *Tachanun* until 14 Sivan); Tishah B'Av; 15 Av; between Yom Kippur and the day after Succos (some congregations do not resume until 2 Cheshvan); Chanukah; Tu B'Shevat; Purim and Shushan Purim (in a leap year this applies also to 14-15 Adar I); or at *Minchah* of the day preceding any of the days listed above.

(e) On Erev Rosh Hashanah and Erev Yom Kippur.

(f) In some congregations, on Pesach Sheni (14 Iyar).

⛾ THE MOURNER'S KADDISH ⛾

TRANSLITERATED WITH ASHKENAZIC PRONUNCIATION

Yisgadal v'yiskadash Sh'mei rabbaw (Cong.— Amein.)
  b'allmaw dee v'raw chir'usei v'yamlich malchusei,
b'chayeichon, uvyomeichon, uvchayei d'chol Beis Yisrawel,
ba'agawlaw u'vizman kawriv. V'imru: Amein.

(Cong.— Amein. Y'hei Sh'mei rabbaw m'vawrach l'allam ulallmei allmayaw.)

Y'hei Sh'mei rabbaw m'vawrach, l'allam ulallmei allmayaw.

Yisbawrach, v'yishtabach, v'yispaw'ar,
v'yisromam, v'yisnasei,
v'yis'hadar, v'yis'aleh, v'yis'halawl
Sh'mei D'kudshaw B'rich Hu (Cong.— B'rich Hu)
l'aylaw °min kawl

(° from Rosh Hashanah to Yom Kippur substitute: u'l'aylaw mikol)

birchawsaw v'shirawsaw tushb'chawsaw v'nechemawsaw
da'amirawn b'allmaw. V'imru: Amein. (Cong.— Amein.)

Y'hei sh'lawmaw rabbaw min Sh'mayaw
v'chayim awleinu v'al kawl Yisrawel. V'imru: Amein. (Cong.— Amein.)

Take three steps back, bow left and say, "Oseh ...''; bow right and say, "hu ya'aseh ...";
bow forward and say, "V'al kawl yisrawel v'imru: Amein."

Oseh shawlom bimromawv,
Hu ya'aseh shawlom awleinu,
v'al kawl Yisrawel. V'imru: Amein. (Cong.— Amein.)

Remain standing in place for a few moments, then take three steps forward.

This volume is part of
THE ARTSCROLL® SERIES
an ongoing project of
translations, commentaries and expositions on
Scripture, Mishnah, Talmud, Midrash, Halachah,
liturgy, history, the classic Rabbinic writings,
biographies and thought.

For a brochure of current publications
visit your local Hebrew bookseller
or contact the publisher:

Mesorah Publications, ltd

4401 Second Avenue
Brooklyn, New York 11232
(718) 921-9000
www.artscroll.com